The Essen...
Financial Empow...

Think Rich!
Get Rich!
Stay Rich!

Karen L. Neilinger, MA, MBA

Francine J. Blum, MA

Book design by Alphagraphics of Pearl, MS - U.S.A.

alphagraphics˙

Paperback ISBN 978-1-938819-27-8
Hardback ISBN 978-1-938819-23-0

First Edition

PRINTED BY ALPHAGRAPHICS OF PEARL, MS - U.S.A.

Tribute:

This book is dedicated to all who are united in the quest to seek financial freedom. Financial freedom empowers more women to help themselves get ahead and stay ahead.
When women are empowered, everyone wins!

Table of Contents

Introduction 1
Think Rich! Get Rich!

PART 1 DEFINING THE REAL FINANCIAL YOU! 7

Chapter 1 9
Finding your Financial Center: Matching your Personality to your Investment Strategy

Chapter 2 27
Find your Financial G Spot!

Chapter 3 37
Smart, Sexy, Savvy, and ...Broke?

Chapter 4 53
Negotiating – Strategies & Tactics:
It's not only what you Know – It's how you Negotiate!

Chapter 5 61
Single & Loaded

Chapter 6 69
The Bag Lady Syndrome

Chapter 7 75
Love & Marriage...go together like Divorce & Prenuptials

Chapter 8 85
Cougar, Trophy, Stepford, Bachelorette & Career-Oriented Women

Chapter 9 91
Financial Infidelity: It's not Lipstick on the Collar!

Chapter 10 103
Life after the 4 D's: Divorce, Death, Disability & Financial Disaster

Chapter 11 117
Timing is Everything in Life!

Chapter 12 123
The Platinum Rules

Part 2 Let's go shopping! 125

Chapter 13 127
   Shop (Stocks) 'til you Drop!

Chapter 14 145
   Bonding with a Bond – 007 Style!

Chapter 15 159
   Commodities: Are Diamonds really a Girl's best Friend?

Chapter 16 171
   Futures, Derivatives, & Options: Are they in your Future?

Chapter 17 183
   Global Exchanges: Travel the World without leaving your Home!

Chapter 18 193
   Cash & Cash Equivalents: Cash is Queen!

Chapter 19 203
   Pension & Retirement Investments: Plan now to enjoy Later!

Chapter 20 217
   Insurance: What is your best Asset?

Chapter 21 227
   Real Estate: Where most Millionaires are born!

Chapter 22 237
   Valuing other Assets: Jewelry, Antiques, Automobiles,
   Collectibles and more!

Part 3 Accentuate the Positive & Eliminate the Negative! 245

Chapter 23 247
   Nip and Tuck your Way to a well-rounded Portfolio

Chapter 24 253
   Where is It going when you're Gone? Estate Planning:
   Wills, Trusts & Greed

Chapter 25 263
   Conclusion: Think Rich! Get Rich! Stay Rich!

Wall Street Jargon 268
The A-Z Guide of Financial Terms 271
Accreditations & Sources 282

Think Rich! Get Rich!

Brunette: You always look so young and refreshed. What is your beauty secret?

Blonde: Honestly, it's because I sleep like a baby at night. And, I use *Karen & Fran's Step-by-Step Beauty Secret.*

Brunette: What is it? How do I get some? I have tried everything imaginable: a glass of red wine at night, counting sheep, reading in bed, sleeping pills, even tried watching late night infomercials and dull monotone news shows to put me to sleep.

Blonde: Nothing worked for me either until I started using *Karen & Fran's Step-by-Step Beauty Secret.* Now I count all the money I made each day through prudent saving and investing. I envision each night the money going into my piggy bank - dollar by dollar. No more nightmares or stress lines. I awake refreshed and looking 10 years younger. It's the best kept beauty secret in the world!

KNL

Introduction:

Think Rich! Get Rich!

We hope to familiarize you, the reader, with the vital tools necessary to successfully shop for investments that will create a well-rounded portfolio and put you on the path of financial success, well-being, and empowerment.

The majority of financial books on the market are dry, text book style with a bias towards the male mentality. In ***Think Rich! Get Rich! Stay Rich!***, we will both use and explain "financial terms" and "financial jargon" used in the marketplace today in an easy to understand feminine format. Not only will you look smarter, sexier, and savvier during cocktail conversations but we will provide you with many of the essential tools of the trade to enable you to outshine and outmaneuver the average investor. By reading this book, you will learn vital life, financial survival, and investing skills and strategies; and in addition, this book will help aid in creating the person you always wanted to be: *financially independent*.

Operate from a Position of Strength & Power

By fulfilling your investment objectives and needs it will enable you to operate from a position of strength and power in your relationships and in general. Instead of being told what to do from your husband, significant other or your financial advisor; you will be able to advise them on how to best invest your money and shared assets. You will see that the investment world is your oyster when it comes to selecting products to invest in.

In life, you invest time, energy, and money into an education. That same time, energy and money need to be funneled into creating investments that can make your life more enjoyable and less stressful. Now is the time to invest in your financial independence! The way to do this is to create a well-rounded (diversified) portfolio made up of not only financial instruments (like stocks and bonds) but also by incorporating insurance instruments, real estate, jewelry, collectibles (like antiques, paintings, Princess Diana dresses, Jackie O's string of pearls, etc.) – you get the picture.

Buyers' Remorse or Exaltation

Purchasing valuables both tangible and intangible to put into your portfolio shopping bag can be truly exhilarating! You can obtain that same shopping high (of "I shopped, I conquered, and I have that pair of Jimmy Choo shoes and Chanel handbag as trophies in my closet to prove it!") by purchasing Tiffany or Saks Fifth Avenue stocks or their corporate bonds instead. (Well, almost!) Especially if that stock doubles! Then you can purchase two of those Prada or Louis Vuitton handbags instead of the knock offs on the street corner. And, consider this, how many of those beautiful designer shoes that you consider an "investment" do you really wear very often once you purchase them? One, they either pinch your feet or give you painful blisters. Or two, you destroy your trophy shoes at a garden party because you (instead of the gardener) were aerating the lawn with your heels and ruined that expensive pair of Salvatore Ferragamo or Burberry shoes. That same amount of money that purchased those shoes and handbags could have been used to purchase stock in many of those same companies. Naturally, you could still lose your "investment". However, stocks have the potential to go up. Those shoes, on the other hand, will only go down in value from the day they walk out of the store.

Just as the smart, savvy shopper discerningly looks for products to purchase that are both desirable and suitable so should you use that same philosophy when purchasing investment products and services.

Have you ever bought an item that you woke up at night fretting and lamenting about? You ask yourself, "Why did I purchase that? Was I pushed into it by a high pressure salesperson? It's really not my style, it doesn't really fit, and it cost an absolute fortune! Can I return it and get my money back?" This same example applies to a bad investment purchase as well.

Why did I purchase that? – Was it impulse shopping? – I had a bad day and sought shopping instead of chocolates and a strong Apple Martini.

I was pushed into it by the salesperson – I was pressured by the broker / investment advisor.

It's really not my style – I'm not a smoker, why did the broker have me invest in Phillip Morris?

It cost a fortune – I bought the stock at the 52-week high and not on sale, instead of at the 52-week low bargain price.

Can I return it and get my money back? – You can definitely sell a stock and you might even make a profit on it.

Platinum Tip: *An investment doesn't begin as a bad investment. You buy it because it's a good investment and then it changes and turns bad.*

When the Going gets Rough....the Tough go Shopping!

When the going gets rough....the tough go shopping! This was the mantra I lived by at university and both graduate schools. I ended up with a lot of cool clothes and was quite the fashionista in college (or at least I thought so). If I had used those same hard earned dollars to go shopping for stocks or even plunked them into a good interest bearing CD instead of all those clothes "investments" (which are now outdated), I would have been better off. Hindsight is always 20/20! Oh the power of time and accrued interest and dividends! (Refer to Section: **The A-Z Guide of Financial Terms** for *The Rule of 72* in the back of this book).

Lucky for me, my college employer and also my father pushed me to look at stocks. I remember coming home one day, because of a credible stock tip from my college employer, and saying to my father, I want to invest in Telefonas de Mexicana (TELMEX) a Mexican telecommunications company. At that time in the 1980's, the stock was trading at about 8 cents a share on the *Pink Sheets* (see **Section: Wall Street Jargon**). My father, thinking, this would be a good lesson learned (because the first time investing in the stock market should be a conservative, blue chip stock instead of a risky over-the-counter foreign security), let me make the investment with my hard earned money. He went to his stock broker, who busted out laughing while asking, "... how many thousands of shares would you like of this stock?" Because of the arrogance of this broker, my father ended up buying shares for himself as well so at least it looked like a respectable amount of shares were purchased. Back then, you neither had the discount brokers like you do today nor the anonymity that you receive from investing online. Also, the commissions at full brokerage houses were very, very high which forced you to "buy and hold" in an attempt to pay the brokers fee and then hopefully eek out a profit in the future. Call it beginners luck but that darn stock ended up paying for much of my business graduate school education! And, I ended up after graduate school going to work for one of the top investment banks on Wall Street – Goldman Sachs & Co. What a lesson learned indeed!

Platinum Tip: *Investing in Penny Stocks is highly risky and we don't suggest you do this unless you are willing to lose your entire investment. Think of it like buying a lottery ticket: it could pay off, but most likely won't.*

We hope this book will put a smile on your face and more than a jingle in your pocketbook, that it will enlighten you and make you focus more broadly about your financial future. We wish you tremendous financial success and happy shopping for investments!

Success comes before work only in the dictionary.

— Anonymous

*There are people who have money
and people who are rich.*

— Coco Chanel

Big journeys begin with a single step.

— Fortune Cookie

Don't wait for your ship to come in. Row out to meet it.

— Anonymous

*You have to find something that you love enough to be able to
take risks, jump over the hurdles and break through the brick
walls that are always going to be placed in front of you. If you
don't have that kind of feeling for what it is you're doing, you'll
stop at the first giant hurdle.*

— George Lucas (Star Wars director)

Part 1

Defining the Real Financial You

This first section will help you make a true self-assessment of yourself and will aid in discovering *who you are* and *who you want to be.* This process is essential in defining your investment parameters. Ask yourself where you want to be in 5 years, 10 years, 20 years, etc.? What type of lifestyle do you feel the most comfortable in? Are you, the red sporty convertible, completely polished type of lady, clad from head to toe in the latest designer fashions? Or, are you most comfortable wearing a pair of flannel PJs, sitting on the sofa with a bowl of popcorn, and enjoy watching old movies such as *Sleepless in Seattle* and *Gone with the Wind* for the twentieth time type of gal? Or are you like most women... somewhere in between?

Find your Financial Center

Yoga Instructor: Ok class, now get into your Financial Warrior position. Stretch and reach for new heights. The stock market opens at 9:30am EST in the U.S.!

KNL

Chapter 1

Finding your Financial Center:

Match your Personality to your Investment Strategy

No two people are alike. In fact, neither are the two sides of your face, your breasts, your hands, nor are your feet identical. So why should the way you think about your finances be the same as someone else? Although we all may possess similar financial needs as discussed in the **Introduction: Think Rich! Get Rich!** of this book, no two person's financial wants, desires and needs are exactly the same.

So many financial advisors have a chart that they try to size everyone up by. Although it is with good intentions; for many people however, it is like putting a round peg into a square hole. Financial advisors use the term *Financial Pyramid* or *Investment Pyramid* to describe this type of "summing you and your financial strategy up." In a nutshell, depending on your *age*, the pyramid will shift from a heavier weighting of *stocks / equity* at the base of the pyramid and a lighter weighting of *bonds / fixed income* at the top to a heavier weighting of *bonds / fixed income* products at the bottom of the pyramid to a lighter weighting of *stocks / equities* up top. *Commodities* and *cash* are also part of the mix.

Think of it this way. If you are a 22 year old, you are more willing to experiment with clothing styles and stiletto heels. You want the latest fashion, and why not? You are young, sexy and want to show it off. You are also more incline to take much higher risks with your financial assets, because you have the opportunity to remake that money if you fall flat on your face with a sour investment. (Younger people tend to invest in high flyer growth stocks like Apple, Google, Facebook, Twitter, Chipotle, and Netflix.) A 75 year old lady, on the other hand, doesn't normally tend to gravitate to the latest fad (unless it is jewelry and that is because the husband picked it out and not her) nor is she wearing 5 inch stiletto heels. She has "already been there, done that," and is quite happy to dress and behave more conservatively. So too, her choice in financial investments are normally more on the conservative side. The reason is simple, she must think about her retirement money - her nest egg. She doesn't have as many years to make back any bad investments and is normally more incline to invest in more secure assets such as bonds, certain preferred securities, and utility companies which behave more like bonds and pay a good dividend.

A good financial advisor will use the *Financial Pyramid*; but in addition, they will also ask you more specific questions which will shift the allocation of *stocks, bonds, commodities*, and *cash* slightly.

Typical Questions asked by Financial Advisors

Some examples of questions asked by *Financial Advisors* are:

• Do you have any specific goals that you are saving for or would like to obtain?

• Are you saving for your own or your child's college education, or private school tuition?

• Are you saving for a wedding? Retirement? Or, change of lifestyle?

• Are you saving for a special vacation?

• Are you saving to make a down deposit on your first apartment or on your dream home?

Diagram of the "Financial Pyramid"

Investment Allocation	*vs.*	*Investment Allocation*
for a 22 year old		*for a 75 year old*

Bonds		**Equity**
Cash		**Commodities**
Commodities		**Cash**
Equity		**Bonds**

Risk Tolerance

A measure of your own individual *risk tolerance level* should tweak your personal *Financial Pyramid* even further. Some women are by their very nature highly risk adverse and conservative no matter what their age is. A perfect example is my own grandmother (now 100) who lived through the Great Depression as a teenager and young lady. She has great "financial scaring" and her outlook on investing in the stock market is far different from other women just two decades younger than her. This is because she personally witnessed seeing her parents and all others around her lose not only their life savings, their homes, but also their jobs. At the age of 99, however, she was looking to move into a retirement community. This move required a specific cash flow to match her monthly expenses. Due to low interest rates on U.S. Treasury bonds and bank CDs in 2013-2014, she chose to invest in higher yielding preferred stocks, some blue chip common stocks, and some corporate bond funds in lieu of bank CDs and bank savings accounts to enable her to maintain her retirement nest egg while generating enough current income through dividends and overall price appreciation to match her monthly expenditures. Many of these securities paid a monthly dividend while the others paid quarterly. Her investment objective has been successful so far: creating a cash flow to help offset her monthly expenses while maintaining a stable principle balance in her investment account. Quarterly rebalancing of her portfolio, making only minor adjustments has also been the key to keeping her investment portfolio in check.

Other women, no matter their age, live on the wild side and embrace risk as exhilarating. You need to decide on a scale of 1 to 5 (1 being *highly risk tolerant* and 5 being *highly risk adverse*) exactly where you fit in to that scale. Perhaps you prefer to have mostly preservation of capital and some appreciation. Then you would be a 4. If you like half and half, some risk and some capital preservation with lower returns, then you are probably a 3. If you tend to like more juice in your investments and seek a higher return on most of your portfolio then you are most likely a 2. If you like the casinos and bet everything on lucky number 7 at the craps table, then you my dear are definitely a 1 – but beware. Just like at the casino, you could lose everything on that high flyer stock. Just make sure you don't bet more than you can afford to lose and consider it a game and not an investment.

Risk Tolerance Levels

Basically, there are five levels of risk tolerance when it comes to investing. Which category do you think you fit into? (Sometimes it can be a combination of two.)

1. Seeking Alpha, Risk Taker, A Gambler — High Risk
2. Higher Tolerance of Risk, Seek Higher Returns — Moderately High
3. Capital Appreciation, Moderate Risk Tolerance — Moderate
4. Preservation of Capital, Low Tolerance for Risk — Moderately Low
5. Highly Risk Adverse — Low Risk

Bulls vs. Bears

The S&P, DOW, and NASDAQ have increased in value since their inception. However, within this time there have been many *Bull Markets* and *Bear Markets* or "ups" and "downs" in the markets. A *Bull Market* is where advancing stocks or bonds lead (outnumber) decliners for an extended amount of time. Generally speaking, a *Bull Market* lasts at least a few months or can go on for many years and is characterized by high trading volume. A *Bear Market* is where declining stocks or bonds outweigh advancers on the big board for several months or years. *Bear Markets* can be triggered by any number of political and economic events such as rising interest rates and political unrest in the U.S. or abroad.

Bubbles & Busts

Over the centuries, there have been many *market bubbles* (booms) and busts in a particular stock, stock sector, or overall market. For example, the 1600s in Holland witnessed the infamous *Tulip Mania Boom & Bust*. Tulip prices surged in price due to demand of the beautiful flower. People bet their homesteads on the bulb. During the 1700s in England, the famous *South Sea Bubble & Bust* occurred. People invested in seafaring voyages that were sure to bring back handsome reward from the South Seas. *Black Friday* in the U.S. (*Gold Crisis, Stock Market Crash & Depression*) occurred 1869-1871 not long after the end of the Civil War, the stock market dramatically sank in the United States. The late 1880s ushered in the *Golden Age* of America with a War of the Titans (Carnegie, Rockefeller, Ford, Astor, Vanderbilt, etc.). *The Panic of 1907* saw a Credit Crunch that crashed the market from 1906-1907.

In the early 1900s the automobile craze (a technology bubble) took America by storm alongside with World War I. The first *Tech Bubble* (caused from the Automobile Sector) ended in the stock market crash of 1919-1921. The *Roaring Twenties* spurred on the flappers, women's short skirts, and bob haircuts. So too, the market followed the hem line up – soaring to new heights! Large construction projects like the first skyscrapers in America (The Empire State Building and the Chrysler Building in New York City), the "coke" in Coca Cola and the "up" in 7-Up all helped to fan the fire. The market soared to all time new highs. Then suddenly and without warning, the music stopped playing on *Black Tuesday*, October 29, 1929. The market plunged and continued to plunge until there was over 24% unemployment in the U.S. and over 33% in some other countries. (Technically, the crash occurred succinctly over a longer period of time.) Quite a few Wall Street people took their own lives rather than face the music. People jumped from newly built skyscraper buildings in the major cities from despair. The U.S. and the world entered into a *Global Depression*. Runs on the banks began; forcing banks to close their doors to the public. People lost everything they had. City people retreated to the farms to scratch out a living and to try to feed their families. Overseas, the German Mark suffered from both *Devaluation* and *Hyperinflation*. Pictures of young people pushing wheel barrows of money just to buy a loaf of bread vividly depict that somber era. The tension and peoples anxiety was similar to that of a hot air balloon. It kept growing and growing until the tension in people's lives finally made the balloon burst into one of the worst wars modern day humanity had ever faced: World War II.

The 1950s became the *Wonder Years* especially in countries like Germany, the United States, and England. Construction boomed again and jobs were plenty. The 1970s saw cars lined up for blocks at the pump during the *Oil Crisis*. The 1980s heralded in a well-deserved market surge after a lackluster 1960s and 1970s but culminated in a *Flash Crash* in 1987. The 1990s ushered in the *Dot.com Bubble and Technology Bubble* which burst in early 2000. The War on Terror took its toll on oil prices and the overall market. Next came the *Housing Boom & Bust, the Credit / Financial Crisis and Great Recession of 2007-2009*: this was the worst recession since the Great Depression of the 1930s. Investors over this last decade (2000-2013) have been whipsawed by the market action.

What will the future bring? History tends to repeat itself: the future will bring more turmoil, more booms and busts, and more investment opportunities! Although history doesn't repeat itself exactly, market historians and statisticians can draw on similarities and make market predictions given how the markets reacted to past events. From studying these statistics you can become a smart, savvy, investor and choose to invest both prudently and wisely.

The 10 most important Rules of Investing for the Smart & Savvy

Rule 1   Never let your investments keep you up worrying all night. If they do, you shouldn't be in them.

Rule 2   Every stock has up days and down days. Expect price fluctuations. Don't panic if the first day you buy the security, the price goes down. Likewise, don't think you're the *Queen of Stock Investing* if the price goes up the first day you bought it. Wall Street, like the game of golf, can be a very humbling game.

Rule 3   Know when to buy. Know when to sell. Study the charts of the security you are interested in, including the stock's 52 week high and low. Do your research and read as much market related and specific security related materials as you can. Look to internet financial websites like Yahoo! and click on the "Finance" section. Read financial newspapers such as *The Wall Street Journal, The Financial Times* or *Barron's*. Use your extra air miles to purchase magazines like *Fortune* and *Smart Money* to get tips on investing and specific securities. Listen to market news and shows on television stations such as CNBC and Bloomberg or specific programs like *The Nightly Business Report* on PBS and *Bulls & Bears* on Fox Network, etc. Get as much knowledge as you can to make an educated decision. Study and do your homework – it will pay off handsomely!

Always think about an entry and an exit point for every position and also for your entire portfolio. Sometimes *Cash is Queen* (not King in this book) and you might choose to exit all positions if you are not comfortable with fickle *Mr. Market*. It's o.k. to set on a pile of cash until you see a comfortable re-entry point to invest again. Also, you might buy the security at a great price, but you also need to sell it for a *higher* price to make money. So many times it is easy to know *when to buy* but it can be much harder to determine *when to sell*. Greed always tries to get in the way of logical thinking. Greed will tempt you with the seduction of higher returns if you just hold on to the security for a while longer. Sometimes this is true; but, sometimes it is not. You must always remember that with gravity – what goes up must come down! Securities act in a similar fashion. Nobody ever went broke by taking a profit; but, you can go broke by taking too many losses!

Rule 4 There will always be another train to catch. If your particular security has already left the station and is powering full steam ahead. It might be too late to catch that particular train. Look for an alternative, or catch it after it retreats slightly, provided you still find the security attractive. It might be retreating for a reason.

Rule 5 Slow and steady wins the race. There will always be momentum and high flyer stocks, but many times they ultimately crash and burn in the end. Look primarily for companies that have a good balance sheet and stocks with a good *P/E Ratio* that look to provide a steady and secure return over time. If you want to take a chance, then invest no more than 5% of your portfolio in a risky security.

Rule 6 Know when to cut and run. Know when to cut your losses. These maxims refer to taking a timely loss before the security experiences a severe downturn or even worse – bankruptcy. It is much better to end up with something (even if it is a loss) than to have nothing by the time you finally throw in the towel and sell.

Rule 7 "Know when to hold them, know when to fold them, know when to walk away, know when to run..." Although these lyrics are from a country western song sung by Kenny Rogers and are originally written about a poker game, they are very applicable to investor psychology in the marketplace. Sometimes it is best to hold on to a security due to short-term capital gains or if you are seeking long-term price appreciation. However, sometimes you need to give up on an investment strategy because it is no longer working. Other times, the trade really isn't there; the stock is going nowhere and is treading water. In this case, you need to walk away without a gain or a loss to take advantage of better investment opportunities. (Always remember the *Time Value of Money* and the *Rule of 72* defined in the **Section: Wall Street Jargon** in the back of this book.) Finally, sometimes you will want to cash out because you lost the bet and the stock lost money; or, you wish to ring the register, cash in on your profit, and take the money and go shopping! (Nothing wrong with that! A girl has got to have some fun in life.)

Rule 8   Wall Street is a form of legalized gambling. (Shhh – don't say it too loud!) Yes, truly it can be. Everyday people place bets whether the price of a security will go up or down. Use it to your advantage! Know the rules to stay in the game. Always live to fight another day by playing it safe and not betting your entire nest egg on the next "hot" stock that suddenly goes out of favor. Remember, the "Trend is your Friend." Fads come and go quickly as with clothing.

Rule 9   Patience is a virtue. Give your investment a realistic time frame to perform the way you are expecting it to. The day after you sell your stock, it will probably go up.

Rule 10 Don't be a pig! Just because some is good doesn't always mean more is better. In fact, don't invest more than 5% in any one individual stock. This way, your portfolio won't become imbalanced. Just like a balanced diet keeps your body fit and helps to reduce outside radicals from attacking it. So too, a balanced portfolio can keep your overall investment portfolio from becoming diseased by outside elements beyond your control.

Platinum Tip: *Nobody ever went broke by taking a profit; but, you can go broke by taking too many losses!*

Soul Searching

Do some soul searching to figure out what types of products and services you have an interest in. You will always do better and feel better about your investment decisions if you actually can relate to the company. That is, you should actually like and believe in a product or service to purchase it. If you particularly dislike a product or service then you might consider selling it short or just not purchasing it. For example, some people view oil and tobacco firms and companies that chop down the rainforest or exploit child labor in developing economies as immoral. Others take views on what they consider politically or socially correct and do not wish to invest in a firm that does not conduct business in a manner which they (the investor) feel is morally, politically or socially correct. For these investors, the Ave Maria Funds or the Eventide Family of Funds could be a good investment choice. This Family of Funds invests according to the ideals and teachings consistent with the Catholic and Protestant faiths. Today, there are also "green" funds and many other funds along these lines to choose from.

Platinum Tip: *Be mindful of insider trading rules. Always remember, as a stock investor, you are a partial owner of that company. Politicians get ousted from their lofty positions for investing in companies and then taking an interest in a company by casting their vote for/against through bills and legislation. Business professionals, like Martha Stewart, have been sentenced to jail for insider trading.*

Diversify using Products you Like, Relate to, and Understand

For example: Make two columns on a piece of paper. In one column are products, services and companies that you like and understand. In the second column are products, services and companies that you dislike, know nothing about and don't ever care to know anything about.

Column 1: What do I Like? (Products, Services or Companies)	Column 2: What do I Dislike? (Products, Services or Companies)
Retail (jewelry, clothing, shoes, handbags)	Oil Refineries
Food (cereal, fast food, Italian food)	Tobacco Companies
Automobiles (Mercedes, Toyota Prius)	Waste Management

Once you think about what products and services you like and can relate to or given your employment position can buy and sell readily without repercussions due to a conflict of interest, write them down on a piece of paper. Now consider how you can balance your portfolio through diversification. This way, if one security goes down, hopefully, the others in your portfolio are different enough that they won't go down as well. Say for instance, you like high-end retailers. Instead of picking one high-end retailer, you loaded up on Tiffany's, Harry Winston, Saks Fifth Avenue, etc. If Tiffany's caught the flu and did poorly one quarter, the entire sector of high-end retailers could go down in sympathy to Tiffany's doing poorly. However the reverse is also true. Tiffany's could hit a home run in the eyes of the analysts and increase its sales and overall market share dramatically. In this case, Tiffany's could lift prices of the other stocks in the high-end retailer sector significantly.

Sometimes, however, securities will go up or down out of sympathy just because the overall market goes up or down. Here we will use the example of The Limited, Ann Taylor, Talbots and J. Crew. The Limited (owner of Victoria's Secret, The Limited and other stores) is currently listed on the New York Stock Exchange (ticker symbol: LTD) and can also be purchased as part of an index of securities called the S&P 500. For example, the U.S. economy begins to falter. People begin to lose their jobs. The S&P 500 Index goes down. Even though all the news and earnings look good for The Limited, the overall market and economy is forcing investors to sell the index and therefore they put selling pressure on The Limited's stock price as well.

Consider also if the asset is *correlated* or *non-correlated*. Tiffany, Harry Winston, and DeBeers demonstrate how highly correlated assets can be. These three companies are highly correlated because all three make high-end jewelry. Saks Fifth Avenue, J. Crew, and Marshalls, on the other hand, are less correlated even though they are in the same industry. Although all three are retailers, one is considered very high-end, one middle market, and the third low-end. A food company such as General Mills, an oil company like Exxon, and Dillard's department stores would be considered non-correlated securities if purchased together because they are considered to be in very different industries.

Next, figure out if the asset is *cyclical*, *secular*, *counter cyclical* or *noncyclical*. Stocks perform in certain patterns. For instance, sales at a gardening company like Miracle Grow will normally increase significantly during the summer months because people are more inclined to spruce up their gardens when it is warm outside as opposed to the winter months. The same is true for most amusement parks like Six Flags. These companies' stocks would be considered *secular*.

Cyclical: stocks tend to rise quickly when the economy turns to the upside and can fall quickly when the economy takes a downturn. Examples include: housing, automobiles, and paper.

Secular: stocks that move in a long-term pattern and follow seasonal trends or cyclical time frames.

Counter Cyclical: stocks that move in the opposite direction to a cyclical stock.

Non-Cyclical: stocks are not as directly affected by an economic change. Examples include: foods, insurance and drugs.

You can't control everything in your life. Investor and analyst sentiment, market sentiment, company profits and outlooks can all take their toll on your security, leave the stock in idle or catapult the stock's price beyond your wildest dreams!

Many securities behave like being on a roller coaster. They will hit 52 week highs (peaks) and 52 week lows (troughs) fast and frequently giving you whiplash along the way. If you can figure out the pattern and timing of when to buy and sell, however, a fortune is yours for the taking. Technology, Biotech, Big Pharma & Drug companies are notorious for this type of behavior. Likewise, many new IPOs (initial public offerings) exhibit this trait as well. The example below shows the stock price pattern of Shoes Unlimited, Inc.

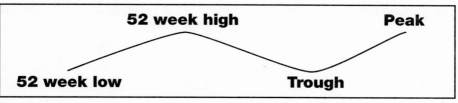

Other securities behave like a slow moving choo choo train. U.S. government bonds, preferreds (preferred stocks), utility and telecom stocks (like Con Ed and AT&T), and even many "Blue Chip Stocks" (like P&G and IBM) generally behave in a slower moving *secular* fashion.

Slow and steady... I think I can, I think I can!

KNL

Some securities are / or perform like a "going out of business sale." This type of behavior can last for years before the stock regains some of its mojo (i.e. Morgan Stanley - stock ticker MS) or eventually meets the grim reaper with a slow death (like Montgomery Ward). The security can also crash and burn; whereby very suddenly, the security can plummet to a zero or near zero dollar price tag (like Bear Stearns and Lehman Brothers).

Rocket to the Moon

A small group of stocks are considered "high flyers." Small biotech drug companies attempting to get FDA approvals fit into this category. In addition, many small companies are listed on the *pink sheets* (named this because the actual paper was pink) in addition to some over-the-counter stocks. But be careful, what goes up usually must come down. These high flyers can fall from their lofty levels just as quickly as they rocketed to the moon. The gravity of ill-sentiment and grave market performance can send them crashing!

Finding your Financial Center

In finding your financial center you should be reflective and intro-spective. Analyze what *your* needs are, what *your* goals are in life, and consider what is really important in *your* life. Everyone has different goals and desires. What makes one person happy won't necessarily make you fulfilled and happy. To achieve your financial goals there are three different investment approaches that you can take: 1. "Hands-Off" Approach, 2. "Laissez-Faire" Approach, or 3. "Hands-On" Approach. Which investment approach best suits you and your lifestyle?

Alternative 1: "Hands-Off" Approach

If watching a financial program bores you, and reading books, newspa-pers, and magazines on investing put you to sleep (of course not ours!);

then, your best investment alternative is to look towards CDs, Insured Money Market Accounts and U.S. Government Bonds. These are normally considered to be safer investments and usually require little oversight and monitoring.

CDs (Certificates of Deposits) vary with maturity lengths and pay a yield or interest rate on your money at an insured bank or lending institution. You can also purchase CDs through a brokerage account as part of an overall investment portfolio.

Make sure the CD is issued from an insured bank or institution. If the company goes bankrupt, your money will be insured by either SIPC or the FDIC and you will at least get your principle back. Otherwise, you could find yourself "up a creek without a paddle!" Also, check the insured limits at the bank or institution. You may need to distribute them between several banks or set up several accounts under the same bank or institution to keep them under the insured limits.

> **Platinum Tip:** *The only free lunch in town! Consider taking some of the cash out of your zero interest earning checking account that you do not really need to pay immediate bills with and stagger the maturities on 3 or 4 different (one month or 30-day) CDs. If you do this, you can have a 1 month CD maturing every week. This way you will never have to redeem one of them before the redemption date and pay a penalty if you need to spend the money in your checking account, although the penalty would be very minimal. The earnings at first glance might not look that significant but if you add up the interest over a full one or two month period of the 3 or 4 CDs that you take out, you will see that it will buy you at least a free lunch every week just from the interest. For simplicity, you can set it up for automatic renewal to make it hassle free.*

IMMAs (Insured Money Market Accounts) can be invested in at your local bank or through a brokerage account. Look to see what type of money market account you are investing in, because the tax repercussions could eat away all of your interest earned. These accounts earn a small amount of interest and should be very liquid to enable you to take your hard earned cash out immediately when you need it.

U.S. Government Bonds (Treasuries or "U.S. Govies" as they are affectionately called on the trading floor) are explained in great detail in **Part**

2, Chapter 14: Bonding with a Bond). U.S. government bonds can be purchased through a commercial bank, online through TreasuryDirect, or through a brokerage account. Basically, they are considered to be a very safe investment alternative and are backed by the U.S. government. Politics aside, the theory is that if the U.S. fails, these bonds would fail, but then, the entire world would most likely be bankrupt as well so it wouldn't matter – would it? Therefore, these securities are as safe as the U.S. government. The maturities range from months to years.

Bills - are short-term securities with maturities of one year or less the Treasury bills are issued at a discount to the face value. Treasury bills have been the primary instrument used by the Federal Reserve to regulate the *Money Supply* through open market operations.

Notes - are intermediate-term securities with maturities of 1 to 10 years. Treasury notes are denominated in ranges from $1,000 to $1,000,000 plus.

Bonds - are long-term debt instruments with maturities of 10 years or longer. They are issued in minimum denominations of $1,000. You can purchase U.S. Treasury bonds on the internet through the U.S. government or by purchasing a mutual bond fund or a non-managed bond fund.

Alternative 2: The "Laissez-Faire" Approach
If, however, you like the idea of dabbling in the marketplace with some of your assets, but you don't want to spend more than a few hours a week doing research and reading up on the companies you choose; then, preferred stock, some fixed income products and utility stocks are probably more to your liking. Make sure that you top up your 401(k) and IRA every year and allocate your money to funds that replicate the major indices like the S&P 500, DOW, NASDAQ, Russell 2000, as well as, investing in some U.S. government bond funds. Watch the news and look to reposition your allocations, depending on longer-term market trends.

Alternative 3: The "Hands-On" Approach
Time dedicated becomes more like a second job or hobby. You find the thrill in investing and the pursuit of finding "that" stock! You look for securities that will set you up for retirement or that will enable you to buy that Rolls Royce (powder blue convertible with the creamy white

interior, and hand stitched leather seats) that you always dreamed of. Setting high investment goals for yourself gets your juices flowing. If you can relate to this, then the "Hands-On Approach" is for you! Seek out the *FT*, *WSJ*, *Barron's*, *Value Line* and financial magazines like *Fortune*, etc. Watch many market focused television shows and imbibe in internet market and company news stories. Sign up for company conference calls that you can listen into as a stock holder. Become a sponge and soak up as much market and company knowledge as you can. Follow the companies you are interested in closely. Study their charts and read the analysts' ratings. That is what the traders do. They are news junkies!

Your Investment Time Horizon

The next thing is to consider your time frame. Are you a patient or impatient person? Again, be introspective. If you are patient, then you can invest for a 5, 10 or 20 year time horizon. If you are a highly impatient person, then you are probably a "day trader" or a "minute by minute trader". Although the term "day trader" was given the scarlet letter to wear in recent years, in reality, most large institutional bond and equity traders do a fair amount of this type of trading.

The patient person will follow the Peter Lynch (a Fidelity market guru) approach to investing. Peter Lynch (the Fidelity market guru) suggests a *buy and hold* approach. This approach emphasizes the logic that the individual / retail investor is at a disadvantage to the large institutional trader. The individual / retail investor will have to weather the storms over a longer investment horizon and reinvest their dividends on the securities they hold to make a profit over time. Otherwise, individuals will euphorically buy at the high and panic sell at the low. They will normally act at the wrong time during the market cycle.

Louis Rukeyser, the commentator of *Wall Street Week*, aired for over a decade on PBS. He was the first main stream show dedicated to picking the brains of the Wall Street gurus. The language used by these Wall Street rocket scientists was put into laymen's terms so the average retail investor could understand the overall concepts and investment strategies. Of all the investment strategies that were aired on his show, Louis Rukeyser always made the point that time is your ally. He always told his audience to forget the market gyrations and short-term rallies and troughs: instead focus on the long-term. It really did not matter if you invested at the top or the bottom of a particular bull or bear market. It only mattered that you invested in the S&P 500 and held it for many years to come – until you were ready for retirement! Louis was a much liked and highly regarded person in this field and his market theory still holds true to this day. The reason is simple. The S&P 500 monitors the pulse of America's larger companies.

Financial Self-Analysis

Be honest and true with yourself. Assess your financial goals, be realistic with your expectations, and then decide on a plan to achieve those financial goals. Naturally going from zero to a million dollars may seem like a pipe dream. However, if you really put your mind and intellect to achieving that goal, it is not impossible. But, you must be very diligent in your savings and investing in order to attain that dream.

Be realistic in your investment approach and know your own strengths, weaknesses, and amount of time you can truly allocate to learning about the markets and investing wisely. A wise decision on your behalf (you may conclude) is to hire a financial advisor that you trust and can speak candidly with. These decisions you make will affect your future lifestyle and financial success. Look at the illustration below and envision yourself as that woman. Which best describes you? (Hint: No answer is incorrect! But, one describes you best!)

The quality of a person's life is in direct proportion to their commitment to excellence, regardless of their chosen field of endeavor.

— Vince Lombardi

Your true passion should feel like breathing: it is that natural.

— Oprah Winfrey

The harder you work, the luckier you get.

— Gary Player

Behold the turtle. He makes progress only when he sticks his neck out.

— James B. Conant

The Financial G Spot

In the film *When Harry Met Sally*, Sally was thinking about something entirely different in that infamous scene.

(Sally was really thinking about her financial windfall from a recent transaction she had received good news about on her mobile phone.)

Sorry Harry!

KNL

Chapter 2

Find your Financial G Spot:

We guarantee Men don't know where to find It Nor know where It is neither!

The History of the G Spot

The origin of the *G Spot* goes back to 1944 in Germany when Dr. Ernst Graefenberg, an obstetrician and gynecologist (OBGYN), collaborated with a prominent American OBGYN, Robert L. Dickinson, whom many referred to as the first American sexologist. They described a zone of erogenous feeling for women.

In 1950, Dr. Graefenberg wrote an article about the existence of this sensitive area in women and he was the first scientist to suggest how important this area could be for women. A German gynecologist, Dr. Graefenberg, described this area in a paper published in 1950 – though his findings were largely ignored. In honor of Dr. Graefenberg, Perry and Whipple named the area the "Graefenberg spot" or simply, the "G Spot." The rediscovery and acceptance of the G Spot opened up a new dimension of sexual pleasure for women and were contrary to earlier researchers' claims.

Fast forwarding a few decades later (John D. Perry and Beverly Whipple both PhDs) in 1980 at a national meeting of the Society for the Scientific Study of Sex, these two delivered a lecture at the conference regarding the Graefenberg Spot referencing Dr. Ernst Graefenberg who was the first modern physician to describe it. Part of their findings as told to the group was that the spot was found in every woman they had examined and as a result of stimulation of the G Spot women often have a series of orgasms. Although this was not the first time that Perry and Whipple had presented their data, it was a historic moment in the field of sexual research because previously the findings were met with tension and discord at earlier meetings of the society. They truly created a stir in the medical field with their research findings.

Then, in 1982, Beverly Whipple and John Delbert Perry collaborated with Alice Kahn Ladas and co-authored *The G Spot and Other Discoveries about Human Sexuality*. The book started a revolution. It single-handedly ushered in a new era of research on female sexuality, radically changed the professional practice of sex therapists, and positively affected the lives of millions of individual women today.

What was so revolutionary about this researchers approach? Simple, rather than telling women what they "should feel", these authors asked women what they "were feeling". Then, rather than assuming women's responses would fit into a model established by men's experiences, they defined women's experiences on their own terms. What they learned was ground breaking! They discovered that far from adhering to a set pattern, women responded in a variety of ways. They learned in short that there is no one way for women to be sexual, and no one uniform pattern of sexual response. Listening to women describe their experiences led the researchers to their first major contribution to the field of female sexuality: the rediscovery of a sensitive spot that can be felt through the anterior wall of the vagina.

Many of today's modern women may be unaware of the scientific origin and historic studies concerning the discovery of the G Spot, however, they surely appreciate the pleasures associated with the G Spot!

Why do we use the G Spot to demonstrate and describe a woman's "Financial G Spot?"

Just as the Graefenberg studies discovered that women don't adhere to a set pattern when it comes to their individual G Spot, women also don't adhere to a set pattern when it comes to their *Financial G Spot* (a term coined in this book) either, according to our study that was performed. Our study conducted on a sample group of women having a range of socio, racial, and economic backgrounds responded in a variety of ways.

What turns one woman on financially can be different from what turns another woman on financially. No two women are exactly the same. Also, many financial advisors tend to dictate "advise" women what they "should" invest in. These same financial advisors should instead be listening to women. They should be asking these women what they would like to invest in, what makes them comfortable, and how they "feel" about certain investment styles and investment products. Hopefully we will start a new revelation in the financial world: the *Financial G Spot!*

The Financial G Spot

The G Spot is what gives *gratification* to women. The G Spot brings pleasure, satisfaction, and resolution as well.

Just as the Sexual Response Cycle, as defined by the book *The G Spot and other Discoveries about Human Sexuality* is characterized by desire, arousal and finally resolution; so too is investing in your future.

1. First, you desire an investment opportunity.
2. Next, you become aroused by the possibility of making a profit or being successful.
3. Finally comes the resolution of success, failure, or mediocrity.

Similar to Graefenberg's findings and his discovery of a woman's sexual G Spot, finding your *Financial G Spot* is also revolutionary. For example, one of the women interviewed, in our study, spent the last ten years buying, refurbishing, and selling older homes at a profit. She felt that her niche in real estate created happiness and gratification for her through the years. She successfully meshed her creative talents with her money making capabilities. Another study participant interviewed revealed that she had worked at the state department almost her entire working career because she believed that slow and steady would win the race in investing for her retirement. She didn't want the stress that went along with many high powered positions and instead sought out an employer that would employ her for life, actually required that she took her vacation time, albeit paying lower wages than many other positions she could have found employment with. She felt that in the end, the security of knowing her job would always be there and the retirement and investment programs that a government job provided brought her financial gratification and job satisfaction – thereby satisfying her

Financial G Spot.

We set out to discover what women viewed as financially satisfying. Rather than telling women what they should feel about their finances and investments, women had very definitive ideas of their own. They were able to pinpoint which investments and styles of investing brought them the greatest degree of happiness and satisfaction. The results of our study are summarized below.

The Investment Satisfaction Study Findings

- Our study revealed that what women "should select for their investments," isn't necessarily "what they feel comfortable, happy or satisfied with."

- Many women went to financial meetings and felt intimidated by financial advisors and were even afraid to ask questions for fear of looking naive or uneducated.

- Rather than assuming women's responses would fit into a model established by men's financial experiences, women define their financial experiences differently by using their own terms.

- Women also define the success of their investments in terms other than money. For instance, does the investment provide great self-esteem or offer social acceptance? For some women, helping other women prosper in third world countries becomes their investment passion. For these women, their investment fulfills two goals: one, a charity aspect of "paying it forward," and second, they invest in a company in an emerging market country that could pay off handsomely in the future.

- Women are more intuitive than men and that reflects in their investment choices as well. Women tap into their "women's intuition" and not only to the facts and figures placed before them.

- We discovered that far from adhering to a set investment style, women responded to a variety of ways. We discovered that there is no one way for a woman to invest; one size does not fit all! Just like clothing and shoes, not all women wear a size 7. Some wear Hush Puppies and comfortable loafers while others prefer killer stiletto heels. So, why should all women want to invest in the same way or in the same company?

- There is no one uniform investment pattern that consistently reaps financial success over time. Instead, there are many. Investment patterns also change over time. So too, women change over time like a fine bottle of wine.

In summary, what we learned in our study was highly insightful. By listening to women describe their investment experiences, this led us to our conclusion: Women's investment satisfaction varies as greatly as their sexual satisfaction!

Platinum Tip: *No two women are exactly alike: women's investment satisfaction varies as greatly as their sexual satisfaction!*

Why Women struggle to achieve Financial Gratification

Women struggle to achieve *financial gratification* for many reasons. Some of the most obvious reasons are outlined below. Once again, they are highly correlated to the same reasons women don't achieve sexual satisfaction or gratification in the bedroom.

- Women too often outsource their investment decisions and let the men do all the work.

- Women sit back and let the men conduct all the business. (Like in bed many women can be lazy and let the man do all the work. You have to be an active participant. If you aren't you can't complain that you weren't satisfied!)

- Women don't participate (enough in financial decision making).

- Women need to be more hands on (with their investments).

- Women should discover what turns them on in investments too.

- Women can and should practice investment strategies before they actually invest with their own money to see if the strategy works. (Experimentation should not just be limited to the bedroom!)

- Women normally choose a spouse or partner to share their life with very carefully. So too, women should be extremely choosey when selecting business partners and financial partners. Women should only enter into "business marriages" by using much of the same criteria that they hold true for a spouse in order for the relationship to work.

Platinum Tip: *There has to be an element of trust. Don't go to bed with just any Tom, Dick, or Harry...or John, Billy or Bob for that matter! Just because they sweet talked you and tried to seduce you, doesn't mean they are the right guy for life. It might turn out to be a one night stand. Likewise, don't invest with someone you don't entirely know or completely trust with your best and most sensitive assets – your money!*

The Effects of Viagra and Investing

Ever wonder what studies have been done regarding the effect on men taking Viagra and then making investment decisions? Do you really want your spouse or your financial advisor investing on your behalf when he could be under the influence? You are likely to end up owning some racy or unmentionable stock in your portfolio!

Undesirable Bed Mates

As the saying goes, "you are responsible for your own orgasm." Translating it into financial terms, you are responsible for your own investment decisions. These choices will culminate in orgasmic and lucrative successes or most likely complete failure if left to chance. Just look at the recent business scandals involving: Madoff, Sandford, Moody, Nadel, etc. Were these bed mates thoroughly checked for financial venereal diseases? They gave everyone a bad dose of financial herpes and other financially transmitted diseases. They infected a great number of innocent people and inflicted them with significant emotional trauma, financial devastation, and losses unimaginable. Some of it was not curable in their portfolios by just a simple penicillin shot. In fact, some people could never recover due to their age and circumstances.

Was the SEC (the financial condom) that should have protected the unassuming public from financial disease, portfolio destruction, and complete ruin? In these cases the SEC "condom" offered little protection to these people whose portfolios were permanently infected and affected.

Platinum Tip: *Investing should be treated like dating: if you don't like the relationship you are in, dump them!*

Money and Sex

The oldest profession in the world (prostitution) revolves around money and sex. Money has a lot in common with sex.

- Men can fail to satisfy their partner's financial desires just as they can fail in the bedroom.

- Money problems are one of the top 3 reasons why couples divorce and so is sex.

- Money, like sex, is a powerful motivator and can force people do things they normally wouldn't do.

- Money, like sex, can entrap you and make you stay in a bad relationship.

- A lot of emotional attachment is given to money and sex. Separation anxiety can occur.

- Money and great sex can liberate you to indulge in more fulfilling relationships.

- Money puts you in the driver's seat. You call the shots. You can end up with a smile on your face. A smile that your cryptic ex-husband would never have understood!

Platinum Tip: *Love, marriage and financial partnerships all require women to "Know when to hold them, know when to fold them, know when to walk away, and know when to run!"*

Discover your Financial G Spot

Although some may consider the comparison of the *Financial G Spot* to the *G Spot* as a bit "odd" especially for women who didn't grow up in the generation that the book first came out in. However, the women from this generation can highly relate to the comparisons made in this chapter. Even if you are not from that generation, I'm sure that you will admit: no two women are the same, we do not think like men, nor are our needs and requirements all the same. So, why should the way we consider investments be the same?

Other comparisons are easy to extract as well and are summarized in this chapter. Emotion, psyche, mood, satisfaction, gratification, feeling happy, comfortable, and yes even "love" come into play when investing.

You can "love" a stock so much that you can't bear to sell it even when the outlook isn't good and the stock has been terrible to your portfolio. Your "love" for the company or product may be so great that you hang on to it. You believe the stock (price) will change over time, come around, and things will get better. Sound familiar to a relationship?

Traders on Wall Street try to take the emotion out of trading a security. They say it is a sure recipe for getting "hurt." This is true. However, most people outside of Wall Street have great difficulty with this concept (as do professional traders). The emotions are always there, even for the trader that tries not to experience any. Sure some of these traders trade in the nanosecond and can be "in and out" of a trade extremely fast and therefore experience less emotion to the actual security. Others, however, hold on to a security trying to capture a trend or price movement in the market. Those that hold onto securities do experience great emotion when buying and selling them, even though they try not to. That is why the trading pits and trading floors are full of great emotion and shouting. I've witnessed personally the good, the bad, and the ugly of traders' emotions running rampant on the trading floors such as: phone lines disconnected to "pull the plug" on a broker, breaking phones in anger, pounding on desks, screaming in joy or anger, jubilant "high fives," etc. If this isn't emotion, I'm not sure what is!

For most individual investors, trading in a short-term time horizon or a long-term time horizon involves "getting married" and having a "good relationship" with their investments, overall portfolio, and investment advisor (so to speak). Individual investors are naturally going to exhibit emotion when ending a long lasting relationship with a good, tried and true friend (stock) in their portfolio or with a financial representative they have used for years.

This book will help to guide you through the world of finance and investing so you can ultimately discover for yourself which financial strategies and choices will turn you on, satisfy your desires, and give you the ultimate orgasmic financial gratification possible! By the end of this book, we hope that you will have discovered your *Financial G Spot*! After all, it's only human to have emotions about investing.

Platinum Tip: *Money knows no loyalty! (...but people do)*

In everyone's life, at sometime, our inner fire goes out.
It is then burst into flame by an encounter with another human being.
We should all be thankful for those people who rekindle
the human spirit.

— Unknown

Get your mind set...confidence will lead you on

— Fortune Cookie

Men are a luxury. Not a necessity.

— Cher

Pleasure of love lasts but a moment.
Pain of love lasts a lifetime.

— Bette Davis

Smart, Sexy, Savvy
& Broke

KNL
&
FBJ

Chapter 3

Smart, Sexy, Savvy, and ....Broke?

Are you, smart, sexy, savvy, and....broke? If so, the following chapter is for you; and if not, these tips may further your financial autonomy and keep you from falling into a financial trap. Debt is most likely the reason you are now broke. Not lack thereof!

How did you become Smart, Sexy, Savvy, and.....Broke?

Whether you are just out of college and saddled with student loans, divorced and penniless because you were taken to the cleaners by your spouse, a victim of domestic abuse and you are starting over from scratch, or the victim of irresponsible spending habits that have led to financial disaster and you've checked yourself into shopaholics anonymous, fret not, help is on the way! Many smart, sexy, savvy women find themselves at one point or another in their life flat broke. Or, at least many women feel that they are broke or barely getting by - living paycheck to paycheck.

In the blink of an eye, life in the big city can easily seduce money out of your wallet. Tempting, sparkling baubles; the latest super, sexy Christian Dior black suede boots; or even the newest trendsetting outfit in pages of this month's Vogue magazine can easily empty your pocket book of all your hard earned cash. Living paycheck to paycheck is no fun! You feel like a laboratory rat on a treadmill, never earning more than you spend. You never even feel able to save a dime to put towards your retirement future or rainy day fund. Life gets in the way and bills accumulate.

Attempting to keep yourself in the lifestyle in which you've become accustomed can be trying at times. Achieving a better lifestyle can be even more financially complicated. Never thinking of paying things completely off on your credit cards, debt begins to mount. The only payment you religiously make is paying off the interest on your credit card. Paying off the principal, interest and fees becomes impossible because there are always more temptations in sight to spend your salary on. Finally one day, you ask yourself, how did I get myself in this financial pickle? Or worse yet, how was I forced into declaring bankruptcy when I am so smart, so sexy, and I thought ever so savvy?

People in real life do make mistakes. Life can throw you a curve ball now and again. Other people can negatively affect your finances too. Having an ex-husband (the louse) who spent all your savings, racked up credit card bills, and leveraged the house on a "no brainer" get rich scheme or losing your fabulous job in the height of your career is like having a financial rug yanked out from under you. Or, perhaps your ex-business partner secretly hid a great deal of your combined assets (unbeknownst to you) while this business partner was in charge of managing the money in the firm. No matter the excuse, the questions still remain: why did you do something this dumb? Why did you let something this dumb happen to you? And how do you dig yourself out of this mess and get your finances back to even?

You need to free yourself from the ties that bind you; namely debt. And, for most of us, it begins with credit card debt because it is too easy to use and forget about until the ominous bill arrives via email or snail mail.

This chapter will help you to learn to forgive yourself, learn from your financial mistakes and prosper.

Single & Broke

Example 1: I have a friend who has lived in a nice neighborhood in the same house for 25 years, belongs to the "in" country club, and has two cars parked in the garage. One car is a sexy convertible and the other a practical work car. She is paying off both car loans plus a mortgage on her house. Now, however, her house is being foreclosed on because she can't make the mortgage payments. Do you see a problem in prioritizing here?

She can resolve her debt problem and keep face in her community by following three easy steps:

Step 1: Sell the impractical car – sorry! She needs to learn to prioritize and that means selling the sexy convertible and keeping the practical car to transport clients to look at real estate for her job.

Step 2: Ask the country club if there are less expensive types of membership: change from a full membership to a social or associate membership to help reign in expenses.

Step 3: Ask a mortgage broker if there is a way to refinance the mortgage payment or inquire whether the mortgage can be extend from a 20 year to a 30 year maturity length. This should result in smaller monthly payments.

By following these three easy steps, she will have additional funds to repay her mortgage, while still enjoying her country club lifestyle and the home sweet home she has come to love. *Lifestyle and finances left intact!*

> **Platinum Tip:** *Be the "Queen" of your cash and castle! Lighten up on the debt that drags you down and that keeps you awake worrying at night. Lack of sleep will age you not only on the inside but also on the outside. You will have fewer stress lines across your forehead, and stress related weight gain. And, you won't have to go in for costly Botox injections to repair the stress lines across your forehead if you take steps to eliminate the financial stresses in your life.*

Married & Broke

Newly married once, twice or thrice? Or, have you been married to the old ball and chain for years? Do you now find yourself in the "for worse" category of the marriage vows and the "for better" category ended quickly after the honeymoon ended? (Yes, it happens to the best of us!) You can help yourself and help your spouse climb out of the money pit you both helped to dig by following some of the helpful tips found in the following 3 examples.

Example 1: Another friend has a husband who has three junk automobiles, two small fishing boats, a monthly mortgage payment, and no job. What a dead beat for a husband (but the sex was out of this world)! His devoted and highly attractive wife "married him for better, for worse." (In this luck of the draw – she got the worse!) He has maxed out his credit cards and owes the IRS for back taxes, penalties and interest. He is thinking of declaring bankruptcy over an amount of close to $60,000, however, he will still owe the IRS for all the back taxes owed. What is the solution to resolve this personal debt crisis? If she divorces him, she inherits half the debt. If she stays with him, she has to force him to pay off his debt. All is not lost, however, if he (with some not so gentle forceful nagging from her) follows the steps below.

Step 1: Sell the extra-curricular activity / hobby items such as boats and electrical gadgets around the house that only collect dust.

Step 2: Get rid of at least two of the junk cars and downsize to one car. Or alternatively, sell all three of the rattletrap automobiles and with those proceeds buy one decent car for going to interviews and potentially a full time job.

Step 3: Make sure the mortgage payment is current so that creditors cannot foreclose on the house.

Step 4: Have an estate sale, garage sale, or tag sale. Use the proceeds from the sale of things he doesn't use around the house to pay off the back taxes owed. (Taxes never go away and they will haunt you to your grave and beyond.) Depending on what items are just sitting and collecting dust around the house, you can take several courses of action. One, you can call in antique dealers or estate sale dealers to determine what his "treasures" are really worth. Two, you can list the items in a local newspaper under the "For Sale" ad section. Three, you can go to a local pawn shop and see what price they will pay for your partner's "treasures." Four, you can market them on the internet auction site EBay.

Step 5: Negotiate with his credit card companies to take off penalties and interest owed. This also applies to the IRS. Also, he might be able to negotiate a settlement amount if he pays off the card and / or the IRS all at once or in installment amounts.

Step 6: Sell items he doesn't really need around the house (or perhaps even items he pays to keep in a storage unit and visit from time to time). He will probably find that he can then pay off a huge chunk, if not all, of the credit card debt he owes. *Debt Crisis averted!*

Platinum Tip: *"One woman's junk is another woman's treasure" and is money in the smart, sexy, savvy woman's pocket book! Never underestimate the treasures that lie around your house. You just might uncover your retirement nest egg. The television show "Antique Road Show" often finds more value in items than the owner knew it to be worth.*

Example 2: A new, fire engine red, Harley Davidson motorcycle just roared into your driveway! Your husband proceeds to tell you that the vacation you both had long planned for is now off because he has just purchased his childhood dream which was more important. What do you do? Although difficult, putting the kibosh on a controlling spouse or significant other is not impossible.

> *Step 1:* First try to reason with him. Tell him the Harley is a depreciating asset. The vacation, on the other hand, would create once in a lifetime memories that the two of you would talk about for a lifetime. And, it could rekindle a sagging romance.

> *Step 2:* Tell him to take the Harley back or you are entitled to spend the exact same amount of money to buy something that you have always wanted. *Dream Buster averted!*

Platinum Tip: *"What is good for the goose is good for the gander." Don't let him rain on your parade. You both worked hard for that money. Just as he is entitled to realize and obtain his dreams, so are you!*

Example 3: Your husband put all your savings in a "get-rich-quick scheme" that blows up overnight. What do you do – cry, scream, or get even? No, you get smart, sexy, and savvy – really quick!

> *Step 1:* Call the Better Business Bureau, your local congressman, senator or attorney general for help. Depending on what the "get-rich-scheme" is, you might want to visit the police station.

> *Step 2:* Seek a lawyer's advice. Be first in line for a claim. An initial consultation is normally free or at a very minimal cost.

> *Step 3:* If no recourse is warranted or granted then you must "pick yourself up, dust yourself off, and start all over again!" The *"Get-Rich-Quick Scam Survival Kit"* consisting of a stiff drink, a box of

chocolates, and jogging can all help to calm your nerves, refocus, and help *"think"* your way out of the mess! *Survived the Scam!*

Types of Debt that can zap your Savings

Debt, very simply defined, is the negative difference between income and spending. If you can increase your income through raises, bonuses, commissions, or a second job – that is a terrific start. If you, like millions, cannot increase your income because you are stuck in a rut at your job, look to your spending habits and try to "nip and tuck" where you can. You're spending must be cut down to make ends meet. Just remember, you cannot spend yourself solvent. And, more debt will just make you feel miserable about yourself.

Dealing with Debt that can make you Broke

First, assess how much debt you really have. Also, assess the due dates on the debt you owe. Make a "T" chart by drawing a large letter T down the middle of a piece of paper. Above the left perpendicular line title it *Assets*. On the right side, title it either *Money Owed* or *Liabilities*. Be honest with yourself. Carefully detail every bank account, house or condo, automobile, piece of jewelry etc. that you can call an asset and that you owe nothing on. Then put down items you have partially paid down. Next, write down all of the credit card balances, mortgage amounts still outstanding, car loans owed, yearly insurance premiums, etc. that you must pay. This will provide you with a quick overview of your *Liabilities* (personal debt) versus your *Assets*. Are you ahead of the game and in the black, barely breaking even, or in the red and losing money?

Assets	Liabilities
House	Mortgage/House Payment
Business	Credit Card Debt
Jewelry	Doctors' Bills
Car	Car Lease Agreement

Types of Debt

Debt can attach itself to you in varying degrees and forms. Types of debt include: automobile payments, student loans, credit card debt, mortgages, new business or professional office start-ups, medical bills, store lay-away programs, home equity loans, margin accounts, personal I.O.U.s, and other unforeseeable types of loans you may have inherited or have incurred.

Automobile Leases & Payments: A sexy new, red convertible or a behemoth, gas guzzling yet "practical" SUV to haul around children and all their paraphernalia may tempt many consumers. In order to help reduce the temptation, consider them as transportation and not an image builder. Shop around for leases versus buying an automobile outright. Sometimes your cheaper option could be leasing the car as opposed to buying it. Leasing can often have business and tax advantages as well. If you lease a car, remember you do not own it. The dealership will usually fix, repair, or maintain your car at some or no cost to you during the life of the lease. This naturally excludes personal damages to the automobile. Dealerships are notorious for trying to talk you into buying new tires for your leased car at some point during your lease. Get a second opinion before you buy a whole new set.

Certain cars due to model type, color, and age may have much higher insurance premiums than others. Make sure you speak to your insurance company agent before purchasing your automobile to make sure you can afford both the monthly payment and the insurance premium. Beware the hot car that is selling for a premium over the asking ticket price. Also, if you purchase the car with cash, you will save on all the interest charges incurred in comparison to if you purchase it with a loan or lease agreement.

Student Loans: Be savvy when it comes to taking out a student loan and make sure you pay off your student loan debt in a timely fashion. Otherwise defaulting on the loan will cause you to carry a bad credit rating for a very long time and will prevent you from obtaining any other financing and loans. In addition, credit reports and overall credit history are an integral part of the hiring process for most companies today. On the other hand, if you pay off your debt obligations, you will be viewed favorably by future employers.

If you are in need of a student loan to fund either your own or your child's education, look towards grant money and scholarships first. It is "free" money and you don't have to pay it back. Go to your local bookstore, Amazon.com or various websites for information. Books will reference all of the different types of scholarships that are available. Websites too offer tons of information on applying for and obtaining many grants and scholarships. Some of these grants include Pell Grants that come from the federal government. Other private scholarships come from departments of education at your local university, numerous business organizations, charities, religious organizations and private family endowments such as the Bill Gates Foundation. The paperwork, application, and selection process can be grueling and should be treated like taking an extra class but it is highly worth it in the end. Not only is it great bragging rights having received such a prestigious scholarship(s); it also looks good on your resume to employers and will open many doors in your future.

There are many opportunities for single moms to go back to university, trade school, and graduate school as well. Look to Women's Resource Centers, YWCAs, college Student Affair offices, and books that focus on scholarship and grant sources at your local book store.

Credit Card Entrapment: Credit card debt is often the financial downfall for many women. Credit card balances are all too easy to rack up but are all so difficult and painful to pay off, due to their exorbitant interest charges. Keep a card with a low credit limit if possible in case the card gets stolen or you become a victim of identity theft. Credit cards should be kept for identification purposes as well as to develop and maintain a good credit rating so you can obtain a loan when you need it in the future. Pay it off each month so you don't incur any finance charges or interest charges. Credit cards should be used for convenience but not to turn you into a "debt junkie."

It's all too easy to become a "debt junkie" because the dealers (the banks behind the credit cards) seduce the average consumer into using their cards. Banks are in the business to make money. They can raise and lower their credit card rates whenever they choose. Although they must legally notify you in writing, who actually reads all those junk pieces of mail with the fine print that get stuffed in the mail box?

Loan sharks and usury rates start at 10% and are considered immoral. How is it legal, that credit card companies, especially many department store credit cards, get by with charging yearly interest rates in excess of 15%? Shouldn't that also qualify as usury?

Write on a piece of paper what your total debt owed on each of your credit cards are. Be honest with yourself and don't merely look at the minimal monthly payments that are due. It's the overall big number that can get you into trouble by lowering your overall credit rating and send you into a financial entrapment if circumstances change for the worse.

When you try to get out of debt, the rate of interest is everything. Consolidation of your debt is not only easier to manage but you should also consolidate and refinance it at a lower rate. Try to consolidate all of your high interest credit card balances into a lower interest rate environment by using a credit union or bank. They will be all too happy to work with you so don't feel embarrassed by asking.

Mortgages: Shop for mortgage rates and terms just as carefully as you would a new pair of shoes! If it is the *first* mortgage you have ever applied for, make sure that what the lender offers really suits your needs carefully, doesn't put a pinch in your lifestyle, or develops a blister on your budget. If you don't, you will be uncomfortable with your selection and won't like what you paid for. Unlike shoes, you will have to live with your bad taste and style choice of a mortgage for a very long time. You will not be able to return the mortgage or throw it away as easily as an ill fit pair of shoes. The bank can't stretch your agreement terms as easily as a shoe cobbler can adjust the ill fit pair of shoes. One size does not fit all when it comes to mortgage terms and agreements!

The monthly mortgage amount needs to be first and foremost an amount that you can easily live with. If it's not, you may want to consider a longer mortgage maturity. For example, instead of paying off your home in 10 years, it may make more sense for you to have a 30 year mortgage. Because the payment is spread out over 30 years, instead of say 10 years, the overall total interest amount that you will be paying is more; however, the principal and interest paid each month is less. If you want to pay less total interest overall and don't mind budgeting your money, a shorter term maturity may be the best for you.

If you already have a mortgage but are unhappy with the rate of payoff or the mortgage rate on the loan agreement, *refinancing* may be a good option for you. However, you will have to analyze *all* costs associated with the mortgage agreement carefully before signing on the dotted line. Make sure you read all documents including the fine print before making a decision. It might be worth checking to see if you can obtain a flat rate fee for a professional accountant or lawyer to review the mortgage agreement before you sign on the dotted line. It could be the best $200 you spend! Also remember, the costs associated with changing a mortgage agreement might outweigh the savings.

Your relationship with a lender is not a one night stand, remember, it is a long-term relationship that you cannot end easily! You will be "in bed with them" for years to come.

Liens: A lien (another four letter word) in general is never good. A lien is a legal claim against property that you own. It encumbers the title and restricts what you can and cannot do with the property. There are different types of liens. For example, most of us are familiar with *mortgages*, but did you know that a mortgage is a lien on your property? And, that it must be paid off, satisfied, or taken over by the new buyer before the property can be legally turned over to a new owner?

Another example of a lien is a *mechanics lien* against your property. This can occur from a handy man who thinks they were not paid for their services rendered on your property. You may have disputed the bill with the handyman, but did not check that he filed a lien on your property with the town (unbeknownst to you). When you go to sell your house, you discover that now you have to remove the lien prior to selling the house. Not sexy, not smart! These types of "surprise" debts can make you go broke! You should have had the handyman sign a statement saying you and he agreed to the negotiated fee so he couldn't come back to haunt you! Another very typical example of a mechanics lien can be instigated from a General Contractor (GC) that you hired to do a renovation or addition to your house. Unfortunately, the GC didn't pay his subs. The subs (electricians, plumbers, gardeners, etc.) file a lien against your property as they were unsuccessful in getting the money from the GC, even though you had paid the GC what was owed to him. Before you can sell your house, the lien must be satisfied.

> **Platinum Tip:** *Want to be smart, sexy, and savvy? Have the GC, subs, and the handyman from the previous example sign a lien waiver before they vacate your property premise. This will save you lots of headaches years later and will keep you from going broke!*

New Business or Professional Office Start-Ups: Great, you are starting a new business! Good for you! This may be money well spent as you endeavor to embark on a new business idea. First, make a budget to determine how much your new venture will cost you, and include the burn rate. Overhead, leases, utilities, décor, insurance, advertising, legal set-up of the business (LLC vs. a Corporation or S-Corp), belonging to trade organizations, etc., must all be factored into the overall cost of the new business.

Although some items are considered write-offs and tax deductions, the rules change constantly. Check with the IRS or a tax accountant to see what is covered and what is not. Even though it may be considered a tax "write-off," the money is still directly coming out of your Gucci wallet to pay for the company expenses in the beginning. Depending on the amount of incoming revenue, you may be the sole source of funding for your business for a very long time before it becomes profitable. You cannot take the tax write-offs until you have revenue to take them against. Some tax write-offs are amortized and depreciated over many years, some must be taken in the same year the expense was incurred, and others can't be written-off at all. Many people forget these simple facts. This is an area where very smart and sexy women go broke: they forget to be savvy! It is good to chase your dreams but you have to be savvy to fund the new business and keep it going. You don't have to have a Donald Trump style office from the get-go. So don't bite off more than you can chew.

Buying on Margin & Margin Calls: We do not recommend you do this as a smart, sexy, and savvy investor! The girl in this chapter's cartoon illustration is a perfect example of what can happen to you if you buy on margin and the stock price goes against you. Some people may like the raciness and the thrill of buying on margin but it can lead to the financial destruction of your hard earned nest egg. You could even lose your house to a margin call and end up on the curb in a tent with your coveted Jimmy Choo and Coach shoes!

The Love Triangle (You, Your Love Relationship, and Your Money): Don't be a love sucker: think with your head and not your heart (uh, or G-Spot!). Boyfriends and husbands come and go but the debt stays with you. Additionally, be careful not to outsource your investment and financial goals to your current flame to obtain for you; he may have his own agenda as to what to do with your money.

```
+-----------------------------------------------+
|                    You                        |
|                                               |
|                   LOVE                         |
|                 TRIANGLE                       |
|                                               |
| Your Love Relationship         Your Money     |
+-----------------------------------------------+
```

Additional Budget Whammies: You are smart and you are savvy but why do you find yourself continuing to feel broke? Is this because others are taking advantage of you and your good nature? Six examples of other *Budget Whammies* include:

Expensive Boyfriend that you are subsidizing: He never seems to have his credit card with him.

Expensive Adult Children: They have not returned to the nest but wish you to fund their nest. (Your children have all the latest computer and electronic models that have been launched in the last six months on your dime while your computer and television are over 10 years old.)

Expensive Husband: He sweet talks you into letting him spend your play money as well as his. (Instead of a spa day for you, he spent mucho money at a strip club.)

Treating or Picking up the Tab: Treating everyone all the time to lunch, dinner, and beyond. Let others treat you, too.

Paying too much Interest on Credit Cards, Mortgages, etc.: You want to own things and not owe things.

Loaning Money to Co-Workers, Relatives and Friends: A loan is a four letter word because you can never expect to get paid back. Wouldn't you rather spend the money on yourself?

The Credit Card Treadmill

Most women like to spend with credit cards because of the advantage of buy now, pay later. Also, it is normally safer not to carry all that cash with you. If your card gets lost or stolen, you can quickly cancel the card. However, if someone steals your wallet because they see all that cash in it, all that hard earned money is gone forever.

The problem with credit cards, however, is that they enable women to fall into a debt trap. This credit card spending scenario entraps many women and happens when women don't pay off the full amount owed each month. Instead, many women tend only to pay off the minimum payment due each month or simply forget to make a timely payment because life gets in the way. Debt, interest, and penalties start to accrue. You feel like you are stuck on a debt treadmill that never stops! This is the treadmill that will not make you skinny! You can't get off this debt treadmill because each paycheck received only goes to pay for past purchases.

The Credit Card Treadmill

Pay off Interest, Penalties, and only some past Purchases

Receive your Pay Check

KNL

8 Easy Ways to jump off the Credit Card Debt Treadmill:

1. Count how many cars you have in your garage and designer handbags in your closet. If you are in debt, get rid of the excess. You only need one car to drive and two handbags: one for spring / summer and one for fall / winter. Give the designer handbags to a consignment shop to sell them on your behalf. You can also sell an extra car or handbag by putting them up for auction on EBay. Or, a close friend or relative might be longing to purchase your cherished handbag and give it a good home.

2. Get a part-time job. Who knows, you may even meet that special someone!

3. Get a handle on your credit card debt. Apply for a loan with a lower interest rate from a bank. Pay off all the higher interest rate credit card debts that you have charged on by using the lower rate loan you have just taken out from the bank.

4. Go back to school to get a better paying job. Apply for grants and scholarships. This is also a great way to meet people!

5. Find someone wealthy to marry! (Sorry, but Bill Gates, Mitt Romney, Bill Clinton, and Mark Cuban are already taken.)

6. Make a diary of your spending habits for two weeks. Analyze where you could cut back. For example, make a cup of coffee at home and bring it to work instead of paying four bucks for a Starbucks. Even two buck chuck wine is cheaper! Check the blow dry bill at your local beauty salon – $40 dollars added in the cost of a color or high-light may entice you to blow your own hair dry at the salon. Think where else you would like to spend that money and set priorities! Rotate getting your nails professionally manicured with doing a quick do-it-yourself manicure. Wait for that latest fashion item to go on sale for a deep discount. You can buy twice as many clothes for the price of one outfit not on sale.

7. Find new forms of entertainment. Instead of a Broadway show or the Opera, take a class at Christies, a local university or continuing education program. Learning a new hobby and expanding your interests also make you more interesting and appealing. You might meet someone with your own interests and then you can eliminate Match.com and eHarmony from your expense budget!

8. Instead of hailing a cab or driving to work and paying for parking, gas, and tolls; why not consider, taking the subway, bus, or get some exercise by bicycling, jogging or walking to work. The ultimate in "multi-tasking" is to exercise and commute all at once. Think of the time you have saved and how fit you will be!

Achieving Financial Autonomy

Financial Autonomy provides freedom and peace of mind. One of the first steps of living a life with financial autonomy can be to rid yourself of debt – *all* forms of debt. Although some debt can be good and allows you to expand your business, purchase necessary and non-necessary items (like that must have piece of jewelry, handbag, or pair of shoes), it is important to always have more assets than debt. At any point in time if the debt is called in to be paid immediately you want to be able to pay it completely without taking out more debt to pay off your current debt.

For most women, living a virtually debt free life means peace of mind. Being able to sleep at night, develop fewer stress lines across the face equates to a younger looking and happier you – now that is priceless financial advice!

Even if you're on the right track,
you'll get run over if you just sit there.

— *Will Rogers*

A diamond is a chunk of coal that made good under pressure.

— *Anonymous*

Good luck is the result of good planning.

— *Fortune Cookie*

There is no future in any job.
The future lies in the person who holds the job.

— *George Crane*

Negotiating 101

The *Research Report* was supposed to have been on the CEO's desk yesterday. I completely forgot because I was on vacation all last week.

I will tell you what Susan, uh uhr I mean Jane... If you get this *Research Report* done ASAP, I'll give you one extra coffee break a day and a $2 raise starting in 6 months.

Hmm... I'm the only one in this Division who has the expertise to put together this *Research Report* for the CEO.

I will raise you. I want 5 extra days vacation a year *and* a 50% raise starting next month. Deal?

Research Assistant

Middle Management

Strategies and Tactics at the Office

KNL

Chapter 4

Negotiating Strategies & Tactics:

It's not only What you Know – It's How you Negotiate!

Negotiating is not a strong suit for many women. Many women have not been raised nor taught how to negotiate successfully on their own behalf. In the past, women were groomed by society not to be confrontational. Still today, women often look toward a male figure to represent them in negotiations rather than negotiate for themselves. Most women have been taught to be nurturers, cheerleaders, and more accepting than their male counterparts. Women often get less than they deserve in life because they are not skilled in the art of negotiation, strategies and tactics.

Successful negotiators are not born with these skills. They are made! Women must learn and train themselves in these skills just as men are trained. Many universities and graduate school programs, like Harvard and Thunderbird, offer three to five day educational programs to executives for development of negotiation skills. Also, books and training programs such as *KARRASS* offer programs to quickly introduce you to the art of negotiating and to refine and hone your negotiating skills.

Platinum Tip: *For a local, low cost training alternative to hone your skills in negotiating strategies and tactics, sign up for classes at a community college, university, women in business type organization (like City Women's Network), women's resource centers, or look into programs at a local YWCA, etc. Check their offerings for day, evening or weekend classes related to negotiating skills that fit into your schedule. Class title might not include the word "negotiating" but many classes such as psychology, business sales courses, anthropology, etc. all delve into the human psyche and can teach you how to better understand and think like the person you are negotiating with. Ask for a class syllabus to see exactly what is covered in the class materials. These types of classes may also teach you how to develop winning strategies that can make the negotiation process easier, more successful, and less confrontational for you and the person(s) who you are negotiating with.*

Dispelling Labels & Stereotypes

Why is it usually considered a positive connotation when a man is aggressive (like a "Go-Getter" or really "On the Ball") in order to succeed in his profession whereas a woman is frequently given a derogatory name (like "Obnoxious," the big "B" or a "Money Grubbing Broad") because she is aggressive in trying to succeed in her profession as well? Negative stereotypical names are actually routinely applied to both genders. Men receive the cache of being a "bully" or "tyrant" whereas women get labeled with the big "B."

Women unfortunately can be labeled with derogatory names because they come across sounding arrogant or condescending when they are only attempting to negotiate and sound confident. Often it is not what the woman is doing but how she is going about it that gives her a negative name and makes her less effective. Does she alienate people by the way she speaks, through her body language, or dress and demeanor? Is she placing emphasis on items that aren't really important in the whole scheme of things? Does she shake a finger and talk down to people like a parent or guardian? Approach, tactic and perception is everything when it comes to winning people over to your way of thinking. The key to successful negotiation, so many times, is not *what you say* but *how you say it* that can successfully persuade people to follow you.

The "Buy-In" Theory

Successful women are enthusiastic team players and possess powerful persuasive skills! They get people to "buy-in" to their ideas with enthusiasm and persuasiveness. They stay focused on their goals and welcome others to participate in the decision making process rather than forcing them under duress to accept their ideas. The "Buy-In" Theory says that everyone will feel happier with the decision if they have a say in the decision making process. Also, they will agree to the decision if they feel that they would have come to the same decision when presented all the pertinent facts. Most people, especially employees, don't like a Dictator Management Style. Employees like to feel that they add value and are important. The "Buy In" Theory addresses this employee versus management concern.

The Harvard Method

According to The Harvard Method, "Negotiators are more effective when they move away from adversarial posturing and instead work jointly to satisfy the interests of both sides." Look at both sides of the issue and address the concerns on both sides. Both sides should feel that they are being satisfied on the majority of their concerns. Although The Harvard Method requires "give-and-take" on both sides, by doing this, the negotiation process will be smoother and less controversial.

Other Effective Negotiating Methods Used

Karrass seminars, as well, focus on "Effective Negotiating" through having "both sides win" and understanding "the *must* and *give* issues." Karrass has also written a book entitled *"In Business As In Life – You Don't Get What You Deserve, You Get What You Negotiate"* by Chester L. Karrass.

The book entitled, *Difficult Conversations: How to Discuss What Matters Most* and written by Douglas Stone, Bruce Patton, Sheila Heen, and Roger Fisher help readers navigate through tough conversations. Whether it be their boss, spouse, friends, kids, or clients, this book shows the reader how to remain constructive and focused without taking a defensive stance regardless of how the other person may respond.

Platinum Tip: *Look on Amazon.com and your local book stores for other titles on negotiating. There are hundreds of books out there and inspirational speakers who come to your community and speak on the topic of negotiating.*

Don't Undersell or Underestimate yourself - Men don't!

Women today in the U.S. are still paid on average 18% less than their male counterparts. Part of this salary discrepancy can be attributed to on the job perks that women never even consider when it comes to salary negotiations. The "Perk Package List" is very long, and depends on how high up you are on the career ladder. There is also a difference in perks offered by various corporations. For instance, some companies may offer day care facilities while others offer a company subsidized cafeteria. The perks listed below highlight many topics which should be considered when negotiating your overall employment package.

- Medical Coverage, Health Care Plans, Dental and Eye Care Plans
- Company Cars, Parking Spot Allowances, and Auto Expenses (Gas etc.)
- Expense Accounts, T&E's (Travel and Expense Allowances)
- Relocation Packages (Moving Expenses)
- Housing Allowances
- Day Care Facilities
- Retirement and Pension Plans, including matching employer plans
- Non-Compete Clauses
- Golden Parachute / Termination Agreements / Termination Clause
- Dry Cleaning Allowances
- Continuing Education Allowances and Scholarships
- Car Services or Limos / Cabs to and from the office
- Business Class vs. Coach Air Fare
- Sabbaticals, Leaves of Absence, Maternity Leaves
- Company Cell Phones and Cell Phone plans
- Life Insurance for Key Men (and Key Women)

When looking for a better position or moving to another corporation, consider reaching out to a "head hunter." Head hunters can help steer you to a company with great perks and benefits and do many of the upfront negotiations in regards to your overall employment package. It is in the head hunter's best interest to obtain the highest financial package on your behalf because they are often paid a percentage of your contract.

Additionally, once you have the employment contract in hand, make sure you have an attorney who specializes in employment law look it over. A good employment attorney will also have ideas on how to best protect yourself and lock in a better salary and benefits. You might also ask the attorney if they have seen in other employment contracts from the same company perks which might be afforded to you in your position.

Negotiating other Aspects of your Life

As Newsweek once said, "Negotiating is the game of life." Other areas in your life demand negotiating as well: relationships, marriages, prenups, and divorces to name a few. Every relationship has "give-and-take". But there is one thing in common when dealing with your significant other: Fight the war, but don't fight every skirmish or battle. It will only exhaust you and cause your significant other to turn a deaf ear to you. In a relationship you are constantly negotiating with your other half. Everybody wants their own way. How you get your way is by *negotiating* effectively on a daily basis.

Relationships & Marriage

Stop arguing about who is right and who is wrong all the time. Instead, try listening to each other over a good bottle of wine and learn to compromise. Learn to abandon blame, anger, and other strong emotions. Never react using these strong emotions, but instead harness these emotions to effectively make your point. *Think before you shout!!!!* What comes out of your mouth, never gains re-entry nor can it be forgotten by the person who heard it. Learn to express yourself with clarity and power. Ask yourself what is really at stake? Does it really warrant an important "talk" or could you be doing better things with your time rather than drumming up an argument?

Platinum Tip: *Remember the World War II mantra: "Loose lips, sink ships!" This applies to negotiating as well. Saying things that you shouldn't have said and expecting others not to take offense or hoping that others will forget what you have said, doesn't work in the real world. Always think before you speak. Otherwise, you will sink your own ship!*

Prenuptials & Divorce

What you gain in your romances, marriages, prenups, and divorces is based on give-and-take, otherwise called *smart negotiating.* If you are negotiating in a prenup or divorce, you should consider who should make the opening offer and how hard a bargain should you drive? How fast should you move? Should you split the difference right down the middle from the start or battle it out with lawyers? And finally, when should you not negotiate or stop negotiating and place your future in the hands of a judge?

Negotiating still not for You?

Everyone must know their own strengths and weaknesses. If after trying, you know in your heart of hearts that negotiating is not your forte; then, don't be shy. Hire a good lawyer to do the negotiating for you. Don't be "penny-wise and pound-foolish!" A good lawyer can often eloquently achieve the goals you are trying to obtain in business or personal agreements. Book a consultation for one hour with an attorney to discuss the issues you would like to address and get the lawyer's view on how you can attempt to resolve them by yourself in an effective manner.

Platinum Tip: *Most lawyers offer a free 1 hour consultation because they are trying to solicit your business. The purpose is for the lawyer to briefly hear your case and for you to interview the lawyer to see if you both feel comfortable working together. Make the best use of that time by having your questions prepared in advance and really make sure you pick the lawyers brain. That free 30 minute to 1 hour consultation might save you from having to hire a lawyer for something so simple you could have done it yourself or from having to hire a lawyer for a lot more money later on.*

Nothing gives one person so much advantage over another as to remain always cool and unruffled under all circumstances.

— Thomas Jefferson (3rd U.S. President, 1743-1826)

Far too often we fail to get what we want, especially in dealing with VIPs, simply because we are afraid to ask or don't ask the right people.

— Al Neuharth (Founder of the newspaper USA Today)

People do not change when you tell them they should; they change when they tell themselves they must.

*— Michael Mandlebaum
(John Hopkins foreign policy specialist,
and quoted in The New York Times 06/24/2009)*

Never tell people how to do things. Tell them what to do and they will surprise you with their ingenuity.

*— General George S. Patton, Jr.
(U.S. Army Field Commander WWII, 1885-1945)*

Single & Loaded

KNL
&
FBJ

Chapter 5

Single & Loaded

How often is a woman defined by what she owns, job title, charitable contributions, or her late husband's financial status?

— *Sophie Tucker*

There is no doubt a woman's financial assets are taken into account as well as her physical assets at the age of 39½ and beyond. Women do it to men, so why isn't it fair game the other way around?

The lyrics of a well-known Steve Miller song, *The Joker*, "I love your peaches want to shake your tree..." could have a double meaning when applied to this chapter. One meaning describes the male suitor who seeks you (the single and loaded female) out due to infatuation, lust, and love. He comes knocking at your door to seduce and charm you into marrying him. The second meaning describes the suitor who sees "your lovely money tree" and wants to shake the best assets out of it. Although gravity may change a woman's physical assets over time (and not for the better), a woman's financial assets can still look quite perky after a financial nip-and-tuck here and there. They can look very enticing and juicy to the opposite sex. Just like when you were a teenager and your parents kept warning you about the unscrupulous nature of the opposite sex saying, "Be careful now, he's only after one thing!" Later on in life, this warning takes on a whole new meaning. "Be careful now, he's only after one thing!" now refers to your money, assets, and overall net worth. Men will always be after your money or your family's money so protect yourself from these types of romantic charlatans.

Are they really after you or are they after – your money! Don't kid yourself. Many men are no less scrupulous than many women in this respect. Call it "women's lib" or "men's lib!" – Men now find chivalry in playing the male escort or the social companion to wealthy older women. Men are no more inclined than women to walk away from a lucrative relationship, marriage, sexual arrangement, or prenuptial with nothing. They expect to get paid for their services just as women do. All is fair in love and war!

Platinum Tip: *Gravity may change a woman's physical assets over time, however, a woman's financial assets can still look quite perky!*

Think Protection

When you think of "using protection," you are probably thinking of birth control, right? We want to highlight a form of protection that can be just as important to your overall well-being: *Financial Protection*. Use it to protect yourself against all kinds of infectious financial diseases!

If you are single and loaded, you want to remain loaded even if your single status changes later on in the future, correct? You may feel pretty good about your financial status and well-being at this point in time. But, what will the future bring? You don't want to be singing the lyrics by Jay Livingston and Ray Evans, *"Que Sera, Sera (Whatever Will Be, Will Be!)"* and later find out that by living such a carefree life it has led to a big fat nothing in your retirement account. Instead, you need to take steps to hold onto it, preserve it, and nurture it. Everyone will be after the extra cash you have. Three simple wealth preservation steps you should take are:

- **Pre-Nups**: You may want to create a legal, protective wall around your assets to protect them from a romance turned sour.

- **Be Careful of Frivolous Spending**: The old adage of, "Waste not: Want not" applies here. Do you really need one in every color?

- **Invest Idle Cash**: An old saying that still holds true today, "The money that money makes, makes money." Invest your extra cash that just sits and collects dust in accounts drawing zero interest into higher yielding securities and interest bearing accounts.

Platinum Tip: *You worked hard to earn your money. Now make your money work hard for you!*

How did you end up Single & Loaded?

People end up single and loaded for a variety of reasons. Six common ways people become both single and loaded are outlined below:

1. Trust Fund Kids
2. Made it on your Own
3. Divorced and left Money
4. Spouse Died and left Money
5. Inherited Money from a Relative
6. Won the Lottery

Whichever way you received your money, you are entitled to it and should want to protect, enjoy and keep it.

> **Platinum Tip:** *The money that money makes, makes money!*

Den of Thieves

People are always trying to rid you of that excess cash you have stashed in your wallet. In the Connecticut community the co-author Karen lives in, she has nick named this unscrupulous phenomenon: "The Fleecing of the Sheep." Living in an area called the Golden Triangle, contractors notoriously hike up their prices in accordance with the zip code and street. It is the "Robin Hood Theory" and they don't see anything unethical or immoral in charging different prices for the same work and services performed to different people according to where they live.

Location, Location, Location – This means that you should expect to be fleeced when it comes to unscrupulous contractors. The better the location, the higher price for services rendered! As an example, a pet groomer in Sarasota, FL charges $30 dollars ($10 per cat for grooming) and comes to your house. Whereas, a pet groomer in Greenwich, CT charges $540 ($180 per cat for the same grooming service)! A second example: Hairdressers in Greenwich, CT charge $280 for a cut, color, and blow dry, whereas hairdressers charge only $130 normally in Sarasota, FL for the same services. See a pattern? If you live in a top location, expect to pay top dollar for all services rendered!

Potential Suitor – Be careful of the sweet talking man who sweet talks you out of all your hard earned money. He thinks flattery will get him everywhere – especially when it comes to your pocket book. Is he right?

Contractors – Negotiate a price for services rendered. Ask for an "all-in" price, stay away from hourly. Otherwise, the interior designer could spend hundreds of hours dreaming up whimsical decorating ideas fit for the Palace of Versailles. All you wanted was a basic design that would have been 20 hours' worth of labor costs. What you got was 120 hours' worth of labor costs.

Auto Mechanics – Do ask for an *"all-in"* repair price; try to avoid hourly labor charges. As with interior designers, this applies to all service providers who provide services for an hourly or a fixed rate for their services. "If you give them an inch, they will take a yard" and why not, it is your money! The auto mechanic is sure to find other items to fix as well on your car, even if you only brought the car in for new brake pads. Automobile Service Departments are notorious for discovering other things you must have fixed on your car. They will also try to scare you into getting things fixed. Make sure to get a second opinion on all these "extras." It will save you a lot of money in the end.

Plastic Surgeons, Cosmetic Dentistry, and the Like – How much is enough? Don't get sucked into thinking you have to change this, that, and the other – you are beautiful just the way you are! A little goes a long way with these doctors, so make sure you get several quotes and credible physician opinions before you spend too much money.

Car Dealers – You should and must negotiate on all new or used cars. Don't be embarrassed, it's expected!

Telephone Marketers – Do get on national and state *Do not Call Lists* if you don't want to be hounded by people soliciting for various organizations and businesses.

Charitable Organizations – Ask the phone solicitor representing the charity to send you something in writing. This puts off a lot of the scam artists pretending to be a charity when it is really their own *for-profit* business.

Banks – Your bank may not always offer the best deals on savings and loan products. You need to shop around!

Advisory Fees – Make sure you ask the price before you hire a financial advisor or any other type of consultant so you don't get sticker shock when the bill or statement arrives. *Financial Representatives, Consultants* and *Advisors* charge a percentage on a per transaction basis or a flat rate transaction fee, a quarterly or yearly "all in" account fee, or a monthly fee.

Jewelers – Definitely negotiate for your bling. Jewelers expect you to. They will also reward good, repeat customers with higher discounts.

Cell Phone Plans – Do check your statement every month. If something doesn't look right, call customer service and ask for it to be removed. Many times you can reason with them.

Credit Cards – Beware of APRs (annual percentage rates) that can suddenly ratchet up. Check and compare rates periodically. Some credit cards have annual fees for services that may or may not be worth it to you to have, if they are not, go for a no annual fee credit card.

Book Keepers – Beware of money that begins to leave your coffers and is transferred into theirs. It's not just in Hollywood movies and *American Greed* stories on CNBC that this occurs. This type of scam happens more often than you think!

Hair Salons – The $40-$60 blow dry hidden in the hairdresser's bill because it is disguised under part of your color and highlights! Check the breakdown of the fees that make up the service of your hair appointment. You may be shocked on what services are worth it and what are not.

Spas – Spas are notorious for trying to sell hair and skin products just as they've lulled you into nirvana with a massage or facial. Suddenly they inform you that you suffer from more defects than you could have ever imagined!

Professional Fees – Many accountants and lawyers expect you to negotiate or at least attempt to negotiate upfront. Some do, some don't. Also, if you receive a bill that will put you in the poor house, try to reason with the person who did your work. Most times a reasonable compromise can take place.

Relatives – Never lend money, you will never see it again. If you do, consider it a gift.

Friends – Never lend money, you will never see it again. It will spoil your friendship if they can't pay you back. Again, consider it a gift and not a loan.

Investment "Deals" – If it sounds too good to be true, it probably is!

Law Suits – Try to avoid legal suits if possible. Normally only the lawyers get rich. Attempt to work out the problem. If this fails, then try to mediate the problem. Mediation and arbitration can be binding or non-binding. It's much cheaper and reaches a quicker solution than going to court with a trial by jury.

Insurance for Protection

Liability Insurance: You may want to take out various forms of *Liability Insurance*. Many *Home Umbrella Policies* contain a liability portion. This could save you if an unscrupulous friend or salesperson "slips on a banana peel" on your sidewalk or in your house. A small premium for a large amount of coverage is nothing to sniff at. Think how many years you would have to work to make back the money lost in a law suit if you are at fault.

Disability Insurance: You have worked hard but become disabled. Medical insurance will cover part of your expenses but not all. You might want to check into Disability Insurance particularly if have a dangerous or risky job such as feeding the lions at a zoo or eating fire in a circus! Seriously though, many jobs can actually be somewhat dangerous especially if you are lifting things. A girlfriend of mine is an interior designer and was working with an antique dealer in Connecticut when a gorgeous albeit extremely heavy marble top table dropped on her foot. She wore a shoe cast for about 6 months. Who knew that would happen? (Food for thought.)

Auto Insurance: You crash into someone else's car and they claim whiplash or much worse. You should have sufficient insurance coverage that would cover liability.

Medical Insurance: Don't play Russian roulette with your health. So many young people think they will never get sick, never need to be in the hospital. It will happen to you sometime in your life. Be prepared or else the hospital bills, doctors' bills, surgeons bills, and medicine could bankrupt you if it doesn't kill you first!

Stay Loaded

"Que Sera, Sera (Whatever Will Be, Will Be!)" can be a good motto to live by. And, it will lower your stress levels. This motto, however, as discussed in this chapter should never be used in relation to your finances or else you will most likely end up in great financial distress and singing a very different tune of *"Down and Out, Busted and Broke."*

You've been lucky enough to either: earn, inherit, or win a large amount of money. Now, it's time to seize the day, invest wisely, and protect your assets. You may not want to remain single, but I guarantee you, you will want to remain loaded!

I've been rich and I've been poor.
Believe me, rich is better.

— *Mae West (actress, lived 1892-1980)*

I'd like to be rich enough so I could throw soap away
after the letters are worn off.

— *Andy Rooney*

Money won't make you happy...
but everybody wants to find out for themselves.

— *Zig Zigler*

Chapter 6

The Bag Lady Syndrome

Bag lady you gone hurt your back
Dragging all them bags like that
I guess nobody ever told you
All you must hold onto
Is you, is you, is you

....If Ya living like a bag lady
(let it go let it go let it go let it go)

Bag Lady Lyrics, sung by rap singer: Erykah Badu

Not to be confused with a collector of fine vintage Hermes Birkin and
Kelly handbags! – The *Bag Lady Syndrome* is a serious phenomenon
that quite a few women suffer from. I think we all can conjure up the
image of Carol Burnett as she sweeps the floor after her show in a bag
lady style, janitor's outfit. Many women fret that they could end up in
that same financial position: poor, homeless, alone, and destitute.

According to www.urbandictionary.com, the *Bag Lady Syndrome* is
a "real psychiatric syndrome experienced by middle-aged women who
feel, at later stages of their lives, financially insecure and would end
up like them bag ladies seen at train stations across the globe with no
money or financial backup."

Characteristics of the "Bag Lady"

"Even earning a six-figure income is apparently not enough to ease the fear, among a whole lot of women, of winding up destitute and alone," according to the *Women, Money and Power Study* by Allianz Life, released March of 2013. Allianz conducted a national survey of 2,200 women aged 25 to 75 with a household income of at least $30,000. Allianz discovered from their research that, "49 percent of those surveyed had a deep-down fear of becoming a *bag lady* with more than a quarter of those women making $200,000 or more a year.

Men, on the other hand, don't tend to suffer from this syndrome because they are genetically wired differently. Eleanor Blayney, a consumer advocate for the *Certified Financial Planner Board of Standards*, explained this difference in men and women as, "Men are cultured a little bit differently around that…They have more of a sense of, well, when it runs out, you go out and make more."

Financial Turning Points

Money (much more than self-worth and self-esteem) is tied to our sense of success, power, independence, and security. It can also be what allows us to, or stops us from, fulfilling our dreams. Unfortunately, for the most part it is something we don't give much thought to until we are confronted with a major life change such as: loss of job, divorce, separation, or death. For those of us who have experienced leaving the safety of our parents' home for the first time, divorce, or the death of a spouse, it may be the first time we are responsible for our own financial plan and security.

Each stage of our life can present unknown challenges and disasters as defined below.

- Leaving the Parental Nest
- Loss of Job
- Mid-Life Crisis
- Divorce
- Separation
- Death

The years following mid-life (the 40's-50's which are endearingly referred to as the Mid-Life Crisis) present its own challenges. Some of us, even those who have been financially successful, walk around convinced that we will end up as *bag ladies* in our final years. We have all seen people who have gone from being on "top of the world" and at the pinnacle of their career to utter financial collapse and devastation.

Whatever your beliefs about money and finance, you own them to the same degree as you own your own unique style of dress and personality. Just like you clean out your closet twice a year to make room for the new and improved fashion forward you and change out seasonal clothes with the new season at hand; so too, you can you rid yourself of the old financial ways of thinking that didn't flatter your inner or outer financial you. You can revamp your financial "wardrobe" into something you feel more secure with, flattering and would suit you better.

Am I a "Bag Lady"?

Many women are afraid of becoming a *bag lady* in their old age and ending up in a state run nursing home or poor farm. You don't have to be afraid, however, if you are financially smart and savvy with your savings!

Steps to take to avert becoming a Bag Lady

Only you can take the proper steps so that never happens to you. By investing wisely you can circumvent the *Bag Lady Syndrome* and never have to wake up in a cold sweat in the middle of the night, scared that your entire investment portfolio and world as you knew it is gone forever.

Whether you are single, married, divorced, working or not, or healthy or not, you get to take ownership of your financial well-being and future. Whatever you create right now will determine your future. Like intelligence, creativity, and work ethic, *money* is simply a tool which can be utilized to help create the life you've always dreamed about.

Smart, sexy, savvy women would take the following four steps to avert becoming a bag lady, and so can you.

1. **Save, Save, Save!** *"The money that money makes, makes money"* and the *Rule of 72* both apply here. The earlier you start, the easier it is to accumulate a nest egg that will see you through any financial turbulence along the road to your "living happily ever after" retirement.

2. **Invest in your Career.** The harder you work, more networking you do, and the more you invest in your education and overall self-development, the more doors presenting opportunity and

good fortune will open for you. For most people, their career instead of their investments and savings are their biggest income generation tool. Keep abreast of industry trends in relation to your chosen profession, sign up for continuing education classes in your community to fine tune your business skills, and maintain and cultivate a network of contacts and colleagues who can help elevate your career.

3. **Pay off your Debts.** Pay off credit cards, car loans and mortgages as early as you can. The money you save in interest every month can go a long way to substantially increasing your retirement savings. It will also bring you peace of mind from becoming a *bag lady*. Generally speaking, your house mortgage eats up the biggest portion of your budget. People who fall into homelessness do so because they fall behind due to a financial mishap: loss of employment, medical costs, disability, etc. If you fall behind on your mortgage, you could be foreclosed upon and forced to leave your "castle." If you can own your home free and clear, there are very few instances where you will lose the roof over your head and become a *bag lady*. So rest easy, and pay off your debts!

4. **Remain Optimistic.** Even when things aren't going the way you planned, if you stay focused, work hard, and concentrate on achieving your dreams, you will achieve your dreams in the end.

Platinum Tip: *Sleep tight and don't let the financial goblins bite! Keep debt to a minimum especially if you suffer from the constant fear of potentially becoming a "Bag Lady."*

Happiness is often the result of being too busy to be miserable.
— *Anonymous*

A wise man will make more opportunities then he finds.
— *Francis Bacon*

Each choice we make causes a ripple effect in our lives.
When things happen to us, it is the reaction we choose that
can create the difference between the sorrows of our
past and the joys of our future.
— *Chenelle Thompson*

Live within your means, never be in debt, and by husbanding your
money you can always lay it out well.
— *Andrew Jackson*

Love & Marriage

KNL
&
FBJ

Chapter 7

Love & Marriage:
Go together like Divorce & Prenuptials

"Love and marriage, love and marriage
Go together like the horse and carriage
Dad was told by mother
You can't have one, you can't have none,
you can't have one without the other!"

Lyrics sung by: Frank Sinatra, Lyrics written by: Cahn / van Heusen

This song in today's world would most likely be changed to *"Love and Marriage, Prenups and Marriage, go together like Divorce and Marriage, Dad was told by mother, You can't have one ... without the other."* Not nearly as melodious or romantic, but it makes a point about today's society and how love, marriage, prenuptials, and divorce are viewed.

To Prenup or not to Prenup – That is the Question!

Prenuptial Agreements are a very emotional topic before many weddings. Who usually initiates the prenuptial (prenup)? In most cases, the person entering the relationship with the most assets wishes a prenup. The reason is simple: they have the most to lose, if things go sour.

To prenup or not to prenup, that is the question! As you review this partial list of reasons to enter into a prenuptial always remember and ask yourself the following questions: Would I like the other person to ask this of me? Will this taint the relationship from the start if I make these demands of my beloved? Will I be able to rest easier at night if I make these requests? Am I right in asking for this? Are lawyers "arm wrestling" me into designing an iron clad, infamous Massey Prenup? (from the film *Intolerable Cruelty* starring Catherine Zeta Jones and George Clooney). Is the lawyer just trying to make a buck by convincing me I need to hire their firm to design a prenup? Or, is a prenup what I really desire and I am just using the lawyers to write up my wishes?

There are many reasons that a prenup is both prudent and a very reasonable request. Some of these reasons to draw up a prenup and protect your best assets include:

1. People who are inheriting family money.

    A. People who are living on a trust fund from a rich uncle, parents, grandparents, etc.

    B. People who have shares in a family held corporation.

2. People on a high annual salary.

3. People who have a long standing established business before the relationship began.

4. People who have the drive and potential to reach the stratosphere in their chosen profession.

    A. Movie stars: starving performers to mega stars.

    B. Business moguls and oil tycoons: rags to riches.

5. People who own unique collections or rare antiques.

6. People who just got wiped out from a previous divorce.

7. People who are entering relationships with children from prior relationships or marriages.

    A. How will your children and new spouse be affected in case of death?

    B. How will your children and new spouse be affected in case of divorce?

8. People who want to preserve what they have worked for all their lives, whether they are 25 or 105 years old.

9. People who came to the marriage with a family estate or fully paid for home.

    A. The previous home has either significant monetary or sentimental value and is owned solely by one person. Family Homesteads and Family Farms that have been in the family for generations fall into this category.

B. The future purchase of a residence using combined assets. Both people, when they enter the marriage, wish to buy a home together. They wish to spell out the financial responsibilities and ownership participation, as well as, "until death do us part" survivorship rights. Divorce issues are also normally spelled out in the prenup.

10. People who want to protect themselves and remain an "Innocent Spouse".

A. If the person you are looking to marry has financial problems you may see about getting a prenup agreement to help shield your assets away from their financial problems. Maybe your spouse is sloppy about filing his tax returns and you don't want to end up in jail with him.

B. The person you are looking to marry has very complicated tax returns and you want to file separately.

11. People who have quirky ideas of what a prenuptial should contain.

A. Husband to be (Fat-a-phobic) slaps a prenup on his sexy, slim wife to be. It states if her weight inverses past his and the weight gain is not caused by pregnancy or comes off after pregnancy, he has a built in "put option" on his wife to get rid of her on the grounds of obesity. (True story!).

B. Sex on a regular schedule: 14 times a week (for Sexaholics) all the way to once in a blue moon (for the Touch-a-phobic).

C. Second flame on the side allowed with a specified visitation agreement.

Platinum Tip: *Smarts before Heart! Prenups set both the tone and language of your "happily ever after." Unfortunately for most couples, the honeymoon stage doesn't last forever. Reality soon sets in and the seven year itch quickly approaches.*

What topics are usually covered in a Prenuptial Agreement?

Hopes, desires, and expectations (whether realistic or unrealistic) can also be addressed in a prenuptial agreement. One crazy Wall Street trader, as previously mentioned, actually wrote up a Prenuptial Agreement which included a *put option*. The *put option* was if his wife gained more than 40 pounds and kept the weight on after the birth of their child, he wanted the right to divorce her and not his money along with it.

Expectations regarding parenthood also become another major topic in prenuptials. To have children, not to have children, or how many children to have can become major points of contention in any relationship. Or, perhaps not, if you already have a prenuptial in place! Not only the number of children born via natural birth, IVF, or through adoption but also which religion, what type of educational system they are to be schooled in (parochial, private, or public) are other battlefields filled with all kinds of emotional explosives. Due to modern science even the sex of the child can be a point of contention between the couple which makes its way into the prenuptial agreement. This is especially true if they live in a country like China that restricts the amount of births per couple. Others might be predisposed to bad genes, while others feel that the world is already overpopulated and wish to provide a needy child from a foreign country a home. Some men and women only will marry if they are going to have a family by natural means or adoption and will stipulate this in a prenuptial contract so there is no question about their motives later on.

Royal families must pass down their lineage to secure and preserve a monarchy. Some examples include: Great Britain's Royal Family – The Windsor Royal Family, The House of Grimaldi in Monaco and The Imperial House of Japan – the Yamato Dynasty. If an heir is not produced in a timely manner, some monarchies could become a Grimm's Fairytale – a once upon a time monarchy! Therefore, these imperial families main function in life is to breed and to breed well.

Family responsibilities, as well as, family size can be another contentious topic on prenuptial agreements. This can range from who cleans the dishes to who brings home the bacon.

Some women may need to look at protecting their own career aspirations if they are marrying someone who expects them to give up their career and move with their spouse to a different city, cross country, or overseas. Many men expect women to follow them. And many women, in turn with fabulous careers, expect men to follow *their* lead. In this case, the underdog spouse should desire to have something put in the prenuptial agreement which will provide them with a golden parachute to eject (instead of a lump of coal) if all goes wrong in the marriage or the couple's relationship.

If your prospective partner needs to work and live in Hong Kong but you have family and work responsibilities in New York, your future living arrangements may have to be spelled out in a prenup to insure future tranquility in the home.

The Underdog Spouse

The person with fewer assets is referred to as the underdog spouse because they are coming to the marriage union with fewer assets and power. The underdog spouse needs protection from being taken advantage of in the relationship and should take note of the following:

1. List all your assets on a Prenuptial Agreement even if they pale by comparison with the moneyed person you expect to spend the rest of your life with. If you own your own home, car, jewelry, or business, make sure to list it under assets that you are bringing into the marriage. Never underestimate what you are contributing.

2. Have your own lawyer who specializes in *family law* review the contract and work to achieve a more equitable solution or compromise. Always remember not to rush into signing any documents. You can always postpone the wedding. If he really loves you, he will wait.

3. Are you the quintessential homemaker or caregiver? This has great value too. Again, don't underestimate your value in the relationship.

4. You have more leverage before marriage than after, especially when it is a first marriage for both of you. Many men think with an organ other than their brain pre-marriage!

If you are presented with an unexpected prenuptial agreement shortly before your first marriage, you have to ask yourself, is this person that I am looking to marry and spend the rest of my life with 110 percent committed to this relationship succeeding? Or, are they all too willing to throw in the towel at the first major argument? You want the other person in your life to be 110 percent committed to the relationship just as you are. Each person always believes they are contributing, or giving more to the relationship. That is only normal. Each spouse will tend to blame the other spouse in the relationship for not extending great enough effort when they march down the divorce aisle.

The Positive Side to a Prenup

A prenuptial doesn't have to be scary or one-sided. Many women, in fact, can feel protected and cherished by their prenuptial.

Example: An article written by Michael Rothfeld in *The Wall Street Journal* on November 15, 2012 highlighted a high profile case involving the family of Bernie Madoff. The following case involves a prenuptial agreement which contained a provision giving Stephanie Madoff the homes and a lump sum payment upon her husband's death (Bernie Madoff's son).

A very high profile case at the time of this writing involves Stephanie (Mack) Madoff. She was married to Bernie Madoff's son Mark Madoff who committed suicide in December 2010 after his father's Ponzi scheme unraveled. Mrs. Stephanie Madoff, signed a prenuptial before marrying Mark Madoff in 2004. She and Mark owned both a loft in the Soho neighborhood in Manhattan as well as a waterfront house in Nantucket in joint tenancy. Joint tenancy means that the two people owned the properties together. However, in joint tenancy with survivorship rights, two or more parties can own a property with the surviving owner receiving possession and ownership of the entire property if the other party (parties) dies. These two Madoff properties where purchased for $6.1 million in New York City in 2005 and $6.5 million in Nantucket, Massachusetts in the 2005.

Mr. Picard, as the trustee, is trying to seize the Madoff family assets to distribute to victims of Bernie Madoff's Ponzi scheme. Stephanie is clinging to her prenuptial. Her lawyers are arguing that it was a contract that predated the disclosure of the Ponzi scheme and therefore must be honored. A legal battle is currently being waged. Mr. Picard's lawyers argue that the decision is irrelevant because it relates to a divorce settlement rather than enforcement of a prenuptial contract after a spouse's death.

In Stephanie's case, however, her claim is complicated by arguments (against Stephanie) that she didn't receive the money in good faith because the fraud was exposed before her husband's death. The following is a direct quote from the article in the Wall Street Journal. "Her knowledge of the fact that her husband was a beneficiary of a fraud is critical," said Richard D. Emery, a lawyer who won a Madoff related case earlier before the same court, the New York Court of Appeals. "If she knew that, then I think anything she got from him is probably fair game for the trustee to get," Mr. Emery said.

Prenuptial Agreements are serious legal contracts which can take many twists and turns, especially since no one knows what the future may hold!

Is a Prenup for You?

Prenuptials are seldom cut and dry. They come with clauses that can change over time and are dependent upon ever changing circumstances. The state that you reside in can also affect the ramifications of a prenuptial agreement. Also, the length of a marriage and the validity of the marriage affect prenuptial agreements greatly. Make sure you get a lawyer, well versed in family law, to review the prenuptial agreement that you either construct and intend to have your significant other sign or are the recipient of and are expected to agree to the terms. Most lawyers require a retainer because it is a costly legal contract that could run anywhere from a few thousand dollars to hundreds of thousands of dollars, depending on the complexity. Financially, this is a major decision and shouldn't be taken lightly. Just remember – *Smarts before Heart!*

Community Property States

As of 2015, when this book was printed, there were nine community property states in the United States. A community property state means that all assets earned during the marriage are split equally or 50/50. The assets acquired before that marriage belong to the person who earned, inherited or won the money in the lottery.

Community Property States

1. Arizona
2. California
3. Idaho
4. Louisiana
5. Nevada
6. New Mexico
7. Texas
8. Washington
9. Wisconsin

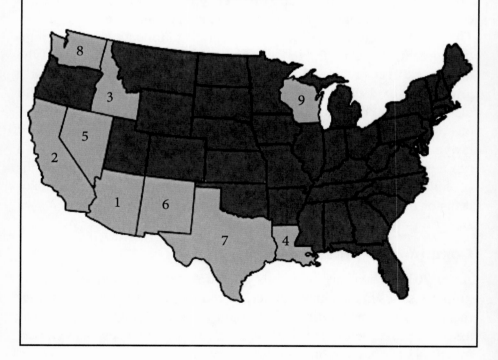

*Many men think there's more protection
in a prenup than a Trojan!*

— Karen & Fran

*Men always want to be a woman's first love.
Women have a more subtle instinct:
what they want is to be a man's last romance.*

— Unknown

*By all means marry; if you get a good wife, you'll become happy;
if you get a bad one, you'll become a philosopher.*

— Socrates

Smarts before Heart!

— Karen & Fran

Which one most describes You?

It's the *Hollywood Squares Show*...
and our guests today are:

Square #1  **The Trophy Wife**	**Square #2**  **The Cougar...Purrr**	**Square #3**  **The Stepford Wife**
Square #4  **The Career Oriented**	**Square #5**  **The Bachlorette**	**Square #6**  **Philanthropic House Wife**
Square #7  **Empty Nester**	**Square #8**  **Divorcee**	**Square #9**  **Widow**

KNL

Chapter 8

Cougar, Trophy, Stepford, Bachelorette, and Career-Oriented Women

Which best describes you?

Women are multifaceted. We don't come in one shape or size either. Our personalities are unique and the complicated circumstances that life throws at us help to shape our persona. Love life, career, and family life adapt to the change. This is a fun chapter that helps to identify what type of woman you *really* are. You will probably find that you are a combination of several types.

The Cougar (Meow!)

The *Cougar* calls the shots. She spends her own money and buys what she wants and when she wants it. She owns her own residence. She vacations when, where, and with whom she wants. She exudes a glowing confidence from within. She plays by her own rules and is able to pick up a younger man, use them, chew them up and spit them out. She can be ruthless but may take a cub (a younger man) and protect and nurture him as well.

Sunset Boulevard, first produced as a Hollywood film and later a musical rendition in the London's West End and New York's Broadway by Andrew Lloyd Webber, focuses on this cougar / cub relationship. The older silent film star who can't act in films anymore because the film industry produces only talkies now, seduces a young handsome, struggling screen writer to live at her palatial Hollywood estate located on Sunset Boulevard. She keeps him well dressed and well fed until he falls for a younger girl.

Two other iconic Hollywood films featuring the *Cougar* in all her colors are: *The Graduate* and *Breakfast at Tiffany's*. *The Graduate*, starring Dustin Hoffman and Ann Bancroft, tells the story of a student seduced by a friend of the parents (who is currently married) and the societal scandal that ensues. The theme song for the film *The Graduate* written and sung by Simon and Garfunkel, "Hello Mrs. Robinson" re-enforces the theme of the cougar / cub relationship.

Breakfast at Tiffany's, written by Truman Capote also featured a cougar and her cub as part of the overall plot. Holly Golightly (played by Audrey Hepburn) falls in love with a writer Paul Varjak (played by George Peppard) in New York City. The writer, however, is a very good looking, albeit kept man – a cougar's cub living in a cougar's den. 2-E (played by Patricia O'Neal) plays the wealthy married woman (the *Cougar*) who has an affair with the younger, very attractive male writer (the *Cub*). She cares for him, supports him, nurtures him and keeps him in apartment 2-E (a well-furnished cougar's den) until he begins to stray for a younger woman.

The *Cougar* possesses an insatiable appetite for domination, strength, and spending power. Although she can't always get what she wants, she is very tenacious, charming, attractive, and will keep trying.

The Trophy Wife

Many made for Hollywood and real life stories feature a beautiful, somewhat younger or substantially younger, trophy wife. Her male counterpart, usually wrinkly and balding, happily escorts and dotes on his gorgeous and great figured *Trophy Wife*. Displaying her like a trophy for all to see, because he wants the world to know he is very successful and his plumbing still functions like that of a teenager's (with a little help from the Viagra he's taking!). A complete ego trip for him, he likes to flaunt his trophy to all his male friends making them believe that this young chick thinks he is hot!

She, the *Trophy Wife*, is quintessentially the type of woman every woman hates because she is viewed by middle-aged married women as a threat, especially to those whose husbands possess a wandering eye or those who are already members in the second wives club! In the back of every woman's mind they think their cad of a husband could attempt to replace them with this type of bimbo bombshell!

A *Trophy Wife*, however, can be compared to a container of yogurt you purchase at the grocery store: they *all* have an expiration date stamped on their bottom! The husband, when the urge strikes, will toss them away for a yummier, newer, fresher and more delicious variety. A new flavor of the week (Passion Fruit) variety will soon replace the boring and aging (French Vanilla) *Trophy Wife* variety.

Trophy Wives often get what they want in terms of clothing, jewelry, and cars because he is trying to show off his wealth and good taste. They are usually made very comfortable but come with a very "uncomfortable prenuptial." These adored women often end up leaving the marriage with little more than the Chanel jacket on their back and the Manolo Blahnik shoes on their feet! Although many books highlight this topic, one prime example *The Pulitzer Prize* delves into a Palm Beach *Trophy Wife's* marriage.

The Stepford Wife

The *Stepford Wife*, often the envy of other men, is normally adored by their "own husbands" but can seem quite robotic at times. Lacking spontaneity, she glides seamlessly from homemaker to socialite on her husband's arm.

The 1972 satirical thriller novel, *The Stepford Wives*, written by Ira Levin first coined the term *Stepford Wives*. This book spawned two Hollywood films and cemented the term *Stepford Wife* to mean that the once independently minded, successful and professional woman had become robotic, poisoned, and brainwashed into male submission in sleepy suburbia.

A *Stepford Wife* usually has holding power within a marriage because her husband becomes dependent on her. In fact, she appears to work hard to anticipate her husband's every need and whim. However, many a *Stepford Wife* has been dethroned when a future sexy, wild and exotic *Trophy Wife* (the *anti-Stepford Wife*) comes along to tempt and seduce the *Stepford Wife's* husband.

The Career-Oriented Wife

Career-Oriented Wives usually fare well on the matrimonial merry-go-round particularly in a bad economy where many husbands prefer a two salary household income. A career oriented wife often has it all – as long as her spouse is supportive of her long hours, work, and helps with the household responsibilities. These wives while working hard must always be vigilant and aware that temptation can strike while she is at the office due to circling *Stepford* and *Trophy Wives* looking for their next prey to devour.

Also, *Career-Oriented Wives* should think twice before hiring an attractive, younger assistant especially if she works from the career-oriented wife's home office. Additionally good looking younger maids, nannies, etc., are a bad idea especially if the husband stays home all day. Or you, the working one in the family, are always away on business trips. The "eye candy" can be too much of a temptation! Arnold Schwarzenegger, the actor and governor of California couldn't resist the temptation of a maid, even though he was married to a very accomplished and attractive wife, Maria Shriver. So why should your adoring spouse be any different?

Many men have left the marriage for their wives' assistants. A book entitled, *Ladies Night Out* written by Mary Kay Lewis is a novel based exactly on this theme. In the book, the heroine discovers her husband and her red-headed assistant doing the "deed" in the garage late at night, and decides to drive his $175,000 car into the pool for a little revenge!

> **Platinum Tip:** *Career-Oriented Wives earning their own money and making their own major investments should consider having their spouse sign a legal document prior to closing or finalizing a major investment. It should state that it solely belongs to her, her efforts, and her money. Marital funds are not the source of funding. Also, be prepared so you don't end up paying alimony and losing your children in a custody battle if you divorce.*

The Many Faces of Women Today

The typical woman is multifaceted and complex: *Cougar, Trophy, Stepford, Bachelorette,* and *Career-Oriented* just to name a few. They can be married or not married. The boring housewife has been replaced in today's society, relabeled and redefined. The *Cougar* in the twentieth century replaces the "scarlet letter" labeling of a few centuries ago. Just like the *Stepford Wife* replaced the boring suburban housewife label. Under the label of housewife and single lady today come many, many more subcategories which further define women. These roles that women play are anything but static and change as society changes. These new roles keep redefining how a woman thinks of herself, defines who she is, and who she desires to be. If you don't like how you are labeled or how people think of you, you can change it. If you do like how people think of you then revel in it and embrace it!

You never find yourself until you face the truth.

— Pearl Bailey

Men always want to be a woman's first love. Women have a more subtle instinct: what they want is to be a man's last romance.

— Unknown

Chapter 9

Financial Infidelity:

It's not Lipstick on the Collar!

Nobody is immune to *Financial Infidelity*! Money can be a very sacred and secretive subject. It seduces you to take care of it, love it and spend it.

According to a December 2011 online poll commissioned by *Forbes Woman* and the *National Endowment for Financial Education*, and covered in a recent *Forbes.com* blog post, "31% of Americans who have combined their finances said they lied to their spouses about money." Shocking? Not really. Such lies often consisted of "hiding cash, minor purchases and bills" and sometimes of "hiding major purchases, keeping secret bank accounts and lying about their debt or earnings," Forbes said.

Meanwhile, according to a survey from the nonprofit *CESI Debt Solutions,* "80% of spouses spend money that their partner doesn't know about. The secret spending occurs in categories such as clothing and accessories, food and dining, beauty and personal care items, gifts and alcohol, among other areas" (excerpt taken from the newspaper article in *The New York Times,* "Financial Infidelity" by Jennifer Saranow Schultz).

Childhood Recollections of Financial Infidelity

I remember when I was 10 years of age, my mother had passed away of a cerebral hemorrhage (a brain aneurism at age 43). My father couldn't part with her clothes. A few years later he finally decided to donate her clothing and started to take the clothes off their hangers when cash started falling out of the sleeves. His darling wife and my saintly mother had been stashing cash – for a rainy day or for that special handbag? Needless to say, it was my first introduction to the now hot topic of *Financial Infidelity*.

Financial Infidelity Pre-Marriage

Financial Infidelity can occur even before the marriage takes place! *Financial Infidelity* at its utmost is when a couple is planning on getting married and doing a prenuptial agreement. A "Prenup" as it is affectionately called is done based on honesty and usually the amount of financial assets each partner has at the time of the upcoming marriage. Many a divorce lawyer will tell you how many future spouses (usually wealthy *men*) will lie or even *underestimate* their assets. Men, particularly, wealthy ones, rarely want a future spouse to know how much money they *really* have. This can backfire years later when the couple is divorcing and the prenuptial agreement gets put aside. (Thrown out by the courts) In this example, the base of assets is considerably less than he declared going into the marriage. The false numbers could hereby be used as a base giving his spouse a greater division of the assets.

This phenomenon of *overstating* one's assets pre-marriage is particularly prevalent in certain states. In community property states, people find it advantageous to over-state their assets. The reason is clear. Whatever you brought into the marriage is yours to keep. Whatever is gained during the marriage is fair game for an equitable distribution.

Men and women who lie on a prenuptial agreement are the ultimate sinners in *Financial Infidelity*. Money is often the last thing talked about during a courtship or engagement. There is this sense that if you need to talk about money in your relationship, you may not really be in love with the other person. No matter how much we avoid this topic, reality will hit sooner than later. We have to deal with the role that money plays in our relationships.

Men and Financial Infidelity

Men are extremely good at financial infidelity and they never think twice about it. In many relationships, they are the bread winner so they truly believe (in their own man frame of mind) that they are entitled to shelter assets away from their spouses. This can be private bank accounts, money for the casino, money for a strip bar, or even a second family on the side. Two lady friends found out that their darling spouses became unscrupulous louses very suddenly when they uncovered the horrible truth that these men were supporting a second wife and family right under their noses!

One a Midwesterner living in New York had a European husband. Little did she know he had a second wife and family over in Brussels, Belgium. When the couple started having marriage difficulties concerning their finances and his prolonged overseas business trips, a family member had a hunch that the root of the problem was due to a second family being supported on the side. After having him investigated, the diabolical truth emerged.

The other, a very attractive and witty friend living in the Northeast discovered her husband had a second family living in Asia. Her husband, an investment banker, was traveling constantly back and forth from America to Hong Kong and Singapore. When the couple decided to divorce, only then did she discover the wicked truth of his other life in Hong Kong.

When we were speaking on this topic, a lawyer told us how he discovered both *financial infidelity* and *sexual infidelity* while reviewing the husband of a client's American Express bills during a divorce proceeding. While living in Florida, the husband frequently went to Texas on business. Although he always stayed at The Marriot Hotel while away on business, the lawyer found bills on the Amex statement for a lawnmower and gardening supplies charged in Texas. Was he mowing the lawn for the Marriot Hotel and trimming the shrubbery? Not unless he took up a second occupation! Shortly after that, the lawyer discovered that the husband had a second family with two children. This man successfully supported this second family in Texas while maintaining his husbandly duties with the first wife of 15 years. This sneaky, little devil of a spouse was able to hide his American Express bills from his wife for 15 years!

The point being, these men successfully hid their spending habits, bills to support another family, and everything that went along with it for many years. These were marital assets used for another family other than yours. If you were a woman significantly affected by this, think what you could have used that money for ...how much better your lifestyle could have been over all those years had he only been honest with you.

One of the most widely practiced aspects of *Financial Infidelity* occurs when the husband asks the wife (usually in a second or third marriage) to visit his financial broker or financial representative with him. Once inside the stock broker's office, the husband adds the wife to the beneficiary or POD (paid on death) form. The wife is happy and feels that she should then do the same for her husband. One month later, however, the wife sees mail from that broker addre ssed to her husband. Her name has been deleted and his adult children from a previous marriage have been inserted along with his new kept girlfriend. Hidden from the current wife, these names had been masterfully inserted in place of the current wife as the new beneficiaries on the account. This is pure deception and *Financial Infidelity* on the part of this "loving and very thoughtful" husband.

Platinum Tip: *Being designated on an account does not make you, the wife, a partial owner of the account. It only makes you a beneficiary which means that the beneficiary can be changed over and over again unbeknownst to the beneficiary.*

Suppose the wife had never seen that statement of the account which named the new beneficiary or beneficiaries? She would have gone on believing that her husband was a wonderful, generous guy. Now that the wife knows that he is actually being a financial sneak, will she continue to trust him in the same way? Will she still desire to give him some of her assets upon her death? Or, will she be better off giving it to her favorite pooch nicknamed Double Trouble? That's exactly what Mrs. Leona Helmsley in Greenwich, CT did just a few years ago! In this case, the heir to the infamous Helmsley estate was dissatisfied with her children and bequeathed a large chunk of her fortune to her favorite dog named Trouble. Many millions of it!

How to Spot Financial Infidelity

We have highlighted a few ways to help you spot *Financial Infidelity* in your own relationship. Although these represent a few obvious ones, be on the lookout for many other devious behaviors that could be a warning sign.

- Your spouse has mail going to a post office box.

- You ask your spouse about a certain bill or transaction and they get defensive, argumentative and belligerent.

- You ask about a brokerage statement that came to the house with only your spouse's name on the address. He then proceeds to tell you that you don't understand finances and to let him take care of the finances in the home.

- Your partner has been promoted at their job. You inquire as to what financial benefits that will bring in addition to a more impressive job title. Your partner brushes you off and tries to change the subject.

- It's the night of April 14 (the day before tax returns are due), and you are rushing off with your spouse to a cocktail party. Your spouse asks you to sign the tax returns without you having a chance to go over them.

- You are given a signature page for a loan agreement and asked to sign as a co-signer, yet you haven't been presented with the 20 page agreement that goes with it. Your spouse says, "Don't worry about it, just sign it, it's nothing!"

- Your spouse out runs you in the fifty yard dash to the mail box immediately after the mailman delivers the mail. He must have something more to hide than you!

- You see a bill for wall-to-wall carpeting for the living and dining room, yet you don't have carpeting in those rooms, nor do you expect to because you have wood floors.

- A priority mail envelope from a financial institution arrives at your door step. Your boyfriend immediately grabs it from your hands and says, "Don't trouble your pretty little head over it." Suddenly, he gets very affectionate and tries to distract you.

Women and Financial Infidelity

Don't think women are immune to *Financial Infidelity*. Nor are women innocent when it comes to participating in this practice. Women save for rainy days on the sly, especially when they suspect that their beloved is a philanderer, too financially controlling, or isn't being entirely honest with them. It can range from $300 hidden in the piano bench to commercial property being held in a Delaware LLC or Corporation.

I'll never forget when my husband and I (newlyweds) moved into our first home, the pet sitter I had hired who had come highly recommended from our neighbor turned to me when my husband was out of the room and said, "Ok, now that we've gone over all the pet stuff, let's discuss the more serious subject – where do you want your bills hidden? That's part of my job. I've heard it all! Don't worry, nothing will surprise me. Do you want them in the oven, the freezer? The only marriages that work in this town filled with all these control freak Wall Street guys are where the wife can get what she wants without having to beg her husband for it. It saves on many arguments later on and keeps the marriage intact." What an eye opener!

Each marriage has a very unique set of financial parameters, circumstances, and rules. After the honeymoon mentality ends, money and the lack thereof can play a very significant role in many marriages and relationships. It is almost impossible to overestimate money's role in a marriage which is why statistically money matters have remained one of the top three marriage killers in the United States.

Examples of Financial Infidelity include:

- Lying about assets on a prenuptial agreement.
- Having financial accounts in another city, state or even internationally that the spouse doesn't know about. And will never find!!!
- Opening new bank accounts locally but unknown to the other spouse.
- Hiding bills.
- What, this old thing?…I've had this outfit forever! I just haven't worn it for a while. (When really you bought the outfit last week! Does this sound familiar?)

- Filling out any financial forms (such as the lease for a car or credit card applications) and underplaying or overestimating your assets.

Extra! Extra! Heard on the Beach

I was lying on a recliner chair sipping a cocktail with my husband on the beach behind a very artsy and Chi-Chi hotel in Palm Beach, Florida. When to our despair, a couple behind us began talking obnoxiously loud. At first, my husband and I were quite annoyed by the banter between the couple because they were encroaching on our married solitude of peace and tranquility on our little carved out section of a beach littered with people on a long bank holiday weekend.

Low and behold their conversation became riveting! The lady began knocking the gentlemen's ex-wife. Between the two of them they unleashed a web of deceit, financial infidelity, and possible money laundering. This was better than reading a gossip magazine at the hair-dresser. Needless to say, my husband's and my ears perked up! We couldn't believe what we we're hearing.

The ex-wife supposedly was an attorney. She with another attorney managed to make a mint illegally from the mortgage lending industry in the last property boom of 2003-2006. She managed to hide her supposed share of the "ill gotten" gains in an overseas tax haven. Her partner in crime went to jail and had to give back most of his money. Meanwhile, she got off scot free albeit her money is now stored in an overseas bank account and untouchable for many, many years to come.

The ex-husband lamented how he got screwed out of all the millions she had accumulated during their marriage when they divorced because she hid all the money in a secret bank account overseas. Was this ficti-tious cocktail talk trying to impress the new gal he was with, like so many men do? Fictitious or not, it's an example of *Financial Infidelity* at its finest! (Or, conversely at its worst!)

Platinum Tips: *One, always watch what your spouse or signif-icant other is doing under your nose or else it could come back to bite you! Two, be discrete with your indiscretions especially in public as you never know who may be listening!*

Financial Infidelity Pyramid

**Lying
on a
Prenup**

**Secretly
supporting
another Family
or Family Member**

**Not disclosing Debts
and Bad Investments
(Or worse—Bankruptcy!)**

**Lying to a Spouse
regarding Beneficiary Status
in Estate Planning**

**Not disclosing Contributions to
Charities, Political Organizations, etc.**

Hiding Credit Card Debt

**Giving an untrue Valuation of a Business,
Net Worth, or Profits Derived from
various Business Ventures**

**Using Marital Funds for Extra-Curricular Activities
and/or Liaisons**

Which have you done? Which one or ones have you caught or suspected your spouse, partner, or significant other to have done?

(Be honest! It's your secret. No one will tell – unless you do!)

How to handle Financial Infidelity

One solution is to set down monthly, quarterly, or even annually depending on your relationship and define your 1 year, 5 year, and 10 year financial goals and aspirations. Define the steps involved to achieve these goals and the strategy to keep you both honest. Factor in a budget for incidentals too. Budget a specific amount to enable each spouse to have a "mad money account." This account entitles each spouse to spend how they wish and without having to report what they spent it on to the other spouse (as long as it's legal!).

The Financial Infidelity Test

*This is a fun and enlightening exercise. Take out your pen and circle either **YES** or **NO** next to each question below. The results might surprise you! Remember: Honesty is the best policy and the only way you will know how you measure up on the scale of Financial Infidelity is to be truthful with yourself. Don't worry; no one else will see it ... if you hide your answers!*

Do you hide your bills from your spouse / significant other?	YES	NO
Do you have separate credit cards that you make "me" purchases on?	YES	NO
Do you ask the sales clerk at the department store to divide up your purchases onto several credit cards?	YES	NO
Do you have a secret account or safety deposit box at a bank?	YES	NO
Do you cut the tags off your clothes at the store before bringing them home so that your husband doesn't see them hanging in your closet with the price tags on them? Or, you pretend like your new clothes just came back from the dry cleaners?	YES	NO
Your husband asks, "Is that new?" You reply, oh this old thing, I've had this for a long time!	YES	NO
Do you stash cash in case of a rainy day inside of clothes, drawers, or anywhere else for that matter?	YES	NO
Does your spouse pay with cash all the time?	YES	NO
Do you give money, stock, or other assets to your children or to other relatives without telling your spouse?	YES	NO

Do you pay for certain items with cash instead of putting them on a credit card so the items can't be tracked?	YES	NO
Do you support other family members on the side without telling your spouse? (For example: underwriting or subsidizing medical expenses, accommodations, transportation, or providing employment for a family member without the approval or knowledge of your spouse.)	YES	NO
Have you ever sought estate planning advice without your spouse's knowledge?	YES	NO
Has your estate planning made deliberate attempts to exclude your spouse financially?	YES	NO
Do you have accounts that are not in joint name?	YES	NO
Do you have beneficiaries on accounts that are unknown to your spouse? Or, a POD Account (paid on death account) with names that are unknown to your spouse?	YES	NO
Have you hurried your spouse to sign tax returns or other financial documents without letting them thoroughly review them?	YES	NO
Have you been extra nice to your spouse, perhaps showing more affection, or imbibing in a glass of wine before approaching the subject that it's just a little document that requires their signature?	YES	NO

Financial Infidelity Test Results:

*Calculate the number of questions you answered **YES** and how many you answered **NO**.*

If you answered **YES** to 10 or more questions, you are without question an infidel on money and finance! You little devil you!! (But who are we to judge! Your secret is safe with us!)

If you answered **YES** to 5 but fewer than 10 questions, you are like most people. A little naughtiness and secrecy can be a good thing.

If you answered **YES** to fewer than 5 questions you have passed the **Financial Infidelity Test** and deserve a gold star for valor and a medal for honesty.

If you answered **NO** to all 17 of the questions, you are an absolute saint and we don't believe you!

*Never trust the man (or woman) who tells you all his
troubles but keeps you from his joys.*

— *Anonymous*

*Financial Infidelity is not as obvious as lipstick on the collar.
To find it, you need to be Sherlock Holmes and
read between the lines.*

— *Karen & Fran*

I know all about cheating. I've had six very successful marriages.

— *Bobby Heenan*

*Every man wants a woman to appeal to his better side,
his noble instincts and his higher nature –
and another woman to help him forget them.*

— *Helen Rowland*
(American journalist and humorist, lived 1875-1950)

Life After the 4 D's

Chapter 10

Life after the 4 D's:

Divorce, Death, Disability and Financial Disaster

Divorce, Death, Disability, and *Financial Disaster*, nicknamed the 4 D's can destroy even the best of portfolios, your love of life, and the future you had originally outlined for yourself. The 4 D's can not only take a toll on your health but can utterly destroy the retirement plan you had in store for yourself. It is not uncommon to see people working long into their retirement years: sometimes by choice, sometimes because they have to in order to survive, and sometimes because their age of retirement got pushed up higher due to unforeseen circumstances.

Divorce

Divorce can come suddenly and entirely unexpected. You never truly know what the other spouse is thinking unless you are a mind reader! A huge chunk of your nest egg will suddenly disappear. Assets like a house, a car, children, pets, boats, campers, etc. can be taken away from you as well. In fact, a divorce could mean that you will have problems obtaining loans or securing loans at as favorable of rates like you used to obtain. This all depends on who is the breadwinner in the relationship and what your credit score is like.

Death

The *Death* of a spouse, partner or loved one, who either financially supported you or contributed financially to maintaining your particular lifestyle, can be devastating. Hopefully, your loved one has taken out a life insurance policy which would provide you with funds to keep you comfortable at least for a while. If not, you could also have many of the same problems facing you as someone getting a divorce because (depending on who the breadwinner is in the family) your yearly household income could suddenly force you to make severe changes to your current lifestyle to stay afloat.

Disability

The third "D," namely *Disability* can affect either you or someone else in your family. It can wreak havoc on your stress levels, your health and make an utter mess of your finances. No matter who becomes disabled, your lifestyle and your finances will both change drastically. The third "D" will be covered in great depth in **Chapter 20: Insurance - What is your best Asset?**

> **Platinum Tip:** *You can always make lemonade out of a lemon. So too, can you make a positive outcome out of a negative time in your life.*

Financial Disaster

Nobody is immune to *Financial Disaster*. Mother Nature when you are least suspecting it can wipe out your home. Investments can turn upside down from global economic turmoil. A bad business venture on your part could force you into paying substantial legal fees, court costs, or force the business to go under. Medical expenses can drain your savings if you don't have enough medical insurance. And, did we mention that identity theft can also play mayhem with your finances. There are so many financial pitfalls that every day should be viewed as walking across a mine field waiting for one to explode or viewed (as per the illustration at the beginning of this chapter) as little and big "Disaster Bombs" raining down on your once blissful life.

Divorce that led to Financial Disaster

Many widows and divorcees have suffered greatly from poor investment decisions. All too often, the divorced woman who has been married to a wealthy spouse tries to use his investment strategies. Sometimes it works and we congratulate these women. However, all too often it doesn't work and even a woman who begins her single life with a mega money settlement can end up in bankruptcy or severely in debt.

Example: The *New York Times* newspaper recently covered the story of Patricia Kluge who was one of the nation's wealthiest divorcees. She was married to the media mogul, John Kluge. Her settlement included the grand Albemarle Estate in Virginia which was over 23,000 square feet with eight bedrooms and thirteen bathrooms. Her jewelry and home furnishings alone raised almost $20,000,000 in two auctions when she went bankrupt. It had been said that she received the income on over $1 billion for life. She also, according the *New York Times*, received $1,000,000 a year for life.

So you ask, what could have happened? How could she have declared bankruptcy, given the amount of such an enormous settlement? Mrs. Kluge said she went down a familiar path learned from the late Mr. Kluge. During the 1980s he sold his highly leveraged media properties to a variety of buyers, most notably Rupert Murdoch for more than $3 billion. Mrs. Kluge always lived with and knew that John Kluge was a high borrower. Her strategy was similar; attract equity investors to pay off the debt, make the business cash flow positive, and then sell.

The Downfall

The downfall started when Mrs. Kluge wanted a working winery. For over a decade, she invested more than $65,000,000 of her own money and then began to borrow more. A winery along with the restaurant business seems to be high on well-heeled investors "Fantasy Wish Lists" (along with owning sports teams). A winery is, in fact, a notoriously risky, capital intensive, and labor intensive business. The winery business is not for the faint of heart!

She aimed high but did nothing to minimize her own financial risk, as she began to borrow more and more money to make the winery, land, and gated community a success. She claims she did a lot of research and found that there was a niche in the sparkling wine market.

She borrowed about $35,000,000 from the Farm Credit of Virginia to further her efforts. By 2008 she had increased production to 30,000 cases of wine. Then, due to the economy, sales plummeted to just 13,561 cases per year.

What happened next in this situation? The banks and the Farm Credit of Virginia closed in on Patricia Kluge. Mrs. Kluge had given personal guarantees for the loans. Bank of America then bought the Albemarle Estate for $15,000,000. Also, in her divorce settlement, she received $1,000,000 a year for life. She was then forced to sell off the rights to these future payments for just $5,000,000. This money then went to the Farm Credit of Virginia, according to Bill Shmidheiser, a lawyer of the bank.

As this tale unfolded, Donald Trump was called by Mrs. Kluge to a meeting since he is known to "buy a lot of very high-end distressed properties." Mr. Trump stated that, "over the years he has worked with many people who have lost their fortunes." Mr. Trump paid $6,500,000 for the vineyard. In 2008, what Mr. Trump originally purchased for $6.5 million was now valued at $75,000,000 by Rothschild Investment Bank. Good for Mr. Trump and salt in the wound for Mrs. Kluge!

Patricia was unique because (at the time the article appeared in the *New York Times* newspaper) she was currently working on a daily basis for Mr. Trump as the general manager and working directly with Eric Trump at the winery. According to the *New York Times*, some wines would continue to carry the Kluge label while others would bear the Trump label. Perhaps in a future episode of *The Apprentice*, there will be an episode featuring the promotion and sale of Trump's wines!

Michael McCarty, who had been running MICHAEL'S Restaurant located at West 55th St. in NYC (when the article appeared in the *New York Times* newspaper) said that the Kluge wines were very good and he carried them also in his restaurant in Los Angeles. He did give his expertise that, "trying to sell a Virginia wine is tough." He further stated that, "If you make a cult wine it can work if you make a very small quantity. But if you make a quality wine in the quantity that Mrs. Kluge was making in a new contemporary wine growing region like Charlottesville, VA like she did, it becomes more difficult to sell."

Lesson of the Day

Women that receive world famous divorce settlements are no different than women who have meager financial divorce settlements. The stakes might be higher and the wealthy woman's name might be splashed across the headlines of a newspaper; but at the end of the day, both groups of women are at risk to future financial disasters unless they are smart and savvy with their money. This rule holds true no matter how large the stakes are.

Emotions often run high for both the newly divorced or widowed woman and can not only effect decisions you make at your workplace, but also decisions you make with your personal finances and social relationships. Most women continue reeling from the emotions still felt from their past relationship and need time to heal. Although some, depending on the relationship, feel like a great albatross has been lifted off them and they are now free to pursue their dreams.

In fact, one of the biggest mistakes women make is selling a house too soon after a spouse or significant other dies because they usually don't get top dollar for it; and then, they spend too much on their new home due to the emotional crisis that they are currently facing. You should always wait at least a year after such a tragic event before you make such a large decision with what is normally the biggest or at least one of the largest assets in your portfolio.

Many lessons apply to *all* women from the previous Mrs. Kluge example:

1. Personal guarantees on loans can be very problematic and could jeopardize your life savings.

2. Savvy, smart female investors should always try to obtain a *non-recourse* loan if possible.

3. Minimize your debt exposure by living within your means. Simply put, don't take on too much debt!

Recourse vs. Non–Recourse

If you have a *non-recourse* loan on a business deal, then only your company is liable for the debt. The company could therefore fail and go bankrupt but your personal assets outside of the company (namely, your home) would remain yours.

If you take out a *recourse* loan, that means you are personally liable. Your home and almost all other assets you own can be seized by the bank and other creditors. These seized assets will normally be sold and used to repay your debt owed to your creditors.

In the previous example regarding Mrs. Kluge, a *recourse* loan was used which was the Achilles heel for Mrs. Kluge. A *recourse* loan puts your personal assets at risk. If you default on your loan, the bank can go after your house, the money in your bank account, and almost all assets you might have your name attached to. A *non-recourse* loan, on the other hand, frees your personal assets. The bank can only attach itself to the underlying property of that which was loaned on. If Mrs. Kluge in the previous example had *not personally guaranteed* (meaning *non-recourse*) her estate as collateral for the debt, the end result would have been much different for Mrs. Kluge. The reason for this is simple: debt remains despite the changes in your business success or failure, unless you pay it off. Even if your business goes bad, you still have to repay your loans unless you are protected via bankruptcy laws. And even then, certain debts (like taxes) still have to be paid off. Plus, you've ruined your credit rating for many, many years to come.

> **Platinum Tip:** *Debt remains despite the changes in your business success or failure, unless you pay it off. So either don't expose yourself in the first place or pay it off in a timely fashion.*

Minimize Debt Exposure

If Mrs. Kluge (in the previous example) had not invested in her fantasy winery; but had instead put all of her divorce settlement money in a cash account or bank CDs drawing little or no interest, she would have remained a very wealthy woman. Sad but true!

The smart and savvy female should use debt wisely and minimize her exposure to debt. Paying back a debt punctually can demonstrate to future lenders that you are a good credit risk. However, it is never a good idea to carry too much debt as that will ultimately lower your credit rating.

A wise policy to women new at handling their own financial futures – keep debt at a minimum and borrow frugally. If you do acquire debt, make sure that you pay back your student loans, car loans, or credit card company loans when the statements come due. Over extending oneself on any of these can spell disaster. Likewise, many small business owners max out on credit cards to keep their businesses a float. If the business owner doesn't pay off the entire debt when due each month, fees and interest charges accrue. These high interest rates charged by the credit card companies can cause the business to collapse like a house of cards.

Adjustable Rates vs. Fixed Rates

Many think debt is static. This is untrue unless you obtained a *fixed rate* loan. Debt can change over time if the interest charged is variable or *adjustable*. For example, a fixed rate mortgage on a home has a constant repayment rate through the life of the loan. An adjustable rate mortgage, on the other hand, may carry a low interest rate and repayment schedule for several years but will then "readjust" after a specific time period. Or, an adjustable rate mortgage can be pegged to an underlying index that fluctuates such as LIBOR (the London Interbank Offer Rate). The interest rate on your loan will adjust accordingly to whether the LIBOR rate goes up or down. There could also be a balloon payment attached to the loan at the end. A *balloon payment* is a larger than normal payment due as the last payment on a mortgage.

In the Mrs. Kluge example, Mrs. Kluge walked out of bankruptcy with nothing according to the *New York Times*. When she and her current husband (a new Mr. Kluge) filed for bankruptcy; they listed $2.6 million in assets and $47.5 million in liabilities. Mrs. Kluge declared bankruptcy in June 2011.

Her vision was certainly grand, but not so different from many women who maxed out their credit cards and home equity loans during previous economic boom times. She didn't do anything different than from many other women; she just had so much more to leverage and lose. She now lives in a rented home and works for someone else instead of herself – Mr. Trump. The moral of the story ... Debt can collapse all dreams: both personal and business.

Once again, some debt can be good. Without taking on debt most small businesses would never grow and reach their dreams. It must be remembered though that debt doesn't alter its numbers because business is poor. Instead, the debt becomes a larger percent of the liabilities' portion of the balance sheet.

Leverage

Leverage can be good if managed properly. It can allow you to live a better lifestyle than you would have been allowed to have done. A simple 30 year mortgage taken out to purchase a house that you plan to live in is considered a form of *leverage*. Almost any form of debt is technically a form of *leverage*.

Men are very good at leveraging their means in order to live a better lifestyle than they could have normally done. Men usually think along these lines so easily and virtually never see anything wrong with this type of thinking. This is why most banks prefer male customers over female customers because banks make their money off of lending to more men than to women. Men are normally the ones in the household who take on and negotiate the loans. Women might sign as a co-signer, however, statistically more men than women take out loans.

Women on the other hand are the savers. Banks don't make nearly as much money off of savers as they do borrowers. Banks use the savers' money (at low interest rates) to lend out money (underwrite loans) at higher rates to borrowers so the banks can make money. The banks use the savers' money to enable the banks to leverage up their books and make more loans which are hopefully profitable to the bank.

Platinum Tip: *It is better to be a lender than a borrower.*

Forms of Leverage

Forms of leverage include: car loans, first and second mortgages on houses and other properties, business loans, student loans, credit card debt, and home equity lines of credit on a primary residence. Once the first mortgage is paid off, a *home equity line of credit* is normally an inexpensive way to finance the update and remodel of a kitchen, bathroom, or an addition on to a home. Yes, these are all forms of debt, however, they are also forms of leverage because you are borrowing what you do not have and using assets as collateral. Just a little "fyi" (for your information): Men normally get into more trouble than women with creditors because they use more leverage then women and then the leverage works against them!

The U.S. isn't immune to over leveraging itself either. In fact, the Financial Debt Crisis of 2007-2009 can be traced back to over leveraging. Bank loans were given to people who either couldn't repay their mortgage on their homes or chose not to repay their loans and simply walked away from their houses because the debt was worth more than the home. This is explained further in the next **Section: When Leverage is Bad**.

Platinum Tip: *Once the first mortgage is paid off, a home equity line of credit is normally an inexpensive way to finance the update and remodel of a kitchen, bathroom, or an addition on to a home.*

When Leverage is Bad

Example: The *Financial Crisis & Great Recession of the 21st Century* began with "over leveraging." It started with a mortgage crisis. Politics played a huge role in fueling the financial crisis, tracing its roots back to the Clinton Administration and easy lending practices throughout several administrations. The idea that all Americans were entitled to *own* instead of *renting* their homes became a priority in Washington, D.C. Regulations over the years on mortgage lending practices were relaxed to the point that it was practically viewed as almost "discriminatory" that a loan officer wasn't loaning to everyone even if they couldn't afford the house on their current salary. A blind eye was turned to matching peoples salaries to the loan amounts and payback schedules on their mortgages. Politics trumped good sound financial business principles and practices.

These loans were originated often using only 0-10% down. In the past, a person had to show a stable, gainful employment track record and put down approximately 20-25% of the loan amount in order to take out the mortgage. Basically, you had to prove to the bank when applying for a home mortgage, that you could afford the property without the loan. Otherwise banks viewed you as too high of a credit risk and would reject giving you the mortgage. These debt obligations (0-10% money down loans) were then bundled up, re-packaged, and sold by Wall Street banks as *Collateralized Debt Obligations*. Wall Street always gravitates to where money can be made.

The financial crisis caught traction when analysts on Wall Street began to thoroughly comb through the loans, obligations, the data of New Housing Starts, and Mortgage Applications. The Wall Street analysts then realized that there was a glut of homes on the market and that it was not first time buyers but instead investors who were flipping the properties to turn a profit. The Housing Bubble burst! Supply grossly outweighed demand. This revelation started to bring housing prices down (due to over-supply) to where the actual market was willing to buy (demand). Simply stated, housing prices began to plummet and millions of people realized that the 0-10% money down loans with high fixed or variable interest rates that they took out at a market all-time high to purchase their homes, meant that they were now underwater on their equity versus the cost of the house. The *loan-to-value ratio* was reversed and people were upside down on their mortgages. Loans which were taken out on homes suddenly exceeded the current market value of the house because the real estate market had tanked. This downdraft in housing prices led to people being forced to walk away from their homes, not paying their mortgages, and declaring bankruptcy in many cases.

The "domino effect" had begun: people began to lose their jobs, refinancing became problematic, the loan-to-value on peoples' homes had reversed. The meltdown on Wall Street and the banking industry led to Main Street employers cutting back on spending and hiring which equated to a huge number of jobs being lost and dreams crushed. When jobs were lost and money was still owed on the home mortgage, people started being foreclosed on, evicted, and short sales started to occur. Many just walked away from their homes and buried their heads in the sand like an ostrich hoping that the big bad world would go away and wouldn't find them!

But that strategy also didn't work. The U.S. Unemployment Rate escalated and the U.S. government found that it was on the verge of more than a Great Recession. We were headed towards another Great Depression if our government hadn't stepped in to back stop the bleeding with a giant "Fed induced Band-Aid."

Debt (a four letter Word)

No one is immune to bad luck and disaster when it comes to leverage unless you don't take out any debt to begin with. Governments, businesses, and individuals can all experience the ill effects of being over leveraged if debt is not used and handled correctly. If debt (normally considered a four letter word) is used wisely and prudently, however, it can be positive. Leverage can be a very useful and wise tool to build and expand your business, provide a better lifestyle for yourself, and can stimulate the overall economy through more hiring and spending.

The Money Wheel
Easy Come... Easy Go...
Depends On Where You Land!

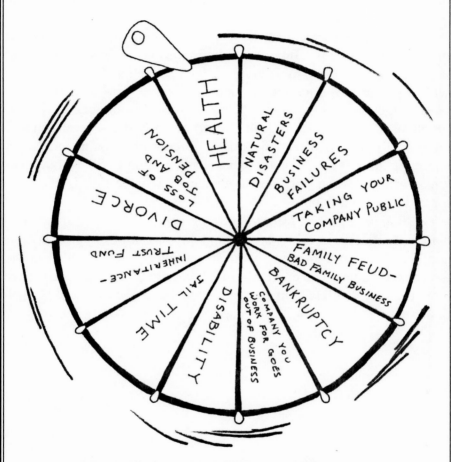

Round and Round We Go
Where It Stops, Nobody Knows!

KNL
&
FBJ

Platinum Tip: *Greatness can come out of a great mess!*

Dial "D" for ...

Just like a bad, scary movie and you are the victim in the tragedy, the 4 D's can and do wield undeniable pain, sorrow and fright. You don't have to be a victim, however. You can be the survivor who triumphs and overcomes the demon.

Talk to a debt specialist, lawyer, tax accountant, and friends who may be able to help. Take small steps to bring yourself out of debt. Restructure your loans by paying off loans having a higher interest rate with one that you have taken out with a lower rate of interest. Put your budget on a diet. Don't feel like you are the only one having debt problems. The E.U. (European Union) recently put several countries' budgets (the PIGS: Portugal, Ireland, Greece and Spain) on austerity slimming diets. Your pocketbook and bank accounts will not only thank you; but in addition, all of your financials will be toned, fit and fab instead of fat and flabby!

Although , *Divorce, Death, Disability* and *Financial Disaster*, nick-named the 4 D's can bring unwanted debt realizations to your doorstep and can do great damage to your stress levels, your health and your finances; greatness can come out of a great mess. If you have the will, there is a way out. Hang in there and read the rest of this book for solutions.

In the middle of difficulty lies opportunity.

— Albert Einstein

I'm selfish, impatient and a little insecure.
I make mistakes, I am out of control and at times hard to handle.
But if you can't handle me at my worst,
then you sure as hell don't deserve me at my best.

— Marilyn Monroe

Failure is Success if we learn from it.

— Malcolm Forbes

Problems are opportunities in work clothes.

— Henry Keiser

Only time can heal your broken heart,
just as only time can heal his broken arms and legs.

— Miss Piggy

Timing Is Everything In Life!

KNL
&
FBJ

Chapter 11

Timing is Everything in Life!

Wall Street's graveyards are filled with men who were right too soon.

William Peter Hamilton (1867-1929)
(Editor of The Wall Street Journal and The Stock Market Barometer)

Timing and Your Love Life

A perfect example in regards to timing and your love life is William Shakespeare's ill-fated lovers *Romeo & Juliette*. They met in Verona, Italy as teenagers who came from families that had long standing feuds. Unfortunately, timing entered into their love affair because they were so young. If they had been adults, and disregarded their parents' wishes, the two could have eloped to another town and lived happily ever after!

A more recent example involving timing and one's love life is the fairy-tale life of Princess Diana. If Princess Diana had not had the misfortune to have been in Paris with Dodi Fayed in a car headed through a tunnel at the exact moment that Paparazzi were chasing after them, what would have been the end to that fairytale romance?

The Hollywood film *An Affair to Remember* and the more recent take off on the film *Sleepless in Seattle* are quintessential examples of *timing is everything*! In *An Affair to Remember*, the love struck couple make a pact to meet at the top of the Empire State Building at a specific date and time. She becomes crippled from an accident on the way to the Empire State building and misses the rendezvous because she is being rushed to the hospital. He waits for hours for her to arrive and believes he has been stood up. Only years later he discovers the truth, the two are reunited and have a happily ever after (Hollywood style). *Timing is everything*!

The *Rhythm Method* form of birth control exemplifies the virtues of *timing is everything*! You get the timing wrong and guess what happens?

The "Timing is Everything in Life" Quiz

What would you do in the following two circumstances concerning "Timing is Everything in Life"? Take out a pen and circle either A, B, or C.

Quiz 1: (Meeting Mr. Right) You just happened to sit down on a 3 hour flight to visit your parents. And, who sat down right next to you, but Mr. Right? Although traditionally he should make the overture to ask to see you while you are visiting your parents, however, if you really feel that this is the fish you don't want to let off your hook, you might have to "step up to the plate" and do the asking before the wheels touch the ground. *Not to be confused with the Secret Service mantra of "Wheels up, Rings off!"* So which would you choose?

A. Do you shake his hand after the flight and say nice to have met you?

B. Give him your business card and say if you are ever close by – let's have lunch?

C. Or do you suggest meeting for a coffee or cocktails while you are visiting your parents?

Timing is everything! If you do nothing, Mr. Right could walk out of your life… possibly forever. Unless of course your life mirrors that of a Hallmark or Lifetime movie! So, what is the right answer for you to hopefully start a relationship with Mr. Right? Is it *A*, *B* or *C*?

Answer: Karen and Fran's choice would be *C* but hopefully he will be man enough and not a mouse and "seize the moment" first and ask you out! If you choose to do nothing, however, you will wonder for years what could have happened, (should have, would have, could have) if only you had initiated the overture to get to know him better. He could be the Mr. Shy type and just needs a little encouragement!

Quiz 2: (Your Biological Clock) Your biological clock is ticking loudly, you are 39½ years old and holding, this is the optimum time to meet Mr. Right but instead you keep kissing frogs? What is a damsel in distress to do?

    A. Do you consider a Mr. Wrong for possible marriage material because of your loudly ticking biological clock?

    B. Go to a sperm bank and design a baby?

    C. Do you do nothing and hope Mr. Right will come along before your clock stops ticking?

    Answer: At this stage in the game, Karen and Fran's choice would be not to panic and continue to date. However, don't go out with anyone more than twice if you know deep down inside that they are not lifetime partner material for you. If at first you don't succeed, then try, try again!

Timing and Your Financial Life

Buy low and sell high: Seems so easy and logical, right? In reality, however, human psychology and ego get in the way for many people. Instead, people buy high (thinking prices will continue to go up) and sell in a panic when prices begin falling dramatically.

> **Platinum Tip:** *Wall Street graveyards are also filled with those who sold too late.*

Winning Lottery Ticket: A winning lottery ticket is nice but can't be counted on for the basis of your financial plans and retirement. Casinos offering slot machines, twenty-one, roulette, and the wheel of fortune are fun to play but also offer slim odds for winning big.

Inheritance: Some people wait with baited breath for that inheritance check to arrive from their rich uncle twice removed. In reality, modern medicine keeps people alive past their normal life expectancy. That enormous inheritance that you were banking on to maintain your lifestyle gradually evaporates into thin air to pay for your 102 year old uncle's home health, nursing, medication, hospital, and other long-term care medical expenses. In more cases than not (as in this example), inheritance can be a pipe dream!

Cycles

Everything from the moon, seasons of the year, real estate, the stock market, crops, and your own life experiences cycles. Within these cycles timing is critical and around these cycles timing is also just as critical. Case in point, the flippers (those who buy and sell real estate quickly to make a profit) in the real estate crash just a couple of years ago did well until the crash occurred. Now, at the bottom of the real estate market cycle they have jumped in again with both feet to make a buck. If the flipper bought at the height of the boom and had to hold the property until the property bust ended, the flipping strategy was a flop for the flipper! (Try to say that 3 times fast!)

All life experiences encounter "*timing is everything.*" For example, a crop was planted at the proper time. All of a sudden, a 50 year flood comes along and wipes out the crop. In this case, the crop couldn't be harvested and is also subjected to *timing is everything.* Another example involves a young girl. The girl meets Mr. Right but would never dream of getting married at such a young age. Then later throughout her life she only meets Mr. Adequate and Mr. No Way. *Timing is everything*!

Luck & Timing

Luck and timing together make for the perfect combination! You make your own luck in the world but proper timing helps dramatically. Although *timing is everything in life* for most circumstances, luck, perseverance, knowledge, and skill all play a huge roll in obtaining your dreams in life.

It wasn't raining when Noah built the ark.

— Warren Buffett, CEO Berkshire Hathaway
(CEO Berkshire Hathaway, investor and philanthropist, born 1930)

It isn't as important to buy as cheap as possible
as it is to buy at the right time.

— Jesse Livermore, Stock Trader & Speculator (lived 1877-1940)

Wisdom too often never comes, and so no one ought not
to reject it merely because it comes late.

— Justice Felix Frankfurter

Winning is not a sometime thing; it's an all time thing.
You don't win once in a while, you don't do things right once in a
while, you do them right all the time. Winning is a habit.
Unfortunately, so is losing.

— Vince Lombardi

The 15 Platinum Rules

1. Never buy anything you don't understand.

2. Volatility always brings opportunity.

3. What goes up must come down.

4. Always shop for sales *(stocks, bonds, and real estate)*.

5. Never sell on panic or emotion.

6. No one ever went broke taking a profit.

7. Timing is everything in life.

8. Be an individual...don't follow the herd.

9. Sometimes you shouldn't delegate. *(Don't outsource your finances to your husband or significant other)*.

10. Beware the warning signs of financial infidelity. *(P.S. It's not lipstick on the collar!)*

11. Never get emotional in investing. Learn to love them and dump them. If it is a good relationship, stay involved.

12. Beauty is in the eye of the beholder when it comes to acquiring and keeping assets.

13. Learn from your mistakes and move on.

14. Follow your dreams. Listen to your inner self.

15. You can't achieve a goal unless you create one!

Let's Go Shopping!

Part 2

Let's Go Shopping!

The following ten chapters will not only define the primary types of investment products available today for the average investor; but will most importantly, also show the smart, sexy and savvy investor in you how to become the well-heeled woman you've always wanted to be!

Although at first glance, you may think this subject matter is boring and makes you yawn, by the end of part two of this book you will get so revved up, you'll be investing your way to financial freedom....and loving it!

Let's go shopping!

Shop (Stocks) 'til you Drop!

Chapter 13

Shop (Stocks) 'til you Drop!

My mama told me, "You better shop around, (shop, shop)
Oh yeah, you better shop around." (shop, shop around)

Lyrics by Bill "Smokey" Robinson & Berry Gordy

Big fortunes have been won and lost in the stock market! Stocks go up and stocks go down. The more turbulent and volatile the market, the more stocks fluctuate in price and the more money that can be made and lost. A penny stock can rise a thousand percent or more and a blue chip stock can crash to zero. Companies can boom and bust and their share prices follow suit.

Stocks come in two varieties: *common* and *preferred*. Owning stock (shares in a company) means that you actually are a part owner of the company. When you buy a few shares of "Big Blue" (IBM), or Apple (AAPL) stock, you are in effect a part owner of IBM and Apple! Common stocks, as the name implies, are very common in most investors' portfolios. Preferred stocks have a preferred status over common shares in case the company goes bankrupt. Common stock may or may not offer a dividend. Preferred stock, on the other hand, always offers a dividend and reverts to par (price $25) when the shares are called / retired. Also, common shares fluctuate up and down in price much more than a preferred normally does.

Why Invest in Common Stocks?

Of all investments, common stocks provide the best return potential and ability to capture substantial dividend and capital growth. Want to make a million dollars investing in the stock market? All it takes is good market timing, a little knowledge, study time to research the stock properly, and honestly – a little bit of luck on your side! Three easy ways to make a million dollars in your lifetime are highlighted below.

---

3 _Easy_ Ways to make a $1,000,000.00!!!

Example 1: You invest $10,000 today, earn a 12% compound annual return, maintain that average return for 49 years, and your initial investment will grow to $1,042,000!

Example 2: You invest $10,000 every year, earn an average of 12% annually, and 22 years later you will have amassed a total of $1,036,000!

Example 3: You invest in the Standard & Poor's 500 Index (SPY). This index has returned on average 11.8% per year since the beginning of 1940. Thus, all you need do is invest $10,000 in a highly diversified portfolio of large-cap stocks, hold that portfolio for 49 years, and you will most likely earn your first million dollars – with a little luck!

Real return is the only true measure of wealth expansion. It's not how many dollars you have; but instead, it's what you can buy with them! If you don't want to take hardly any risks, then Treasury bills are for you. Your investment will be safe and relatively free of risk, however, your gains will normally be more modest. This is one major reason stocks are so popular among investors.

History tells us that over the long run, average stock pickers can expect to earn between 10-12% annually on their investments gross (before subtracting all brokerage commissions and income taxes). Slightly more aggressive stock pickers earn between 12-14% annually. Aggressive stock pickers with exceptional ability may earn annual compound returns up to 18%, but this is quite unusual. Hardly anyone can earn over 20% year after year. And if they do – watch out as they might be privy to insider information and end up in jail like Martha Stewart! Or, the returns might be made up like in the case of Bernie Madoff.

When you buy a share of common stock, your _return on investment_ (ROI) is composed of _dividend returns_ (the stock's dividend yield) and the *rate of growth of share price* (capital appreciation). This relationship is illustrated in the following step-by-step equation outlined below:

Total Return on your Investment

Step 1: Dividend Yield (Y) is simply the current cash dividends (D) divided by the current share price (P). $D/P = Y$ and is calculated as follows:

$$\text{Dividend Yield} = \frac{\text{Current Cash Dividends}}{\text{Current Share Price}}$$

Step 2: Capital Appreciation is the rate of growth (G).

Capital Appreciation = Rate of Growth

Step 3: Total Return on Investment (ROI) is the dividend yield added to the capital appreciation. $ROI = Y + G$ and is calculated as follows:

Total return = Dividend Yield + Capital Appreciation

Using this formula, suppose you want to earn at least 13% annually on your investment in Karen's Cupcakes Inc. and it is currently trading at $20.00 a share with a 3% annual dividend (or $0.60 a share). Assume for the moment that the future share price and sales growth will mirror the company's historical earnings and sales growth (about 10% per year). Now try substituting these values into the preceding equation. Using these numbers, we have the following outcome:

Total Return on your Investment in Karen's Cupcakes Inc.

Step 1: Dividend Yield (Y)

$$\text{Dividend Yield} = \frac{\text{Current Cash Dividends}}{\text{Current Share Price}} = \frac{.60}{\$20} = .03 \text{ or } 3\%$$

Step 2: Capital Appreciation (G)

Capital Appreciation = Rate of Growth *or* 10%

Step 3: Total Return on Investment (ROI)

Total return = Dividend Yield + Capital Growth *or* 3% + 10% = 13%

Diversification

Rule of time diversification. This rule states that you should purchase an equal dollar amount of shares in different types of companies and industry types over time. Because of the ups and downs in the market-place, if you spread out your investments, you are more likely to not always invest at the top of the market. Suppose you have $12,000 to invest. You could invest $3,000 into: a financial company, an oil company, a technology company, and a food company. By investing in these four different types of industries, this would help to create a diversified portfolio. Now, in addition to picking out four companies to invest in, spread out that $3,000 investment into each company over time. For instance, perhaps $1,000 is invested today, another $1,000 invested in 6 months, and another $1,000 is invested in 12 months.

You will have a better chance of making a profit if you also buy these stocks just after the market takes a dip or the market makes a significant correction of 5-7%. In the case of a general stock market decline, remember that the prices of the stocks of good companies go down with the bad – at least temporarily.

> **Platinum Tip:** *You will have a better chance of making a profit if you buy stocks after the market takes a dip or the market makes a significant correction of 5-7%.*

Rule of portfolio diversification says that you should own stocks of firms in unrelated industries. For example: IBM, Coca Cola, Exxon, and Stifel Financial. If you selectively pick only a few companies for your portfolio (called cherry picking a stock), you must continually worry about permanent capital losses if the share prices of these two compa-nies were to fall and never rebound. However, well-diversified inves-tors know that although a few companies may not be able to survive prolonged periods of recession or excessively high interest rates, others prosper and will increase your total portfolio value over time.

> **Platinum Tip:** *Cherry picking stocks can either destroy or elevate your portfolio to new heights. A better strategy is diversification. Try to own stocks of firms in unrelated industries with little or no correla-tion. For example, PepsiCo and Google are in two different industries.*

Risks Associated with Common Stocks

When you buy common stocks you assume company specific risks in addition to overall market risk. Company specific risks result from the line of business the firm is in, how it finances its operations, competitive forces, and risks involved in the company's day-to-day operations. Some firms are more risky than others merely because of what they do (i.e. public utilities vs. internet stocks). Firms that borrow money to finance their operations are generally more risky than those that only use owners' (equity) capital. Also, sometimes unexpected events that affect only one company can drive down investment returns even though other firms in the same line of business are doing well. Investing in common stocks is risky because investment returns are not guaranteed and are subject to often wide price variations from period to period. The overall variability of return, called total risk, is the sum of company specific risk and market risk. You can eliminate a significant amount of risk just by not "putting all of your eggs in one basket." Try to invest in 8 to 10 companies from non-related industries to decrease risk. The risk reduction obtained from proper portfolio diversification cannot be emphasized enough. More than 2/3 of the total risk (or total return variability) of a single stock is company specific, whereas only 1/3 is market related. Thus, well diversified investors take far less risk than those who hold only one stock.

The prices of risky assets, such as individual common stocks, are highly volatile – they can rise and fall by significant amounts in a short period of time. Some stocks fall in price, never to rise again (such as Lehman Brothers – may it rest in peace!) But stock prices, when taken in aggregate (i.e. the Standard and Poor's 500 Index) have always moved to higher ground – even after significant drops over prolonged periods of time such as after The Financial Crisis of 2007-2008 which many economists feel was the worst financial downturn since The Great Depression. The S&P and the Dow in 2014 have now surpassed previous record highs, whereas some individual stocks have been left in the dust!

Dividend Paying Stocks vs. Non Dividend Paying Stocks

Stocks that pay dividends can be your best friend; whether they are *preferred* or *common*. While you sit and wait for the stock to make its price move, the dividend can outpace the annual inflation rate. A dividend stock can pay you to patiently wait. The example below demonstrates the power of dividends.

Calculating the Return on a Dividend Paying Stock	
Dividend Yield	4.5%
Price Appreciation	+ 7.6%
Total Return	12.1%
Annual Inflation Rate	- 4.3%
Total Real Return (*before* taxes)	7.8%

Types of Common Stock

Common stock comes in five sizes just like clothing: Extra Small, Small, Medium, Large, and Extra Large. And, just like clothing – one size does not fit all! In this book, we will concentrate on the most popular types of stocks in the stock market. Common stock is normally placed into three main categories of *small-caps*, *mid-caps*, and *large-caps* (although *micro-caps* and *mega-caps* exist too). Caps pertain to the market capitalization size of the company – or how large the company actually is. There is also usually a risk factor assigned to each market cap as shown below.

Small-Caps	=	Higher Risk
Mid-Caps	=	Medium Risk
Large-Caps	=	Lower Risk

Small-caps, mid-caps, large-caps can be bought and sold in many forms. They can be purchased as a single security or lumped into a group such as in an ETF or a Mutual Fund.

Penny Stock

Just as the name implies, penny stocks are small companies. They are normally traded *over-the-counter* (usually not on an exchange) and customarily off of the *pink sheets* (so called because the stocks and share prices were written on paper that was a shade of pink). Penny stocks are not for the faint of heart.

In 2013, the Singapore Penny Stock Crash completely devastated many Singaporeans to the point of financial ruin. The market crash was over a 3 day time period. Many times, very little information is available on these companies because they are small and few analysts follow these companies. When the company matures and grows in size the share price increases. Analysts then begin to track the stock and offer their opinions and forecasts on the company performance for the future. Before this time, little information on the company is available.

Penny stocks are quite risky but can offer a huge financial reward (almost like the lottery). Biotech and internet stocks are prime examples of the huge rewards, risks, and losses that are associated with penny stocks: great fortunes have been both made and lost.

> **Example 1:** A biotech stock could be in *Phase 3* trials, attempting to gain approval with the FDA (Food and Drug Administration) when it becomes apparent that the placebo given to test subjects had the same effective rate as the drug itself. Guess what? The stock will plummet in price!

> **Example 2:** A biotech stock that is supposed to treat hair loss ends up in a *Phase 1* trial showing that although it treats hair loss, the main effect of the drug cures a form of cancer. Guess what? The stock will skyrocket in price!

A typical penny stock can be summed up as being a very small company with highly illiquid and speculative shares. The company is subject to fewer filings, regulatory standards, and fewer listing requirements. Fraud runs rampant with penny stocks so *caveat emptor* (let the buyer beware)! A recent example of this is the stock Cynk Technology (CYNK). This company had no assets, no revenue, and only one employee. Yet for one hour in July 2014, the company had a market value of more than $6 billion! How you ask? In 2013, Cynk claimed to operate a social network and was trading for a few cents a share. On June 17, 2014 Cynk shares spiked from 6 cents a share to $2.25 a share (a gain of 3,650%). Then shares spiked further to a gain of 36,000%! Can you smell something fishy here? Cynk's shares sunk soon after this enormous spike. *Call it "Pump & Dump!"*

Small-Cap Stocks

Small companies' stocks known as *small-caps* because the market capitalization of the company is small compared to other companies. Small-cap stocks normally take a much larger beating during bear markets (economic downturns) than their large-cap counterparts. For this reason, small-caps are generally considered to be a riskier investment than either mid-cap or large-cap stocks.

Small caps normally show their largest gains in the years following bear markets. During the four years after the great bear market of 1929-1932, the Standard & Poor's Composite Index gained 200% while small firm stocks gained nearly 600%. During the period following the 1962 bear market, small firm stocks outperformed big company stocks by more than two to one. And after the 1973-74 shake down, small cap stocks outperformed the S&P Composite Index (SPY) by more than 4 to 1! From 2009 to the beginning of 2014, small-cap stocks have outperformed the S&P Composite Index as well.

Small-Cap Funds

The Russell 2000 Index measures the performance of U.S. small-cap stocks. Two examples of small-cap funds include: SPDR S&P 600 Small Cap Value ETF (SLYV) and the Vanguard Small Cap ETF (VB). And, iShares even offers a Micro-Cap ETF (IWC). There are many, many types and fund families to choose from if you are looking to invest in a small-cap fund. Let your fingers do the walking on a financial newspaper like *The Wall Street Journal*, financial magazine like *Barron's*, or a financial website like *Yahoo!* – It's a snap!

Mutual funds use the phrase *small-cap* or *emerging growth* in the description of their investment objectives contained in their prospectuses. Other examples include: Discovery, Frontier, Small-Cap Growth, Special Growth, Opportunity Value, Special Equity, Special Value, Special Investment, Value, Small Capitalization, New Horizons, Over-the-Counter Securities, OTC, and the like.

Mid-Cap Stocks

A *mid-cap* stock is generally defined as a company stock having a market capitalization between $2 billion to $10 billion. The market cap is calculated by multiplying the number of a company's shares outstanding by its stock price. Mid-cap is simply an abbreviation for middle capitalization. These companies have established businesses that are still considered to be developing.

Mid-Cap Funds

A stock fund that invests in mid-sized companies (firms generally ranging from $2 billion to $10 billion in market cap). These funds tend to offer more growth than large-cap stocks and less volatility than small-cap companies. Two examples include: The Vanguard Mid Cap Index

Inv. (VIMSX) and the Russell Mid-caps (EWRM). There are so many different types of mid-cap funds to choose from! – Just remember to do your homework first if you are planning to invest in one of these.

Large-Cap Stocks

Large-cap stocks are generally defined as having a market cap (capitalization) value of greater than $10 billion. The market cap is calculated by multiplying the number of a company's shares outstanding by its stock price per share. Examples of large-cap stocks include: General Electric (GE) and Microsoft (MS).

Large-Cap Funds

Large-cap funds are comprised of large-cap stock with market caps of more than $10 billion. The Russell 1000 Index measures the performance of U.S. large-cap stocks. There are many large-cap funds. Two examples include: the Russell 1000 (EWRI) and the iShares Russell 1000 ETF (IWB). With so many to choose from – what is a girl to do! (No, not buy one in every flavor and variety! But instead, shop wisely! That is what the smart, savvy shopper does!)

Mutual Funds

Mutual Funds offer investors a different style of investing. Although not quite passive, mutual funds can relieve you of a lot of the day to day investment activities and anxieties. The greatest benefit of investing in common stocks via a mutual fund is not selecting the stocks yourself; but, having an experienced investment professional making the decisions for you. The fund manager will also be responsible for deciding when to buy and when to sell. Risk can be reduced by owning a fund that holds diversified assets. Diversified mutual funds that hold common stocks normally exhibit much less price volatility than do individual stocks. Proper portfolio diversification eliminates most company-specific risk. Another benefit is simplified record-keeping. Management receives and reinvests dividends and interest payments from its investments and ultimately pays out this investment income to fund shareholders. Rather than placing buy or sell orders for 20-50 stocks in an individually managed portfolio, a fund investor can get in or out of the market with a single buy or sell order. Lastly, the presence of low-cost professional management can be a big benefit. But look closely because some mutual funds charge higher fees than others. By investing in a mutual fund, investors in that fund obtain full-time management governed by a strict investment strategy as outlined in the fund's prospectus.

Platinum Tip: *Beware, beware! Mutual funds vary with cash out restrictions, management investment styles, and fees charged. Make sure you do your homework before you invest!*

REITs

REITs (Real Estate Investment Trusts) invest in real estate. REITs are put under the stock section of this book because they trade with a ticker symbol and are listed on stock exchanges. For example, Annaly Capital Management (NLY), Gladstone Capital Corporation (GLAD) and Chimera Investment Corporation (CIM) just to name a few are simply a trust that is set up to invest in real estate whether it is residential or commercial. Most of the money (usually 90%) flows directly to its investors through this investment vehicle thereby providing juicy and attractive dividend yields. Many REITs yield more than 10% and some yield over 20% a year. The security, like the dividend can go up and down in value. Be careful if a REIT is not doing well, it can also shrink or cut its dividend as many did during the last financial crisis.

Like any other investment, there are varying degrees of risk depending on the REIT and what they invest in. Mortgage REITs earn their money on the spread: between low-interest, short-term borrowing and purchasing high-interest, long-term securities. Mortgage REITs typically borrow at low rates and lend in the mortgage markets at higher rates. This is done usually by buying mortgage-backed securities. By purchasing bonds guaranteed by the government, analysts argue that these companies take on "no risk" of default, with the principle concern being an interest rate risk instead.

Hybrid *mREITs*, on the other hand, are moderately riskier as they own mortgage-backed securities (MBS's) or any debt obligations which do not have an implicit guarantee by the U.S. federal government.

Restricted Stock

Like the name implies, these stocks are restricted from the shareholders buying and selling the stock freely. These shares are given to owners and board members of a company in lieu of cash for services rendered and cannot be bought and sold freely. Nor, are these stocks freely traded on the exchange due to their restrictive nature. Often times, they can only be sold after a specific amount of time has elapsed (i.e. 2-3 years), etc.

For example, the CEOs of Alibaba (BABA) and Facebook (FB) received "gazillions" of shares of their respective company's stock in lieu of their bonuses and salaries for compensation purposes in these two recent IPOs. Many other CEOs when bringing their companies public do the same, as it is standard practice. After the shares trade on the exchange for a required number of months (i.e. 6 months), the restriction of selling the shares is then lifted. The CEO could then begin selling his/her shares to buy their McMansions and other billionaires' toys (such as Ferraris, yachts, private islands, jewelry, and the like).

What should you do in a Bear Market?

The inclination of most individual investors is to sell out at any price. However, the best course of action is actually the reverse. During bear markets, the stocks of financially sound growth-poised companies are normally priced far below their underlying values. Of course, as stock prices drop so does the value of your investment portfolio and you may feel that it is quite foolish to throw good money after bad. Even though bargains are easily recognized, very few investors have a strong enough stomach to snap them up. Most investors are feeling quite queasy by this point in the downturn! This is especially true of those investors who abandoned sound investment practices during runaway bull markets. These investors include those who assumed more risk than they could tolerate, those who held highly concentrated portfolios, those who bought stocks without assessing their underlying values, and those who failed to apply sound cash management techniques. These are the investors who are typically forced to sell; and thus, have created bargain basement buying opportunities for other investors to take advantage of.

What should you do in a Bull Market?

Buy, Buy, Buy! But do it wisely. There is a saying on Wall Street that, *"the rising tide lifts all boats."* This saying pertains to stocks during a bull market. The overall positive wave of information and buying demand for stocks will lift the share price of most stocks. Some, however, can perform just the opposite. A smart, savvy, and relatively conservative choice is to invest in the indices like the S&P 500 Index (SPY). The indices have to go up if the overall market goes up, however, an individual stock does not. Just be careful of extreme exuberance. When this occurs, it is normally the sign of a market top. A sell-off or correction will be soon to follow.

Is a Stock priced High, Low, or just Right?

Stock theorists, market mavens, traders, and strategists use many important calculations when considering whether a stock is a good investment, or not. They must decide whether the shares are priced too high, too low, or fairly priced. Assessing the value of a company's stock is paramount before buying that company's stock. Two of the most important calculations for assessing the value in a company's shares and the quality of a company are the *Price to Earnings Ratio (P/E Ratio)* and the *Earnings per Share (EPS)*.

The *Price to Earnings Ratio (P/E Ratio)* is one of the most important formulas used before investing in a stock and deciding when to sell a stock. This equation evaluates the result of taking the current market price per share and dividing that number by the last 12 months' earnings (or last 4 quarters). Let's use the company Karen's Cupcakes Inc. as the example to illustrate this. The company, Karen's Cupcakes, has a current price of $30.00 a share and the company earns $2.00 a share. Or put another way, the company has a $30.00 stock price and the company's earnings over the last 4 quarters were $2.00 a share. The *P/E Ratio* for Karen's Cupcakes would be calculated as follows:

$$\frac{P}{E} = \frac{\text{Current Market Price per Share}}{\text{Earnings per Share (EPS) over the last year}} = \frac{\$30.00}{\$2.00} = \$15.00$$

The P/E is also called the *multiple*. So in this example, Karen's Cupcakes is selling at a P/E or Price to Earnings of $15.00. This company is also selling at a multiple of 15 times its earnings.

Is this considered a high or low share price? Is it considered to have a high or low multiple? This entirely depends on several factors: the type of industry the company is in and also where the company fits into the *Industry Life Cycle* as shown below. The P/E of an individual company's stock should only be considered high, low, or fairly priced after comparing it to its competitors, the overall stock market, and in relation to itself. New IPOs, fads, and market sentiment can also contribute to the change in the *P/E Ratio*.

The second important calculation is the *Earnings per Share (EPS)*. The EPS is a portion of a company's profit that is allocated to each outstanding share of common stock. Think of it as an indicator of a company's profitability that also helps determine the overall quality of the company. The formula to find Fran's Fudge Inc.'s *Earnings per Share* is outlined below.

EPS = <u>Company's Total Earnings for 1 Year</u> = <u>$20 million</u> = $4.00
        Number of Shares Outstanding $5 million

Many market theorists consider the Standard & Poor's 500 Index to be an excellent barometer of U.S. companies and the U.S. stock market overall. When the S&P 500 (SPY) trades far above the average EPS of around $16 dollars a share, the market is too expensive and could be ready to take a breather or correct significantly. When the S&P 500 trades around $16 dollars a share it is considered fairly valued. When the S&P 500 trades far below a $16 EPS, the market is considered cheap.

Life Cycle of an Industry & How It pertains to Stock Price

To understand how and why a firm's rate of growth changes over time requires an understanding of the overall *life cycle of an industry*. This is highly relevant because it easily explains how and why a stock changes in price and why the stock's P/E Ratio changes in value.

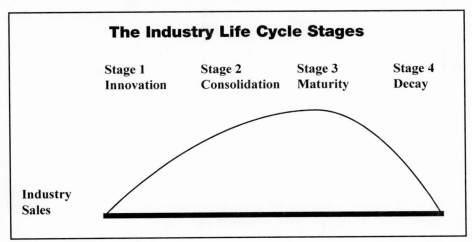

Chart demonstrates the sales of the company increasing, peaking in Stage 3, and then declining.

Stage 1
In many young industries, management expertise is low. The competition is high, and many companies first struggle just to get beyond their break-even points. Investment risk is extremely high. During this embryonic stage of the industry life cycle, the *innovation stage,* the casualty rate for newly organized firms can be horrific. The common stocks of these firms which have managed some degree of profitability tend to sport very high P/E ratios. Cash dividend payments are generally nonexistent for these firms and sales growth rates in excess of 100% per year are quite common.

Stage 2
The second stage of the industry life cycle is the *consolidation stage.* This stage is commonly marked by a significant reduction in the number of firms in the industry. Many firms are forced out of business. Other firms with acceptable product innovations but having inferior production capabilities or firms having an inability to raise capital to expand output are acquired by stronger firms in the industry at this stage. The level of management expertise and the firm's production and distribution efficiency also increases. These surviving firms are normally still growing at a rapid pace, and their need for new capital continues to remain high. As a result, these firms retain most of their earnings for reinvestment. Many engage in secondary common stock offerings to raise additional capital. Investment risk remains moderately high during this stage of development. The P/E ratios of these firms are also considered to be relatively high and commonly range between 20 to 40 times the expected per share earnings. Or, they can be much higher such as in the social network sector. For example in 2014, Facebook (FB) a social network company, had a P/E ratio of 83 and an EPS of 0.92.

Stage 3
During the third stage, the *maturity stage*, the industry is dominated by only a few very large and seasoned firms. Since much of the product demand is replacement demand, sales and earnings growth tends to slow to a rate paralleling the growth rate of the overall economy. The need for new capital diminishes and firms pay out a higher percentage of their earnings in cash dividends. Payout ratios of 50% or more are quite common. The P/E ratios for these firms fall considerably and most will sell at a multiple of 5-15 times next year's estimated per share earnings.

Investment risk is considered moderately low and institutional share-holders tend to dominate the trading in the shares of mature companies.

Stage 4

The fourth stage is the *decay stage*. Naturally, most firms try to avoid this. Demand for output declines in this stage and these firms in *Stage 4* begin to liquidate their production facilities. Firms with good management normally try to acquire firms in *Stage 2* of the industrial life cycle and attempt to replace their dated product lines to avoid industrial decay.

> **Platinum Tip:** *Try to wait until the industry has moved from Stage 1 to Stage 2 of its life cycle. Although large returns can be earned by investing in firms within the innovation stage of the cycle, corporate mortality rates and investment risks are many times too high to justify the potential rewards.*

Investing in firms that reside in the consolidation stage of the industrial life cycle can provide handsome returns with far less risk. Investment in growth firms at this stage of their lives can provide investment returns that average approximately 15-20% per year. Investing at this stage means paying higher than average P/E multiples (from 10-30 times estimated EPS) and sacrificing some current dividend yield. These firms are still relatively small and have not as yet gained a large following among institutional investors. Usually 15% of their outstanding common shares are held by institutions.

Shop (Stocks) 'til you Drop

"Shop 'til you drop!" has been a favorite saying for many women over the years. We shop enthusiastically for clothing, shoes, handbags, makeup and accessories. We relish in a good sale and get a shopping high and feel euphoric when that purchase suddenly becomes the "best buy of the century." We look at the same pair of designer shoes very differently when priced full retail versus when those same shoes are at a 20% discount or then marked down to 40% off. When these shoes become an enormous bargain and reduced by 60%, our perception of those shoes changes even more. Then finally, these designer shoes get placed on the metal discount racks, adjacent to the shoe department and labeled "final markdown." The smart and savvy buyer instinct comes out in all of us. The huntress of a shopper begins circling her prey and swoops in for the kill (purchase) around the 80% off bargain discount racks, salivating over the potential fantastic "steal of a deal" that can be picked up. We become giddy with excitement when that $500 pair of shoes finally becomes $125 or the $150 pair of shoes suddenly becomes a mere $20. It's exhilarating! These shoes no longer become a luxury item, but instead, practical, prudent and a "must have." They become…. an investment in your future? The answer is: maybe yes and maybe no.

Stocks perform in much the same manner as the bargain huntress shoe example above. Stocks can be fully priced, bargain priced, or reduced to downright fire sale prices. Just like a pair of shoes may come with a seductively, reduced price; there may be a defect in the shoes. Stocks are no different in this respect. A pair of shoes may warrant a significant price reduction due to: the stitching could be off, they may pinch your feet, the heel immediately breaks off the first time you wear them, or the company manufacturing the shoes went out of business, etc. Stocks too may come with a bargain price attached to them for similar reasons as well. The company may be "broken" and the stock is thereby defective. The company might be going bankrupt. Consumer sentiment may have changed and the company and the products it produces are out of fashion and so too is the stock. Momentum seekers and hungry buyers are no longer interested and instead shift their attention towards something else to purchase. The economy may have changed and with it the desire and abundance of loose cash chasing these once desirable items has dried up. Demand dries up and pushes the price down. That basement bargain price could now actually be priced correctly. And, that "steal of a deal" that you thought you had now makes you feel as if you were suckered into buying them.

The alternative can also happen. Going back to the designer shoe sale example, the shoes you selected to purchase suddenly become iconic. Princesses and movie stars around the world all of a sudden begin wearing the same designer shoes and the price skyrockets. Weren't you the smart, savvy, and sexy shopper! You spotted those gorgeous shoes on the final sale rack at Nordstrom or Dillard's for $25 when a year later that same designer's shoes could only be purchased for $650 a pair at Neiman Marcus and Saks Fifth Avenue! This same philosophy holds true with stocks. The stock could be broken but the company isn't. This means that the sale on the stock is not warranted and is only a temporary price reduction. It really is the deal of the century! Your investment really is an investment in your future! Your smartness and *"savviness"* paid off!

Begin to invest –
it does not matter how slowly you go
as long as you do not stop.

— Confucius

It's said that when Albert Einstein was asked what man's greatest
discovery was, he replied, "Compound interest!"

— Albert Einstein
(Small Stocks Big Profits, Pg. 14, by Gerald W. Perritt)

In my experience, selling a put is much safer than buying a stock.

— Kyle Rosen
(Boston Capital Management as featured in Barron's on 8/23/04)

The stock market is that creation of man which humbles
him the most.

— Anonymous

To know values is to know the meaning of the market.

— Charles Dow
(Co-founder, Dow Jones & Co., 1851-1902)

Bonding with a Bond

But which 007 Bond do I really prefer? Sean, Roger, Barry, George, Timothy, Pierce, Daniel or... _Raymond?_

(A girl's best friend is one that sticks around for a while: a Raymond James Bond!)

KNL

Chapter 14

Bonding with a Bond

007 Style!

There may be no such thing as 007 on Wall Street as in Hollywood but you can still be a sexy Bond Girl! And the men will not only respect you but they will revere you as the "Bond Goddess" when they see how smart you are in preserving your principle investment and how savvy you are by earning a good yield on that principle investment. You will suddenly become even sexier to them when you not only attain a good yield; but in addition, the prices of your bonds go up considerably in value. Now that is smart, sexy and savvy!

Smart women like to feel financially secure. It's nice to have a "nest egg" that continues to grow – even if it is slow and steady. Bonds used to be thought of as security investments designed for larger institutional investing and for retirees because of the stable income they can generate.

Bonds, however, are no longer just for the stogy, retiree investor type. Since bonds come with varying degrees of risk, maturities and yields, ranging from 1 year to practically infinity (*perpetuals*) and from triple A (AAA) backed by either an extremely stable government or corporation to high yield and junk bonds that offer a high amount of yield for more risk; bonds can be appropriately placed into almost any investor's portfolio as a smart investment asset class.

Today, many types of bond funds including *ETNs* and *mutual bond funds* offer investors a much greater variety to choose from. Additionally, they can provide more:

- Flexibility
- Versatility
- Diversification

Bonds Defined

A bond is simply a form of a loan or an IOU. The *holder* of the bond is the lender (creditor), the *issuer* of the bond is the borrower (debtor), and the *coupon* is the interest. Bonds are instruments of indebtedness of the bond issuers to the holders. Bonds are classified as a debt security, in which the issuer owes the holders a debt. And, depending on the terms of the bond, is obliged to pay them interest (the coupon) and / or to repay the principal at the maturity date. Interest is usually payable at fixed intervals (semi-annual, annual, and even monthly). Very often the bond is negotiable whereby the ownership of the instrument can be sold in the secondary market.

Bonds provide the borrower (corporations and institutions) with external funds to finance long-term investments. Governments, on the other hand use government bonds to finance current expenditures. Bonds and stocks are both called securities. Stockholders have an *equity (owner's)* stake in the company, whereas bondholders have a *creditor (lender's)* stake in the company. Being a creditor, a bondholder will have absolute priority and will be repaid before a stockholder (who is technically an owner) in the event of bankruptcy. Another difference is that bonds unlike common stocks almost always have a defined term or maturity, after which the bond is redeemed. An exception is an irredeemable bond (*perps* or *perpetuals*). An example of this is Consols, which is a perpetuity bond with no maturity.

Types of Bonds

Bonds come in many forms. This chapter will explore four common types of bonds: government (govies), corporate (corporates), municipal (munis), and high yield (junk).

Government Bonds

Governments as a rule spend more money in a year than they raise in revenue. Consequently, they are obliged to borrow money to cover their debt. Government debt markets are the largest markets in the world. A government bond is simply an "IOU" by the government with the promise to repay the debt at some date in the future. Over the life of the bond the holder receives interest, referred to as the coupon. At maturity, the loan (the principal) is repaid. The major government bond markets today are: the United States, Japan, Germany, France, Italy, the United Kingdom, the Netherlands, Canada, Belgium, and Spain.

Government bonds or "govies" as they are affectionately called by many bond traders come in a variety of flavors. Firstly, government bonds are distinguished by country such as Japanese, U.S. or German. Secondly, they are distinguished by maturity, for example a 20 year, 10 year or 1 year.

Platinum Tip: *If you think the U.S. stock market is going to falter, take your money out of stocks and put it in U.S. government bonds. It's normally considered a safer haven.*

Since August 1, 1986, U.S. Treasury notes and bonds have been issued in book entry form only. This means that the bondholder cannot physically keep the piece of paper anymore. The U.S. Secretary of Treasury is authorized to issue Treasury securities (bonds, bills, and notes).

Treasury Bills: are issued with maturities of 13, 26 and 52 weeks. They are auctioned at a discount. Bills are in book entry form held for investors through the Treasury direct system, and by financial institutions and Federal Reserve banks through the commercial book-entry system. Minimum purchase is USD $10,000 with larger amounts in multiples of USD $1,000.

Treasury Notes: are coupon-paying securities normally issued with maturities of 2, 3, 5 and 10 years. All notes have fixed coupons and bullet maturities. The minimum denomination is USD $5,000 for 2-, and 3-year notes and USD $1,000 for 5-, and 10-year notes.

Treasury Bonds: are coupon-paying securities issued with maturities over 10 years. The 30-year maturity is no longer issued today and has been replaced by the 20-year. All bonds have fixed coupons and bonds issued since 1984 carry bullet maturities. The minimum denomination is USD $1,000 with larger amounts in multiples of USD $1,000.

Callable Treasuries: The U.S. Treasury may decide to call in their debt and pay bondholders in advance of the maturity date.

Savings Bonds: The U.S. Treasury issues non-marketable securities such as Savings Bonds.

Government Agencies: like GNMA (Ginnie Mae), TVA or the Small Business Administration. Government agencies can issue marketable debt or guaranteed debt.

Government Sponsored Enterprises include the Federal National

Mortgage Corporation (Freddie Mac), Farm Credit System, the Federal Home Loan Bank System (Fannie Mae), and the Student Loan Marketing Association (Sally Mae). Government sponsored enterprises also issue marketable debt and guaranteed asset-backed securities.

Eurobonds: Eurobonds are issued in *bearer form*. The first Eurobond issued was in U.S. dollars in 1963 for Autostrade, the Italian road building company. The U.S. dollar has been the dominant currency for Eurobonds. However, other currencies especially JPY (Japanese Yen) are also popular. Eurobonds are traded globally, but the market is centered in London, England. Examples of Eurobonds include: Italian Eurobonds and French Eurobonds.

Eurobonds are bonds that are denominated in different currencies and sold to investors outside that country whose currency is used. Maturities are generally up to 10 years. They include FRNs and MTNs.

Global bonds are a subset of a Eurobond. They are issued in registered form. They are more liquid than a Eurobond and are globally distributed. Global bonds have a larger issue size.

Corporate Bonds

Want a larger coupon and a higher yield? Then, purchase a corporate bond. Corporate bonds (Corporates) are issued by large companies and institutions anywhere in the world. It could be a bank, insurer, utility or any large corporation that issues a bond to raise money to expand its business.

There are two types of corporate debt: *secured / unsecured debt* and *senior debt / subordinated debt*. Generally, *secured debt* is favored by an investor over *unsecured debt* and *senior debt* is favored by an investor over *subordinated debt* because they are perceived to be safer and have a stronger claim to the company's assets in the event of a default.

Corporate bonds will vary in their yield due to the perceived risk associated with a particular company and its financial viability (ability to repay its own debt). For instance Big Blue (IBM) and Proctor & Gamble (PG) are extremely stable, bell weather companies that have been around a long time. Investors have learned to trust them over the decades because of their ability to pay back debt in a timely fashion. Companies, on the other hand, that are in financial turmoil have bonds that typically exhibit a high yield. For this reason, the yield (reward) should match the risk. For instance, the yield on a risky corporate bond will be much greater than the yield on a "blue chip" corporate bond.

Finally, corporate bonds can be issued as very plain vanilla and straight forward or they can be issued with a little twist. The twist can come in either the form of a *call option* or as a *convertible bond.*

Call Option: allows the issuer to redeem the debt before its maturity date.

Convertible Bonds: allows the bondholder the ability to convert the bond into the equity of the same company. (Think of it as a bond with a stock option hidden inside.)

When compared to government bonds, corporate bonds are usually perceived to have a higher risk of default and thus command a higher yield to compensate the investor for investing in their company. This risk, however, depends on the particular corporation issuing the bond, the current market conditions, the particular government to which the bond issuer is being compared, and the rating of the company. A large, stable corporation can be a much safer bet than an unstable, small government.

Municipal Bonds

Municipal Bonds ("Munis") are issued by state, city, and local government entities. *Munis* can preserve your capital while generating a tax-free income stream. Basically, when you buy a muni, you are loaning your money to the issuer in exchange for a set number of interest payments over a predetermined period. Upon maturity of the bond, the value of the bond will revert to its par value. Municipal bonds are issued in both taxable and tax-exempt status. Tax-exempt status can mean free of federal, state, or local tax.

Two types of municipal bonds are not only tax exempt but are considered to be particularly attractive to risk-averse investors due to the high likelihood that the issuers will repay their debts. These two types of munis are called: *general obligation bonds* and *revenue bonds.*

General Obligation Bonds: General obligation bonds are issued to raise capital to cover expenses and are supported by the taxing power of the issuer. Examples include: parks and equipment, public parking garages, and roads and bridges that are meant to service the entire community.

Revenue Bonds: Revenue bonds are issued to fund infrastructure projects and are supported by the income generated by those projects.

Examples include: toll bridges and toll roads that service specific populations and are repaid through collecting user fees.

Purchasing a municipal bond normally is viewed as a conservative investment strategy. As with all bonds, however, some risks do exist with municipal bonds such as *credit risk* and *interest rate risk.*

Credit Risk: exists because the issuer is sometimes unable to meet its financial obligations. The issuer may fail to make scheduled interest payments and/or be unable to repay the principal upon the maturity of the bond. Many municipal bonds are backed by insurance policies guaranteeing repayment in the event of default.

Interest Rate Risk: The interest of most municipal bonds is paid at a fixed rate twice a year. The rate does not change over the life of the bond. If interest rates in the marketplace rise after you purchase the bond to 7% and your bond is only paying 3%, you are not keeping up with the rate of inflation. Also, if interest rates rise, the price on your bond will fall (a yin-yang relationship).

Junk Bonds

A junk bond is slang for below investment grade. High-yield bonds are also bonds that are rated below investment grade by the credit rating agencies and may or may not be labeled as junk status. Investors expect to earn much higher yields on both high-yield and junk bonds due to these bonds being associated with a higher risk of default.

Most people would not touch these securities with a ten-foot pole, unless you are someone like a Michael Milken who made his fortune by trading junk bonds in the 1980s. The average investor can get very hurt by dabbling in these bonds because their value could drop dramatically overnight. Junk bonds can either be a bond issued by a corporation (that is financially troubled) or a government (like Greece that was cut to junk status in 2010, because it was about to default on all of its debt and relied on the European government leaders to help bail them out). Junk bonds can also be a once viable company that has lost its financial footing (i.e. General Motors) or a government (i.e. an emerging markets country) and has slipped on the rating scale and is now considered trading at junk status. The rating (credit rating / worthiness) of the issuer is normally stated as "BB" or lower by Standard & Poor's or "Ba" or below by Moody's.

Platinum Tip: *Greater the risk, greater the reward. However, a company can default on its debt and you could end up losing everything. Sometimes the higher risk doesn't always justify the danger you face in a high yield product.*

Other Types of Bonds

Many, many more types of bonds exist. Although this book explores only the primary types of bonds that you the smart and savvy investor might invest in, other types of bonds worth noting include:

Zero Coupon Bonds: don't receive interest until maturity. These bonds are bought at a discount from their face value.

Convertible Bonds: can be converted into a fixed number of common stock.

Index Linked Bonds: the price fluctuates according to the index it is linked to.

Floating Rate Notes (FRNs): an example of an index linked bond. It is linked and floats according to LIBOR (the London Interbank Offered Rate), interest is reset every 3 months.

Medium Term Notes (MTNs): MTNs were first established in the U.S. during the 1980s by the two major auto companies. A large majority of MTNs are book entry and settle through DTC. They are normally senior *unsecured* debt obligations and rank *pari passu* with all other senior obligations. MTNs can be fixed-rate, floating, zero coupon, or have index-linked coupons.

Platinum Tip: *TIPS or Treasury Inflation-Protection Notes and Bonds can offer some inflation protection because their principal value is adjusted by the Consumer Price Index (CPI).*

Bond Pricing

A bond upon its maturity will always revert back to its original face value of 100 (par or par value). The price of a bond will be shown in newspapers, magazines, newsletters, and television shows as normally trading (or priced) at below 100 or above 100. For example: 98.57 or 102.85. The first example of 98.57 is said to trade at 1.43 below par. In the second example of 102.85, this bond is said to trade at 2.85 above par. Upon maturity or when the bond is "called in" prior to maturity the bond holders will be paid $1,000 per bond plus any interest on the bond. In other words, the price of the bond will go back to 100 or par value. The owner of the bond whose face value is 98.57 will make 1.43 (equating to 1.43% or $14.30 per $1,000) and the owner of the bond whose face value is 102.85 will lose 2.85 (equating to 2.85% or $28.50 per $1,000) upon maturity.

Example 1: How much would I earn at maturity on a $1,000 bond that currently trades at 98.57 to par?

Step 1	*Step 2*
100.00 par value at maturity	$1,000 face value
- 98.57 current price	x 0.0143 gain
$1.43 gain at maturity or 1.43%	$14.30 gain per $1,000 bond

An Inverse Relationship

Think of a bond relationship as a seesaw with price on one side and the yield on the other. This up/down relationship can be seen as a steamy hot/cold, love/hate, or yin-yang relationship. The simple reason for this is that when you are loving the yield on the bond at say 8%, the price has probably sunk – or vice versa. Or, the price of the bond increased 5% but the yield has now tanked to 3%. This is called the inverse relationship of the bond: high price, low yield; low price, high yield. It is only at maturity that the investor is made whole. In between that period is when a lot of trading happens for quick profits.

Platinum Tip: *An easy way to envision the price to yield relationship of a bond is to imagine a seesaw. On one side sits price and on the other side sits yield.*

"Clip the Coupon"

Are you a coupon clipper? Then you will like bonds. The coupon is actually a term used long ago when people received a bearer bond and actually kept the physical bond (under their mattresses or in a safe deposit box at a bank). The bond holder would physically clip the attached coupon on the bond and bring it in to get the money. Today, the lingo of a "coupon" is still used but most people have it automatically applied to their account electronically as part of the service that online brokers and full service brokers supply.

Interest

Interest on a bond is stated as a percentage and is normally paid on a semi-annual basis.

Issuer

The issuer is the company (i.e. Goldman Sachs, Morgan Stanley, or Ford) or it could be a government (i.e. United States, Germany, or Japan) that needed to borrow the money through the debt market and issued the bond.

Yield

The yield is normally slightly different than the interest. The yield is the rate of return received from investing in the bond. It usually refers either to the *current yield* or the *yield to maturity*.

Current Yield: also called the *running yield* is simply the annual interest payment divided by the current market price of the bond (or clean price).

Yield to Maturity: also referred to as the *redemption yield*. It is a more useful measure of the return of the bond, taking into account the current market price and the amount, timing of all remaining coupon payments, and the repayment due at maturity. It is equivalent to the *internal rate of return* of a bond, which is the true annual return on a bond if it is held until it matures.

Rating

Just as a student is rated with a grading system of A+ to an F, bonds are similarly rated on a grading scale from Moody's, S & P, and Fitch. 'AAA' by S&P and Fitch being the best and 'Aaa' by Moody's for the long-term. The worst long-term rating is a 'D' meaning *in default by* S&P and a 'C' by Moody's. Even as a student, Cs and Ds were never considered good grades! So why would they be any different for a company or government?

Factors that determine a bond's rating include: how well the issuer has paid off its debt in the past and the current economic conditions. Although they (the company or government) used to pay off their debt/ loan, a rating agency may think that they won't be able to do so in the near future because of current economic, company's management, or geo-political conditions. Greece, Portugal, Spain and Italy are all currently facing problems concerning their ratings. Even the United States dropped slightly in its credit rating because of global and domestic economic conditions during the last financial crisis.

Rating Agencies

Just like individuals are assigned their own personal credit ratings (from Equifax, Experian, TransUnion, etc.) due to personal savings and spending habits, bond issuers (companies and governments) receive their own individual credit ratings from Moody's, S&P, and Fitch which are based on a similar criteria. The ratings of a company or government can go up or down just like your own personal credit score. Rating agencies also look at the timeliness of paying back the bondholders, just like creditors look at the timeliness of an individual paying off their credit cards, mortgages and other debt.

To evaluate an issuer's creditworthiness, ratings agencies (such as Moody's Investors Service, Standard & Poor's, and Fitch) analyze a bond issuer's ability to meet its debt obligations. They issue ratings for the long-term from 'Aaa' or 'AAA' for the most creditworthy issuers to 'C' or 'D' for those in default depending on the credit rating agency's own criteria. Bonds rated 'BBB', 'Baa' or better in the long-term are generally considered appropriate investments when capital preservation is the primary objective.

Default

Just as you might default (not pay a loan back on a credit card, a car loan, or student loan payment on time), a government or company might not be able to make their payments to the owners of their bonds on time. They are termed to be *in default*.

Bond Holder

If you own a bond in your portfolio, you are a bondholder. Normally, the bond is "held" in your account at a brokerage company.

Types of Risk associated with Bonds

As with any investment, bonds are not without a certain degree of risk. The risks associated with bonds are highlighted in the following points.

Default Risk: the risk that the government or corporation could either go bankrupt or out of business. Or, they could simply stop paying the interest on their debt until they have money to do so.

Credit Spread Risk: the risk that the extra yield paid in order to compensate investors for taking greater default risk becomes insufficient compensation for the default risk that could deteriorate further. Since the coupon is fixed, the only way the credit spread can readjust to new circumstances is by the market price of the bond falling and the yield rising to such a level that an appropriate credit spread is offered.

Interest Rate Risk: Government bond yields may change and thus bring about changes in the market value of fixed-coupon bonds so that their *yield to maturity* adjusts to newly appropriate levels.

Liquidity Risk: A continuous secondary market may not exist for a bond, thereby leaving an investor with difficulty in selling the bond at, or even near to, a fair market price. This particular risk could become more severe in emerging (developing) markets, where a large amount of junk bonds are originated.

Supply Risk: Heavy issuance of new bonds similar to the one held may depress prices.

Inflation Risk: Inflation reduces the real value of future fixed cash flows. The perceived anticipation of inflation by the bond markets, or the reality of higher inflation, may depress prices immediately.

Tax Change Risk: Unanticipated changes in taxation may adversely impact the value of a bond to investors and consequently its immediate market value.

Bond Buying & Selling Tips

How are bonds priced? As already discussed in this chapter, bonds are priced using a par or par value. Par value equals 100. If a bond is priced at 97, it is selling below (or at a discount to par). If a bond is selling at 101.5 for instance, it is selling above or at a premium to par.

Market Price: The market price of a tradable bond will be influenced amongst other things by the amounts, currency, and timing of the interest payments and capital repayment due, general level of interest rates, the quality of the bond, and the available redemption yield of other comparable bonds which can be traded in the markets.

Clean vs. Dirty: The price can be quoted as clean or dirty. "Dirty" most commonly used in European markets includes the present value of all future cash flows including accrued interest. Whereas "Clean" most often used in the U.S. market does not include accrued interest.

Issue Price: Typically, the issue price at which investors buy the bonds when they are first issued will be approximately equal to the nominal amount. The net proceeds that the issuer receives are thus the issue price, less issuance fees. The market price of the bond will vary over its life: it may trade at a premium (above par, usually because market interest rates have fallen since issue), or at a discount (price below par, if market interest rates have risen or there is a high probability of default on the bond).

When to Buy: Normally you want to purchase a bond under par, not over par (par value) if you are holding the bond until maturity. Upon maturity, the bond will revert back to par or par value (always 100).

When to Sell: As an investor, you can either hold the bond until maturity. At maturity, you will receive the par value of the bond, meaning 100 percent of the face value of the bond. You may also sell any time before the maturity date. The bond can fluctuate above and below the par value. Naturally if you bought the bond at par 100 and sold the bond at 95. You would lose $50.00 or 5% of its par value. On the flipside, if you sell the bond at 102 and you bought the bond at 98, you have a nice little $40 dollar profit or approximately 4% on a $1,000.

How can I bond with a Bond?

You can purchase bonds direct from the U.S. Treasury on the internet or you can purchase them through your broker. You can also invest in mutual bond funds with Vanguard, Templeton, Dreyfus, Fidelity and the like. In addition, you can find ETFs and ETNs that focus on bonds.

Bonds can fit well into anyone's portfolio because they come in so many varieties and carry far less risk than common stocks. If you are just starting out, a bond fund might be more appropriate in your portfolio because they offer an easy and affordable way to buy and sell bonds. However, they may or may not have a manager overseeing the overall investment strategy of the fund. Remember, ETN and other Bond ETFs don't usually have financial managers but mutual funds do. Bond funds also provide diversification and hopefully less downside risk than buying just one bond. These will allow you to bond with as many bonds as you so wish!

> **Platinum Tip:** *Bonds have a yin-yang relationship when it comes to their price and yield.*

I'm not nearly so concerned about the return on my capital
as I am the return of my capital.

— *Will Rogers*
(American humorist & showman 1879-1935)

In investing, the return you want should depend
on whether you want to eat well or sleep well.

— *J. Kenfield Morley*

Experience is helpful, but it is judgment that matters.

— *General Colin Powell, b. 1937*
(Chairman Joint Chiefs 1989-1993,
Secretary of State 2001-2005,
quoted in The New York Times 10/22/2008)

Success in a free country is simple.
Get a job, get an education, and learn to save and invest wisely.
Anyone can do it.

— *William J. O'Neil*
(Founder of Investor's Daily)

Old McDonald had a Farm...

While old McDonald was out farming; Mrs. McDonald, the financially savvy one in the family, was trading commodities on her computer to hedge against a possible corn crop failure because old McDonald didn't have much of a green thumb!

Later in the day while old McDonald was out feeding the chickens and collecting eggs, Mrs. McDonald was checking the Wall Street Journal and buying winter wheat contracts to fund the new addition to their home sweet home on the range.

KNL

Chapter 15

Commodities:

Are Diamonds really a Girl's best Friend?

Old McDonald had a farm…and on his farm he had a commodity…
with some live cattle here and a pork belly there,
a corn stalk here and winter wheat there.
Here a trade, there a trade everywhere a commodity trade.
(And that's how commodities got started and old McDonald got rich!)

Farm girls across America recognize that for every season there is a crop and that equates to money – either gained or lost (depending how the crops and weather cooperate). City girls can also take advantage of these harvest cycles and capitalize on them too! All you have to do is think about what and when you consume food items in your fridge. Do you gorge on chocolate at Valentine's Day? Knock yourself out from all the tryptophan in turkey on Thanksgiving? And eat ham leftovers for a week after Easter? (Just to name a few holidays and eating customs). If this is the case, trading commodities might be an easy and very understandable investment strategy for you!

When imbibing in that Sauvignon Blanc, Chardonnay or Cabernet at 5pm (or at least 5 o'clock somewhere), just remember, that if it is a glass of vino worth remembering, it might just be that the futures might be worth investing in too! Case in point, I was running out of creative ideas on what to buy my husband as a birthday gift so I bought him some futures on Rothschild wine. He had to wait two years to get his cases of wine, but by then the price of the gift had tripled in value and he had fun keeping track of how much his wine was worth along the way.

If you are strictly a city girl and believe that *milk* (a commodity) doesn't come from a cow but from a plastic jug at the grocery store, you can surely relate to jewelry and the value people place on owning nice pieces of jewelry. Did you know that *diamonds, gold, silver, copper* and *platinum* all used in making jewelry are all considered to be commodities?

What is a Commodity?

Generally speaking, commodities are bulk goods such as grains, metals, and foods:

- **Grains** (such as Wheat – Summer Wheat and Winter Wheat, and Soybeans, Oats, Rice, and Rapeseed)
- **Metals** (such as Gold, Silver, Platinum, Copper, Palladium, Lead, Zinc, Tin, Aluminum, Steel, Cobalt, Rare Earths, and Nickel)
- **Foods** (such as Milk, Cocoa, Coffee, Frozen Concentrated Orange Juice, Palm Oil, Lean Hogs - pork, and Live Cattle - beef)

These bulk goods are then traded on a commodities exchange or on the spot market. Farmers use commodities as a hedge often times to guard against falling prices on their own crops and livestock (i.e. hogs and cattle). Speculators, traders, and investors see commodities as a way to potentially make money. Also, they see it as a way to diversify and hedge their investment portfolios.

More defined categories of commodities include:

- **Energy** (such as Crude Oil, Heating Oil, Brent Crude, Natural Gas, Ethanol, Gasoline, and Propane)
- **Softs** (such as Cocoa, Coffee, and Sugar)
- **Meats** (such as Live Cattle, Lean Hogs, and Pork Bellies)
- **Currencies** (such as the U.S. dollar, Euro, Swiss franc, British pound, and Japanese yen)

Commodities are Everywhere - Just look around You

Women across the world recognize diamonds as a good investment. Most of us grew up hearing the song, *"Diamonds are a Girl's best Friend"* written by Jule Styne and Leo Robin and then memorialized and sung on Broadway by Carol Channing and also in the Hollywood film with Marilyn Monroe, entitled, *"Gentlemen Prefer Blondes."* Some of the lyrics are on the following page.

Men grow cold as girls grow old
and we all lose our charms in the end.
Diamonds are a girl's best friend

He's your guy when stocks are high
but beware when they start to descend.
It's then that those louses go back to their spouses
Diamonds are a girl's best friend.

Diamonds have the cache of lasting forever: unlike many a spouse! Diamonds never lose their sparkle (although they do tend to shrink in size over time while wearing them!). And, normally diamonds will go up in value over the years (provided they were of good investment grade and quality to begin with). If treated as a part of your total asset portfolio, they can also be a very good investment. Again timing is everything, as diamond prices trade up and down in value just as other tradable commodities.

Women also are drawn to the luminosity of other gem stones such as rubies, emeralds and sapphires; in addition to, the jewelry designs created by molding *gold, platinum*, and *silver* into beautiful creative designs. But did you know that these are also considered to be commodities?

You use another well-known commodity every time you fill up your gas tank at the pump. Your house is probably built from another commodity, namely *lumber*. And you eat commodities each and every day such as: *beef, pork, chicken, sugar, wheat, corn, cocoa, coffee, soy (soybeans), etc., etc.*

Look at the clothes you love to wear: *wool* for your winter coats and sweaters, *leather (live cattle)* for your jackets, shoes and handbags, and the *cotton* t-shirts, dresses and shorts for summer. Everyone uses *cotton* towels in the bathroom and kitchen and most people sleep in *cotton* sheets at night. Petroleum products are used in many spandex type outfits and elastic types of clothes: stretchy cotton jeans; undergarments (from "mentionables" such as Under Armour (UA) and Victoria's Secret (LTD) to "unmentionables" from Madam X, and the like); yoga and athletic work-out clothes (i.e. Lululemon Athletica (LULU), Nike (NKE), and the like); and so on and so forth. We wear commodities, eat commodities and live in commodities every day!

Diamonds – A Girl Investor's Best Friend?

Women wanting to invest in diamonds have several choices at their fingertips: stocks, funds or the stones themselves! Stocks such as miner Rio Tinto (RIO), jewelry seller Tiffany (TIF) and online diamond merchant Blue Nile (NILE) are well-known names in the diamond arena. Funds such as JP Morgan Global Natural Resources and First State Global Resources offer some exposure to diamonds, while an exchange-traded fund (ETF), the Gem Shares Physical Diamond Trust, may be arriving soon. More exotic prospects include the U.K.'s Pink Iguana Enterprise Investment Scheme. A direct way to try and profit on diamond prices is simply to buy the diamonds directly. Investors need to pay special attention to the pricing, origin of a given diamond, the expertise of a jeweler who's selling it, and how it measures up in terms of the Four C's – clarity, cut, carat weight, and color.

The Diamond Concierge Service based in Manhattan's Diamond District utilizes suppliers in New York, India, Israel, and Belgium. They find diamonds for individual buyers, basically operating as a match-maker.

The diamond market has a wide range of participants ranging from wholesalers, middlemen, and retail. Like all industries some partici-pants are better than others. Normally, you want the highest quality you can get (and can afford) for the least amount of money: highest quality for the lowest price.

Research & Basic Fundamentals on Diamond Investing

The *rapaport.com* and *idexonline.com* are two industry trade publica-tions that report on trends and pricing. *The Rapaport* also publishes a diamond price list for the industry to which diamonds' prices are bench-marked.

It would be advisable for diamond investors to look at historical data and future forecasts of the diamond market as a whole, then research the niche markets (i.e. blue, pink, and yellow diamonds), because price trends and liquidity differ dramatically between niches. For example, pink diamonds from the Argyle mine in Australia have increased in price over the last few years due to waning available supply from that particular diamond mine. (Once again, this is the simple economic rule of *supply & demand*.) Therefore, investing in pink diamonds now may be too late. Instead, you might want to bide your time and wait for a pullback in prices. For white diamonds, the Asian and Indian markets have grown dramatically over the past decade and forecasts continue to show an upward trend. These markets demand diamonds of higher clarity. For this reason, buying a diamond that is flawless to VVS [very, very slight inclusions] in clarity could be considered a "safer investment" for return on your capital than an SI1 for instance.

The Gemological Institute of America (GIA) located in the U.S. is the largest, most well-known, and most internationally accepted institute which grades stones (including diamonds) and issues certificates. The "Four C's" were developed by the GIA. Other respectable companies, however, grade diamonds. A few examples include: the European Gemological Laboratory (EGL International), the European Gemological Laboratory (EGL USA) located in the U.S., the American Gem Society (AGS) in the U.S., and Gublein in Switzerland.

> **Platinum Tip:** *Don't invest in physical diamonds if you need quick liquidity. Instead, invest in stocks, funds and ETFs. The selling process on a physical stone can be compared to real estate (a tangible asset) – the right buyer is out there somewhere, but you must be patient.*
>
> *One way to maximize the number of potential buyers is to choose a diamond that has ideal characteristics and has investment grade carat weight, cut, color, and clarity. A non-ideal diamond will have a smaller realm of buyers within the wholesale market when you are looking to resell your diamond(s).*

Types of Commodity Products

There are many types of commodity products in the market place today that enable smaller investors to purchase commodities. You can diversify your portfolio through the use of *ETFs, ETNs, Commodity-Backed Bonds* which are tied to the price of an underlying commodity, and *Commodity Paper* which are secured by commodities. *Mutual Funds* also specialize in commodity funds, either bundling them all together or separating them into categories of commodities.

Easily traded examples of ETFs and ETNs include: XLE, IYE, DBO, DBA, MOO, JJG, GLD, SLV, OIL, and UHN. Just to name a few!

Platinum Tip: *Always do your homework. There is a plethora of commodity based ETFs and ETNs out there and some are riskier than others. Make sure you follow the market while invested in any product because some markets and securities trade with wider fluctuations and volatility than others and experience higher peaks and lower troughs.*

How can You make Money from trading a Commodity?

For every *season* there is a commodity. Commodity prices rise and fall according to the season. *Summer wheat* and *winter wheat* are examples of commodities that trade according to planting, growing and harvests. These commodities are said to trade on a *seasonal* basis.

Commodities make seasonal highs and lows each year. Commodities also follow *cycles* and these cycles can be very short or span many years. Sky high gas prices and long lines at the pump caused by a lack of supply in the 1970s is a perfect example of a *market cycle*.

Holidays and Holiday Seasons can all significantly affect the prices of specific "food" commodities and also the price of oil. Summer road trips cause an increased demand on fuel for your car. Summer BBQ Season and Fourth of July celebrations mean more hot dogs, hamburgers, fried chicken, and ice cream being consumed. Thanksgiving creates mega demand for turkey, green bean casseroles, and pumpkin pie. Wedding Season in India triggers a much larger demand for gold (for jewelry). There are many holidays both religious and secular that significantly affect the prices of commodities around the globe.

Summer Road Trip Vacations translates to more gasoline consumption.

Heating Oil, especially in the Northeast, sees higher consumer demand in the winter months rather than in the summer months. Companies that supply heating oil to its customers must purchase heating oil months in advance to lock in prices.

Platinum Tip: *Did you know that you too, as a customer, can lock in a winter contract price with your heating oil supplier! You just need to watch the price of heating oil and then call your company and negotiate a price for the winter months in your area. It could save you money!*

Housing Starts, Stops & Bubbles. Spring ushers in more housing starts. Just think of all the commodity products like lumber, copper, steel, and aluminum that are used in building a house! You can take advantage of the next housing boom by investing in commodities that go into building a house as opposed to the home builder stocks!

Farmers' Harvest & Planting Schedules. *"The Wheat Cycle"* has a very definite seasonal pattern. Winter wheat is planted in the fall and harvested in midsummer. The harvest is normally around June-July. Supplies are normally most abundant (supply high = lower wheat prices, supply low = higher wheat prices). Wheat prices normally decline in February due to the "February Break" as more supply from the southern hemisphere enters the market place.

Do you love chocolate? Then trading *"The Cocoa Cycle"* might be your favorite way to make money. Cocoa also trades in a seasonal pattern and has a strong tendency to peak in March and bottom in June. Although cocoa butter is derived from the cocoa bean and is used in numerous products, ranging from cosmetics to pharmaceuticals, the main use is still that of chocolate candy and confections. It is no wonder that Valentine's Day and Easter create more demand for chocolate thereby triggering increased demand in cocoa and a spike in cocoa prices. (demand high = higher cocoa prices)

For all of you Starbucks, Dunkin' Donuts, and Costa coffee fans out there, you can learn to make money off your coffee addiction by trading the *"The Coffee Cycle."*

Commodities also rise and fall in price due to changes in supply and demand. An oversupply of orange juice left past its expiration date in the refrigerated section of your local grocery store will be disposed of because it goes bad. So too, commodities have a defined date on the contracted bulk amount. The price goes up and down during this time according to the perceived demand of the product and the undersupply or oversupply of the product.

Mother Nature with her earthquakes, tsunamis, hurricanes, tornados, and volcanic eruptions all disrupt the mining, growing, and shipping of commodities that, in turn, either positively or negatively affect the prices of commodities. Weather plays a very large role in forecasting the price of many crop related commodities. Weather can freeze orange crops. Drought or flooding can destroy wheat, corn, and soybean crops.

Too hot or too cold of weather can wreak havoc or produce a bumper crop. Bumper crops aren't necessarily good if the supply completely outstrips the demand because prices of these commodities will then fall. Balance is needed as with everything in life!

Political upheavals can prevent shipping of commodities across the ocean. A perfect example of this are oil shipments from the Middle East. How many times in the news do you hear about the cargo and oil tankers being held up near the Suez Canal? Likewise, political upheavals and border disputes can and do shut down the mining of gemstones and diamonds in Africa, India and Burma just to name a few places. Rare mineral mining that goes on in Tibet is subject to border disputes and political upheaval.

Where are Commodities traded?

Just as stocks trade on stock exchanges, commodities trade on commodities exchanges. Some commodities are more readily available to the public than others. For instance, diamonds are traded on a diamond exchange but are not readily packaged up in a tradable form for the retail investor. Oil and gold, however, can be easily traded by an individual investor.

Just like the SEC (Securities & Exchange Commission) regulates the U.S. stock exchanges, so too, commodities trading is also regulated in the U.S. by the government. The CFTC (Commodities Futures Trading Commission) was established in 1974. Commodity futures that include all commodities traded in organized contract markets fall under the jurisdiction of the Commodities Futures Trading Commission.

Commodity exchanges are where both commodities and derivatives products are traded. Commodities exchanges usually trade futures contracts on commodities. These contracts can include spot prices, futures, forwards and options on futures.

Example: A Kansas farmer wishes to hedge her next crop of wheat. She therefore sells a futures contract on the wheat, that won't be harvested for several months to come. This contract guarantees her a specific price in the future for her wheat.

A national cupcake and bread manufacturer located in Ohio buys the contract now to guarantee (lock in) a price so that the cost of making the different varieties of cupcakes and breads won't go up when the wheat is delivered.

In this example, the use of a *commodity futures contract* is intended to protect both parties: the farmer and the cupcake manufacturer. The farmer is protected from a potential drop in wheat prices. Whereas the buyer, the cupcake and bread manufacturer, is also protected from the possibility that wheat prices may rise in the future.

The following list consists of commodity exchanges found in the U.S. and are categorized by location. However, the exchanges are constantly changing due to mergers and acquisitions of the major commodities exchanges.

Short Name	Commodity Exchange Names & Products Traded	Location
ICE	Intercontinental Exchange Energy, Emissions, Agricultural, Biofuels	Atlanta
	Hedge Street Exchange Energy, Industrial Metals	California
CBOT	Chicago Board of Trade (part of the CME Group) Grains, Ethanol, Treasuries, Equity Index, Metals	Chicago
CCX	Chicago Climate Exchange Emissions	Chicago
CME	Chicago Mercantile Exchange (part of the CME Group) Meats, Foreign Currencies, Euro dollars, Equity Index	Chicago
	Nadex Exchange Energy, Industrial Metals	Chicago
USFE	U.S. Futures Exchange Energy	Chicago
	Flett Exchange Environmental	Jersey City
KCBT	Kansas City Board of Trade Agricultural	Kansas City
	Memphis Cotton Exchange Agricultural	Memphis
MGEX	Minneapolis Grain Exchange Agricultural	Minneapolis
NYMEX	New York Mercantile Exchange (part of CME Group) Energy, Precious Metals, Industrial Metals	New York

Commodities exchanges are located all over the globe. The above list only represents those located in the United States of America.

The Skinny on Commodities

Commodities in general can offer another type of diversification to your overall portfolio. Some smart women understand the tangible aspect of a commodity better than say a stock or a bond. Other savvy women understand the patterns of commodity trading better than other types of investments. If either of these scenarios best describes your way of thinking, commodities could be an excellent way for you to make money the smart, sexy, savvy way!

Platinum Tip: *Like other investments, beauty is in the eye of the beholder and there lies the value and upside potential of a commodity. The more people want and desire the product (commodity), the higher the price will rise because the supply diminishes and makes the product harder to come by. Likewise, some people might not see that investment as a thing of beauty. Instead it may be fraught with ugliness and warts! That is what makes a market: a buyer and a seller. Some love the product and buy it, while others hate the product and sell it.*

If you bet on a horse, that's gambling. If you bet you can make three spades, that's entertainment. If you bet cotton will go up three points, that's business. See the difference?

— Blackie Sherrod (Sportswriter, born 1919)

If the market does not rally, as it should during bullish seasonal periods, it is a sign that other forces are stronger and that when the seasonal period ends those forces will really have their say.

— Edson Gould (Stock Market Analyst, lived 1902-1987)

Commodities tend to zig when the equity markets zag.

— Jim Rogers

It's not the strongest of the species (think commodity investors and traders) that survive, not the most intelligent, but the one most responsive to change.

— Charles Darwin

Futures, Derivatives & Options

KNL
&
FBJ

Chapter 16

Futures, Derivatives and Options:

Are they in your Future?

The Big "O" - Options

Many years ago, I had a friend called April who was a stay-at-home mom. After a disastrous second marriage, she found herself in the midst of an ugly divorce. Her estranged husband even had the audacity to book an engagement party with his girlfriend at a top New York hotel while divorce proceedings were on-going between him and April. Instead of getting mad, April decided to get even. She began investing in herself instead of commiserating in her misfortune. My friend stayed home and kept watching CNBC and Bloomberg, learned a great deal about the stock market, and began to successfully trade options. April turned out to be extremely gifted in options trading and later worked professionally in this field to hide her successful trading profits and capabilities from her soon to be ex-husband.

Options opened another door for this lady and it can do the same for you, if you do your homework and use them wisely, options can be your best friend!

Options Defined

Options can be a useful way to help generate income and potentially increase returns. Options can also be used as an instrument to decrease downside risk in a portfolio. One of the major attractions of options is also their versatility. They can be used individually or combined in various ways to create strategies that modify an investor's risk/reward ratio. Options come in two types: *calls* and *puts*. However, there are many varieties of call and put options, and strategies that combine both.

Simply put, (no pun intended!), an option is either the *right to buy* or the *right to sell* a security at a given price at a future date in time. An option gives you just that: the *option*. You can: buy, sell, or do nothing and let the option premium expire worthless.

There are four components of an option: the *option premium* or *contract price*, *contract size*, the *strike price*, and the *expiration date*. The *premium* is the market price of the option. The *contract size* is 1 to 100 shares of a company's stock. This means that 1 option contract can be bought on 100 shares of Apple stock. The *strike price* is the price at which the option's owner can buy or sell the underlying investment. All options contracts have *expiration dates* after which time they are no longer in effect. Options expire on the Saturday immediately following the third Friday of the month, nicknamed *witching* and *triple witching*. Sound scary? Sometimes they can be scary. These witching days or option expiration days have a reputation of creating higher volatility in the marketplace. Options also have settlement terms that specify whether the writer of the option must deliver an underlying asset, cash, or a combination of the two.

There is one more vital component in options, namely *volatility*. The more volatile the share price of the stock; the more money that can be made by trading options.

Options generally are traded during normal daytime business hours on U.S. options exchanges and for a short period afterwards. However, trading in options is not confined to those hours. Trading of options in the evening and night trading sessions occurs in foreign currencies and overseas markets. Moreover, when there are unusual market conditions, an options market may authorize trading to continue for a substantially longer period than under normal conditions. Additionally, options on foreign currencies and debt securities are traded in international markets and are virtually on an around-the-clock basis.

Types of Calls

There are basically *two* types of calls:

1. a ***covered call*** (sensible and conservative)

2. a *naked call* (very risqué and risky as the name implies! – ooh la la!)

A *covered call* is one of the most common option strategies. This means you sell a call option on shares you actually own. Whereas, the writer of a *naked call* option does not own a long position in the stock on which the call has been written and is therefore completely exposed.

How a Call Option Works

Say for instance, you own 50 shares of Nirvana Chocolates stock because you like its tasty, steady dividend of 3.5% in addition to the scrumptious chocolate that they manufacture. Even though you are creating sizeable demand for their chocolates by consuming some each and every day and your waistline is beginning to show it, the stock's share price just hasn't been as cooperative in its performance as you would have liked. In fact, the stock hasn't increased much over the last few years. What could you do to possibly enhance the return on your Nirvana Chocolates stock?

Option 1: You can either, do nothing and hold onto the security and collect the dividends because you think eventually the stock could go up significantly. After all, you and all your friends are communicating using Facebook and Twitter and other forms of social media that you simply adore Nirvana Chocolates and can't get enough of it. You are confident that your friends will tell their friends and spur on a rapid demand increase for the chocolates in the hope that some Wall Street analysts catch on and will raise the target price of the stock.

Option 2: You can potentially generate income by selling a call option on your Nirvana Chocolates shares of stock but first you will have to purchase an additional 50 shares. (This is because options are sold as 1 option per 100 shares of stock and you only own 50 shares at present.) This will give the investor who purchased the call option (that you sold the option to) the right to purchase your Nirvana Chocolates shares from you at a preset price on or before a preset date, assuming your share price triggers the option strike price during the contract period. In this case, you must hope your shares don't reach that price during that time period so you can keep selling call options and receiving the premiums in addition to the 3.5% yearly dividend. While you are waiting for the stock to break out of a trading range, this could offer a nice way to make a profit.

Option 3: You purchase the call option on your 100 shares of Nirvana Chocolates. However, the stock price rises above that preset price and triggers the strike price on the option for your stock to potentially be called away by the investor who purchased the call option (that you sold to them). You can hope that this person doesn't really care for chocolate and forgets that he/she owns the option. Although not likely, it does happen. You can see how this strategy can limit the upside potential of the underlying stock position, as the purchaser will likely exercise the option and take ownership of the stock from you at the present price, also known as the *strike price*. In this case, you will receive the small stock price appreciation, the option premium, and the dividend (provided you didn't have to sell the security before the ex-date for the dividend payment).

Strategies & Examples on Calls

Purchasing a call option gives you the right to buy 100 shares of a particular stock or stock index at a predetermined price before a preset deadline, in exchange for paying a *premium*. For instance, buyers who think a stock will go up dramatically but can't afford to purchase a lot of the shares because it would be too costly, have another option. Namely, a call option when purchased by an investor permits that person to purchase a lot of shares for a very small price in relation to purchasing the stock itself. Call contracts are cents on the dollar compared to purchasing the stock itself. In addition, purchasing a call option instead of the stock can limit your downside risk. If the stock price on 100 shares first rises past the strike price but then plummets from $1,000 a share to $10, you as the shareholder would be out a lot of money. However, you as the option holder would only lose the premium (provided you chose not to exercise the option).

Example: Sale of a Call Option

You own 1,500 shares of Fashionista Corp. worth $10,000. You can sell a call option contract for a premium of $3 per share and collect $1,500.00. If the stock price of Fashionista Corp. drops or does not reach the call's strike price within the time limit of the contract, the option would expire, and you would pocket the $1,500.00 premium, less your transaction cost of $15 for selling the option.

$3.00 x 1500 shares = $1,500.00
$1,500 - $15.00 commission = money in the piggy bank

Types of Puts

A *put* is the opposite of a call. It means that you have the right to *put it to* or *sell it to* someone else by exercising your right.

There are basically *two* types of puts:
1. a *covered put* (sensible and conservative)
2. a *naked put* (very risqué and risky as the name implies!)

The buyer of a put option expects that the stock price will be going down in the short-term and purchases the right to "put" the stock to someone else by exercising the option under the terms of the option contract. The put option grants the right to sell but not the obligation to sell, at a specified price, a specific number of shares by a certain date. The put option buyer gains this right in return for payment of an option premium.

The seller of the put option is obligated to buy the underlying shares at the agreed upon price within a specified time limit, if the strike price is reached. A put option seller grants this right in return for receiving the option premium. The put option seller hopes the stock will remain stable, and will neither rise nor drop by an amount less than his or her profit on the premium.

The writer of a naked put option does not have a short position in the stock on which the put has been written. Naked options are extremely risky but can potentially offer significant financial rewards to the investor.

> **Platinum Tip:** *Being caught naked is never a good idea! The same applies to option trading! Always make sure you have something on underneath like a good solid stock.*

Strategies & Examples on Puts

Options can be used as a hedge to reduce risk in much the same way as an insurance policy can provide protection against a catastrophic loss. If an investor owns stock and does not want to sell it, even though it may decline in the near future, a put option could be bought as temporary insurance against a large decline.

Example: Buying a Put

Your Glamourama stock is trading at $50 a share. You own 100 shares of stock plus boxes of their lipsticks and eye shadows in every color. After trying their makeup you've decided that you don't like their cosmetics because it makes you breakout and fear that the stock you purchased might go down significantly in the short-term until the company fixes their formula. You could buy a *put contract* on them for $3 a share, with a strike price of $45 ($5.00 below the current share price). If the stock drops below that, you can exercise your contract. You will have limited your loss to $5 per share, plus the premium, fees, and commissions, which in this case equal $510.74. For peace of mind it might be worth purchasing the put option.

($5.00 x 100 shares + $9.99 commission + $0.75 premium) = $510.74

Lipstick on the Collar – Not this One Baby!

A more sophisticated option strategy is *the collar.* This type of option trading strategy is frequently used to limit risk. Think of it like the collar on a shirt. It wraps itself around the security in both directions to protect the underlying security from huge price fluctuations in either direction. The purpose of the collar is to protect the buyer from a massive decline in share price while earning an option premium from selling (writing) the covered call on the underlying security. Usually both the purchased put option and sold call option expire within the same month.

Example of a Collar

Say you own the stock Trophy Handbags and its current price is $10 a share. You simultaneously buy a put for protection and sell a call option. By selling a call option with a strike price of $13 for $.50 per share premium and buying a put option with a strike price of $7 for $.50 per share premium, the collar would ensure that the gain or loss would be no more than $3 per share (plus fees and commissions).

$10.00 share price + $3.00 = $13.00 *and*
$10.00 share price − $3.00 = $7.00

It's your Option

The following techniques sound risqué but they are actually in the Wall Street vernacular! Who ever said Wall Street is boring never worked there! They must have gone to a cabaret show or kinky night club to have come up with these option strategies: *the straddle, the vertical spread,* and *the strangle* (no joke!) And there are more like these. Leave it to a bunch of men on a trading floor to come up with these names!

The *straddle* consists of an equal number of puts and calls purchased or written simultaneously with identical strike prices *and* expiration dates. The purpose of the straddle is to enable the buyer to profit from a major price change in either direction while limiting the risk to the total combined premiums paid.

The *vertical spread* is formed by simultaneously buying and selling options on the same underlying stock with identical expiration dates *but* different strike prices.

The *strangle* is related to the straddle. This option strategy uses option derivatives on the same underlying security. There are *long strangle* strategies and *short strangle* strategies. Sounds a bit kinky, doesn't it?

> **Platinum Tip:** *The world is your oyster when it comes to the many varieties of option strategies available. Be choosey. Just like a bad oyster can make you sick, a bad option strategy can make your portfolio reel with pain!*

Buying the Exchange

Instead of buying a particular future, option or derivative, you can also take advantage of this sector by "betting on the house" itself. For example, you can purchase shares of the CME Group (CME), the owner of the Chicago Mercantile Exchange which exclusively lists interest-rate derivatives. The CBOE Holdings (CBOE), owner of the Chicago Board Options Exchange, exclusively lists options and futures on the CBOE Volatility Index (VIX). The International Securities Exchange (ISE) operates a leading U.S. options exchange and has merged with the Eurex Exchange owned by Deutsche Boerse AG to form one of the largest transatlantic derivatives marketplaces. Buying shares in the actual exchanges offer smart and savvy investors a side door entry way to profit from interest rate volatility and also stock market downturns.

Do you see Options in your Future?

It's really your call (again no pun intended!) if options are for you or not. Options can be complicated. In fact, many people have a difficult time understanding them. Options aren't for everyone so don't feel badly in any way if you prefer not to dabble in them.

Options strategies come in many more varieties than described in this chapter. This book has only touched upon the basics in options trading because of the complexity around options and options trading.

If however, you particularly take a liking to them then stay focused, do your homework, and learn everything you can about options. Keep investing wisely and make sound investments based on your time horizon, risk tolerance, income, and financial needs. You can create your own financial future. Good luck and good fortune!

Terms used in Option Trading

Call Option – A contract that gives the owner the right to buy an investment at a specified price within a specific time period.

Expiration Date – The date on which an option and the right to exercise it cease to exist.

Extrinsic or Time Value – Any part of the option price that is not reflected in its intrinsic value.

In the Money – A call option is in the money when its strike price is lower than the actual market price of the stock. A put option is in the money when its strike price is higher than the stock's current market price.

Intrinsic Value – refers to the "in-the-money" portion of an option's price. A call option has intrinsic value when its strike price is lower than the actual market price of the stock. A put option has intrinsic value when its strike price is higher than the stock's market price.

Multiple-leg Options Order – An order to simultaneously buy or sell two or more different options. Multiple-leg option strategies can entail substantial transaction costs – including multiple commissions, which may impact any potential return – and often involve greater risks than a basic option trade.

Naked Call – is a strategy in which the investor writes a call option without owning the underlying security. (It does not mean that it is nude!) This strategy, however, does subject the investor to unlimited risk.

Options Contract – A contract that gives the buyer the right to buy or sell an investment, such as a stock, bond or commodity, for a certain price by a certain date.

Out of the Money – A call option is *out of the money* when its strike price is higher than the actual market price of the stock. A put option is out of the money when the strike price is lower than the stock's market price.

Premium – The total price of an option contract includes the premium, or the cost paid if you are buying the option, or cash received if you are selling the option.

Put Option – A contract that gives the owner the right to sell an investment at a specified price within a specified time period.

Settlement Terms – This part of the contract specifies whether the writer (or seller) of the option must deliver an underlying asset, cash, or a combination of the two.

Strike Price (also called the Exercise Price) – is the price at which the option's owner has the right to buy or sell the investment.

In my experience, selling a put is much safer than buying a stock.

— Kyle Rosen
(Boston Capital Management as featured in Barron's on 8/23/04)

I'm a great believer in luck,
and I find the harder I work the more I have of it.

— Thomas Jefferson

Investment strategies that worked yesterday may not work tomorrow –
a good reason to do something today.

— Anonymous

Travel the World without leaving Home

Chapter 17

Global Exchanges:

Travel the World
Without Leaving Your Home

What is an Exchange?

An exchange is a market or marketplace. Simply put, it is where people come to buy and come to sell. It is where they can make a market in something either tangible or intangible. Exchanges and markets have existed since the beginning of time.

The History of the Stock Exchange

The dynamic history of the stock exchange spans well over 2,000 years and is forever evolving. Taking many twists and turns through the centuries to finally morph into what we now know as today's stock market, bond market, commodities, and options and derivatives exchanges, these exchanges located around the globe continue to change as the needs of its users continue to change.

Ancient Mesopotamian clay tablets record interest bearing loans. The Roman statesman Cicero in 390 B.C. wrote that people had *partes* or *shares* and stated that, "these shares had a very high price at the time." Fast forward over 1,000 years later and history records that back in the 9th century (the 800s A.D.) a letter by Emperor Louis the German to hold free trade fairs evolved into the beginning of the Frankfurt Stock Exchange in Germany. By the 1500s, Frankfurt had already developed an economy based on trade and financial services. In 1585 a *boerse* was established in Frankfurt to set up *fixed currency exchange rates*.

Meanwhile, the authorities of the Republic of Venice in 1171 concerned about their war-depleted treasury decided to pay 5 percent interest per year on a forced loan (called *prestiti*) with an indefinite maturity date that had been drawn from all of their citizens, thereby starting the origins of the *bond market*. Many believe that the modern day exchanges took root in Venice, Italy in the 1300s. The Venetians were the leaders in the field of moneylenders in Europe and filled important financial gaps by trading debts between each other. They were also the first to start trading securities from other governments. They would carry slates (instead of laptops) with information on the various issues for sale and meet with clients in hopes of selling the securities. Similar to *brokers* today, these lenders began to sell debt issues to their customers (the first *individual investors*).

As far back as 1531, Belgium had a *stock exchange* in Antwerp (but without stock). Brokers and moneylenders would meet to deal in business, government and even individual debt issues. Only *promissory notes* and *bonds* were exchanged.

By the late 1500s, English merchants were experimenting with *joint stock companies* that were intended to operate on an ongoing basis. One example, the Muscovy Company tried to force trade away from Hanseatic League dominance and in favor of Russia. In 1571, The Royal Exchange was opened by Queen Elizabeth I in London. During the 1600s, however, *stockbrokers* were not allowed in the Royal Exchange because of their rude manners. Instead, these stockbrokers had to operate from other establishments in the vicinity, such as coffee houses. These brokers and investors did their business in the various coffee shops around London. *Debt issues* and *shares for sale* were written up and posted on the shops' doors or mailed as a newsletter.

Several big steps in the evolution of the stock market happened in the 1600s. First, the Dutch East India Company was formed in 1602 as a *joint-stock company* based in six locations with *shares that were readily tradable*, thereby starting what we know today as the modern stock market. However, since stocks were not allowed to be traded with multiple addresses for a company, the stocks were re-designated as coming just from Amsterdam. Second, by 1636, tulip bulbs were traded on the stock exchanges of numerous Dutch towns and cities, encouraging all members of society to speculate in the markets. Many people traded or sold their possessions to participate in the tulip market mania. Unfortunately like any bubble, it all came to a horrible end in 1637, when prices dropped, panic selling began, and people lost their fortunes. Third, the Dutch, British, and French governments in the 1600s all gave charters to companies with East India in their names. Sea voyages that brought back goods from the East were extremely risky. In order to lessen the risk of a lost ship ruining their fortunes, ship owners sought investors who would put up money for the voyage (outfitting the ship and crew) in return for a percentage of the proceeds if the voyage was successful. Investors spread their risk by investing in several different ventures at the same time. When the East India companies formed, they changed the way business was done. These companies had stocks that would pay *dividends* on all the proceeds from all the voyages the companies undertook, rather than going voyage by voyage. These were the first modern *joint stock companies*. Because the shares in the various East India companies were issued on paper, investors could sell the papers to other investors. Unfortunately, there was no stock exchange in existence, so the investor would have to track down a broker to carry out a trade (much like a *private placement*).

It wasn't until 1773 that the first stock exchange in London was officially formed. Soon after, in 1790 the "Board of Brokers" in Philadelphia was located at the Merchants Coffee House, now known as the City Tavern, at the corner of Second and Walnut Street. Two years later, in 1792, the New York Stock Exchange (NYSE) began by twenty-four stockbrokers and merchants who gathered in front of 68 Wall Street under a Buttonwood tree and signed the Buttonwood Agreement.

Today, exchanges exist in many major cities around the globe and are listed in the back of this chapter. In fact, there are well over 250 exchanges worldwide but many are very small.

The New York Stock Exchange

Out of all the exchanges formed throughout the centuries, the most famous exchange worldwide today is the New York Stock Exchange (NYSE). This exchange like all others is constantly changing with the times. Some of the history of the NYSE includes the ringing of the opening bell that has long been a symbol of the NYSE and is aired on television stations throughout the world each day. The very first "guest" to ring the bell was Leonard Ross, who at age 10 won a quiz show answering questions about the stock market. 1967 ushered in the first woman member of the NYSE, named Muriel Siebert. After being turned down by the first 9 men she approached for sponsorship, she finally successfully became a "member" and then crusaded to have a ladies room installed, although you had to walk through a telephone booth enclosure to gain access to the ladies room! In 1970, Joseph L. Searles III became the first African-American to become "member."

Technology has continued to improve the stock exchange. In 1918 pneumatic tubes, containing stock orders, were installed to allow floor brokers to send order slips quickly to clerks. The original ticker tape machines were retired years ago and handheld terminals, flat screen panels, and fiber optics have all been tremendous upgrades.

Successful mergers and acquisitions have likewise continued to transform the NYSE. In 2006 the NYSE converted "member seats" (1,366 seats) into shares and the NYSE began trading as a public company. Then in 2007 the NYSE merged with Euronext, a large pan-European exchange to become NYSE Euronext (NYX). The NYSE then purchased its rival the American Stock Exchange in 2008. The Intercontinental Exchange (ICE) then acquired the NYSE Euronext in 2013. Today, the NYSE is the home to stocks, options, and derivatives trading. However, derivatives volume far exceeds stock trading volume.

Why Invest in an Exchange?

By investing in exchanges, you can gain exposure to a specific economy, the success of a specific region of the world, and a specific type of market. Or, you can gain some exposure to one country or many countries, depending on the type of exchange.

For example, you believe that Africa is going to boom over the next 5 to 10 years. Instead of buying the stock of a particular individual company in Africa that is listed on an exchange, alternatively you can invest in an exchange in Africa. There are 29 exchanges in Africa, representing 38 nations' capital markets with the Johannesburg Stock Exchange (JSE) being the largest. The Egyptian Exchange (EGX), Casablanca Stock Exchange, Namibian Stock Exchange and the Zimbabwe Stock Exchange are also in the top 10. By investing in an exchange, you can gain some exposure to that region instead of *cherry picking* an individual company listed on one of the African exchanges.

Perhaps instead, you believe that the European continent is going to boom in the next 2 years. You decide to invest in Western Europe as opposed to Africa. The Euronext might be the perfect investment opportunity as this pan-European exchange is based in Amsterdam, Brussels, London, Lisbon, and Paris.

Everyone can find something that they understand or can relate to when it comes to investing. Perhaps you found the commodities or options chapters in this book too complicated or felt uncomfortable about investing in bonds. Don't worry, investing in an exchange could be much simpler and could offer quite a bit of global exposure as well. For example, orange juice futures require an investor to have a thorough background of industry knowledge, technical ability and instinct to be a brilliant trader in that field. However, anyone can buy a share in the CME which is the exchange for trading commodities.

Stock Exchanges as an Investment

In recent years, privately held stock exchanges in the United States and around the world have gone *public*. These stock exchanges sell shares just like any corporation (IBM, Starbucks and Pfizer, and the like) through *IPOs* and *public offerings*. Many public stock exchanges now even list their shares on the NYSE as well as the NASDAQ. Many investors have been rewarded handsomely for investing in the exchanges because of all the merger and acquisition activity.

Explosive Growth of Derivatives Markets

The derivatives market is growing faster than the stock market! Based on the value of the underlying securities, it is already larger than the stock market. Because options and derivatives exchanges have become a very profitable business for the exchanges, many exchanges trade options and derivatives in addition to stocks.

The advent of electronic trading for stocks has significantly contributed to, as well as, being a major driving force of this explosive growth. Faster "fills" for larger volumes of stocks allow options traders (and their computers) to implement new strategies and offset greater options positions through hedging the underlying securities.

Mergers create Efficiencies and Increase Value

Securities exchanges derive their value from the economies in which they operate in. Also, they tend to perform best when they focus on the geographical region in which they are located. As a result, their value increases exponentially when regional equities and derivatives markets are merged under one exchange. This enables the merged entities to offer a wider spectrum of financial products at a lower cost, providing benefits to the capital markets of that country or region.

Platinum Tip: *Mergers, acquisitions and stock buy-back programs by corporations can all unlock shareholder value and increase the price of your shares.*

Exchanges and their Locations

The list on the following page shows many of the world's largest exchanges and their locations. There are hundreds of many, many smaller exchanges scattered across the globe that are not listed. Also, due to the creation of new exchanges and constant mergers and acquisitions between the exchanges, the list of world exchanges continues to change. The world's exchanges remain dynamic, ever changing with the times. The chart on the next page by the World Federation of Exchanges found on Wikipedia.org lists the top 21 stock exchanges ranked according to market capitalization as of June 30, 2014. Eight of the largest commodity exchanges and the largest options exchange are also listed at the end of this chapter. This will help get you started on your quest for finding the right exchange to invest in!

World's Largest Stock Exchanges
Ranked by Market Cap.

Exchange Name	Headquarters	Economy
New York Stock Exchange (NYSE)	New York	U.S.A.
NASDAQ	New York	U.S.A.
Japan Exchange Group comprising comprising the Tokyo Stock Exchange and Osaka Securities Exchange	Tokyo	Japan
Euronext combines Euronext France, Netherlands, Belgium, Portugal	Amsterdam	Europe
London Stock Exchange Group	London	U.K., Italy
Hong Kong Stock Exchange	Hong Kong	Hong Kong
Shanghai Stock Exchange	Shanghai	China
Toronto Stock Exchange	Toronto	Canada
Deutsche Boerse (DAX)	Frankfurt	Germany
SIX Swiss Stock Exchange	Zurich	Switzerland
Shenzhen Stock Exchange	Shenzhen	China
National Stock Exchange of India	Mumbai	India
Bombay Stock Exchange	Mumbai	India
Australian Securities Exchange	Sydney	Australia
Korea Exchange	Seoul	S. Korea
BME Spanish Exchanges	Madrid	Spain
BM & F Bovespa	Sao Paulo	Brazil
JSE Limited	Johannesburg	S. Africa
Taiwan Stock Exchange	Taipei	Taiwan
Singapore Exchange	Singapore	Singapore
Moscow Exchange	Moscow	Russia

Eight of the Largest Commodity Exchanges
(in alphabetical order)

Exchange	Headquarters
Chicago Board of Trade	U.S.A.
Chicago Mercantile Exchange (CME)	U.S.A.
Hong Kong Mercantile Exchange	Hong Kong
Kansas City Board of Trade	U.S.A.
London International Financial Futures and Options Exchange	England
London Metal Exchange	England
New York Mercantile Exchange	U.S.A.
Tokyo Commodity Exchange	Japan

World's Largest Options Exchange

Exchange	Headquarters
Chicago Board Options Exchange (CBOE)	U.S.A.

Seize the Day!

You are the master of your own destiny. Investment opportunities are endless. Find the ones that best suit you, your personality, and your risk tolerance. By following your intellect, woman's intuition, and having a bit of luck, you too, can conquer the world of investments, one trade at a time. Every country experiences their Golden Age at some point in history. *Carpe diem!*

When you change the way you see things,
the things you see change.

— Anonymous

Confidence is the hinge on the door to success.

— Fortune Cookie

Every country experiences their Golden Age
at some point in history. Invest in their success!

— Karen & Fran

Cash is Queen

Chapter 18

Cash & Cash Equivalents:

Cash is Queen!

Ever heard of the saying, "Cash is King!" There is a reason cash is considered the "King" of all transactions. It is easy to transfer, spend, and transact with. As long as the cash is not counterfeit, most people prefer cash to checks, credit cards and IOUs. Cash and cash transactions can be much harder to trace. Every person no matter their age can spend cash but not every person can have checks or credit cards. Because this is an empowerment and financial investment guide for women, naturally "Cash is Queen!" in our book!

Cash Defined

Cash is classified as an asset, namely a liquid asset on a balance sheet. Cash represents paper currency, coins, negotiable money orders, checks, and also bank balances that you can easily withdraw on short notice.

Cash & Cash Equivalents

In the financial statements of annual reports, cash is usually grouped with *cash equivalents*. Cash equivalents are defined as all highly liquid securities with a known market value and having a maturity of less than three months. They are known for their safety and are virtually as good as cash.

> **Examples include:** Money Market Funds, Checking Accounts, Traveler's Checks, Foreign Currencies. Some CDs, Commercial Paper, and Treasury bills (depending on length of their durations / maturity lengths) are also included in this category.

Foreign Exchange

The only exception to cash not being the "King or Queen" but instead the "Jester" is when the currency is devalued against other currencies. When your U.S. dollar suddenly plummets in value against other foreign currencies and is now worth a third or half of what it was 6 months ago, you feel like a poor American abroad. Hotels, food, transportation and tours are now deemed very expensive. Don't you feel like the Jester? Instead of the Queen doling out your greenbacks for trinkets and souvenirs, you feel like the poor foolish American holding onto a worthless currency. Instead of haggling for sport with the local vendors, you barter because the item is really too expensive. That cheap vacation to Mexico just got *very* expensive. Instead of having a toast with champagne, you have to toast with the champagne of beers!

Example 1: Daisy the Camel in Egypt

My husband, also a Wall Street banker, and I learned all too well that our U.S. dollar was undesirable and virtually worthless in comparison to the British pound and the Euro when we took a trip to Egypt a few years back. We were riding a camel named Daisy, as you do, around the three pyramids just outside of Cairo. The camel owner said we had to "pay before we dismounted the camel." (Camel owners are very sneaky when it comes to the art of negotiating.) Although we had previously negotiated a price for the two of us before we got onto the camel's back, the camel owner had asked enough questions while we were riding to know we were living in London and not in the U.S. at the time. My husband proceeded to pull out the greenbacks from his "Big Mac" sized wallet, stuffed with various currencies. The camel owner spotted our British pounds and Euros in the wallet in addition to our U.S. dollars. The camel owner suddenly refused to take the American greenbacks. He said every day the currency was devaluing more and more. (This was true!) When he would go to the bank at the end of the day to make the exchange into Egyptian pounds, the money was worth less and less. Even the camel owner got it – that "cash is only king or queen" when the currency is stable or going up in value! Don't get me wrong, the U.S. dollar still had value, just considerably less than the other two currencies we had in our wallet. As the British pound and Euro were appreciating in value the U.S. dollar was depreciating in value! A lesson in foreign exchange well learned.

Example 2: German Hyperinflation 1919-1923

Germans experienced a horrible devaluation of their currency between 1919 and 1923. Germany had abandoned the gold backing of its currency in 1914, lost WWI and much of their manufacturing and industrial area, and was forced to make reparation payments in gold-backed German marks under the Treaty of Versailles. The Germans began to lose confidence in their Weimar Republic government. The currency became unstable and plummeted in value.

In January 1919, Germans could buy 1 ounce of gold for 170 German marks. By November 30, 1923, that 1 ounce of gold cost 87,000,000,000,000 German marks. No joke! The German mark had devalued so much during those years that it required a wheelbarrow or suitcase to carry the small denominations of German marks to buy just a loaf of bread! The Reichsbank (central bank) came out with the 1,000 billion German mark in 1923. In 1923, the exchange rate between the U.S. dollar and the German mark was 1 U.S. dollar to 1 trillion German marks!

Example 3: Fear & Panic of Currency Devaluations and Cash Crises

Germany isn't the only country to suffer huge devaluations or the fear and panic of currency devaluations. The U.S. after the 1929 Stock Market Crash entered into the Great Depression which spurred bank runs (run on the banks) because people were afraid their money wasn't safe anymore. The now infamous classic Christmas film by Frank Capra *It's a Wonderful Life* was adapted from a short story written in 1936 by Philip Van Doren Stern. The Hollywood film released in 1946 portrays how a bank run can happen. Jimmy Stewart who plays George Bailey attempts to run a small-scale local bank referred to as a Building & Loan (Savings & Loan). The bank is denied capital that it was reliant upon and chaos soon begins. The Bedford Falls people, fearful that the bank is about to crash, all arrive at the bank to withdraw their savings: a typical depiction of a run on a bank during the Great Depression.

In 1994 the Mexican Peso Crisis (the Tequila Crisis) was caused by the sudden devaluation of the Mexican Peso. Argentina suffered the Argentine Peso Crisis and Argentine Economic Crisis between 1998 and 2002. Argentine people also believed that the Argentine Peso would be devalued and people rushed to the banks to convert them to U.S. dollars.

The Zimbabwe Hyperinflation between 2008 and 2009 caused

Zimbabwe in 2009 to abandon its currency. As of 2014, Zimbabwe still does not have a national currency but uses other countries' currencies. Currency devaluations and crises can happen to any country and it does happen!

When is sitting on Cash a good Idea?

If you have children in school or college and need tuition money to fund their educations, keeping cash in a savings or checking account is recommended to meet those financial demands. Just think if little Harry or Harriet couldn't go to school for 6 months because their mother didn't have the cash on hand to pay their tuition and books?

You should also keep enough cash in either a checking or savings account to easily match your spending habits each month. Paying off credit cards in full and other monthly expenses such as utilities, house and car payments is a must with all smart, sexy, savvy women. Why pay extra amounts in late fees and interest payments when the savings rate is so low anyway?

Medical bills and caregiver costs for you, your aging parents, husband or child can rack up too. And, insurance doesn't always cover these expenses. Likewise, healthcare premiums (if not automatically deducted from your pay check) will need to be paid with cash or cash equivalent funds.

You may decide you have had it with your current profession and boss. With some cash on hand you can comfortably make that lifestyle and career change you have always dreamed about. Or, you might wish to take a 6 month long sabbatical from teaching and travel to Africa and live amongst a village group of people with the Peace Corp. The world is your oyster when you have that cushion of cash!

Make a list of *all* your monthly expenses and match your expenses to your cash on hand. It is always a good idea to keep *at least* 3 months' worth of cash on hand to cover those expenses. The rest of your money can be put to use in other investments and purchases.

Platinum Tip: *Decide what gives you bliss and go for it! With some cash on hand, the world is your oyster!*

The Rainy Day Fund

The *Rainy Day Fund* is a doomsday scenario. You lose your job. Your significant other runs off with another woman (or man)! Little did you know! Perhaps you, a relative, or a pet needs emergency surgery. A tornado, hurricane, tsunami, flood, lightning bolt, or earthquake destroys your home sweet home and the fine print in your insurance policy doesn't cover you for that particular type of disaster. Murphy's Law!

Rainy Day Funds can also be less dramatic but just as necessary. Your spouse just pulled into your driveway with a new, shiny blue Corvette. You want pay back and drive in the next day to your home with a new, racing red Jaguar convertible. Touché! You look in the mirror one day and decide a few nip-n-tucks are a worthwhile investment in yourself, but your significant other disagrees and refuses to give you the money for the procedure out of your joint funds. Or, perhaps you want to take a college course, exercise class, painting and jewelry making class or another type of self-improvement or hobby course. Maybe, you want to get a manicure every week and your spouse thinks that it is money ill spent, or you want that little black dress at the department store you've had your eye on for a month. Perhaps, you just got dumped by your boyfriend and you need chocolate, strong alcohol, a box of tissues and large pizza with extra cheese. Don't worry….that is where the *Rainy Day Fund* comes in!

This fund can be tucked secretly away in a cookie jar, coffee can, home safe, or coat pocket in your closet. Alternatively, you can set up a checking or savings account at a local bank with just your name on it. The *Rainy Day Fund* can be a life saver in times of need!

Cash: a Four Letter Word?

Admittedly cash doesn't earn much sitting in a bank account these days, however, cash is not considered a four letter word (even if it is four letters: **c-a-s-h**). Although investment advisors will try to sell their services and say that they can earn you more money than if your money is just sitting in a bank account drawing little or no interest; they can also lose your money or tie it up in a long-term investment vehicle that is hard to get out of. Nothing should keep you from comfortably squirreling away 6 months' worth of cash to keep you safe from the curve balls life can throw.

Waiting for a Stock Market Correction

Every good investment advisor will tell you to keep some cash on hand to jump into the market after there has been a 5-7 percent correction. After all, the mantra with the markets is "buy low and sell high." These corrections are normal and healthy. In fact, they happen quite periodically. Less frequently, 10-15 percent corrections and even much deeper 40 percent corrections happen within market cycles. Fortunately, deeper corrections occur much less frequently than the normal 5-7 percent corrections. Keep some cash on the sideline, listen to the market news, and get ready to pounce on the stocks you want and have researched to be a good investment… and make more cash!

Platinum Tip: *The money that money makes, makes money!*

How to Double your Cash

In order to find the number of years required to double your money at a given interest rate all you have to do is to divide the compound return into 72. This is called the *Rule of 72.* The result is approximately the number of years that it will take for your initial investment to double.

The Rule of 72

Formula: Divide the compound return into 72. This will equal the number of years required to double your money.

Examples:

- If the bank pays a 1% interest rate, divide 1 into 72 and you get 72 years that it will take to double your money.

- If the bank pays a 4% interest rate, divide 4 into 72 and you get 18 years that it will take to double your money.

- If the bank pays a 10% interest rate, divide 10 into 72 and you get 7.2 years that it will take to double your money.

Plan your Vacation around Foreign Exchange

Planning on a vacation abroad? You may want to investigate which country offers the most value for the U.S. dollar? This fluctuates daily, monthly and yearly. If you are planning to take a vacation in a foreign country, ask your local bank for a list of currency exchange rates. Many are posted on signs that fluctuate as the prices change. Foreign exchange bureaus, kiosks and offices are located across the country including many shopping malls and local banks.

By taking advantage of *currency cycles,* it could enable you to have a "champagne taste" vacation on a "beer budget." Everything from hotels, meals and tours cost much less when the foreign currency depreciates (is weak) against the U.S. dollar. Your U.S. dollar will stretch a lot further if you shop around. You may take a view that this year I will go to Spain and Italy instead of Australia or Canada because Spain and Italy's currency is the Euro. The Euro is currently extremely cheap versus the U.S. dollar. Likewise the Mexican peso might be trading at a premium to the U.S dollar this year so I will take my holiday in Argentina instead because their peso is weak against the U.S. dollar. You could get a 30% discount on your vacation just by playing the currency market!

Where can I get the best Exchange Rate?

ATMs, credit cards, currency exchanges, local banks or exchanging at the hotel front desk all offer foreign exchange transactions. Get the most purchasing power for your U.S. dollar by shopping these rates as they can vary greatly. Normally ATM's and local banks will offer you the best exchange rate rather than a foreign exchange kiosk set up at an airport, but not always. Currency exchanges have also been known in certain places to offer better rates than the big bank around the corner. Many credit cards now waive the transaction fee to become more competitive in their rates as well. You shop for a good price on food at the grocery store and the best price to fill up your gas tank, so why wouldn't you shop for a good rate on your foreign exchange transaction?

Cash reigns Supreme

Cash is Queen in our book and reigns supreme especially when the going gets rough. No one expects the rough years to happen but they always do. But you, the smart, sexy, savvy woman that you are, can easily prepare in advance for these times. Be the "Queen" with your stash of cash. Ignore anyone who tries to intimidate you by saying you are foolish for keeping *at least* 6 months' worth of cash on hand at either a bank or in a brokerage account. You may decide your comfort level is greater or smaller than a 6 month stash of cash. That's ok too! Everyone's comfort level is different.

Cash may technically be spelled with four letters,
but cash is not a four letter word in our book!

— Karen & Fran

If your money devalues against another currency,
then cash is a four letter word!

— Karen & Fran

The money that money makes, makes money.

— William D. Gregg
(Words of Wisdom from my father, lived 1933-2014)

Cash is Queen!

— Karen & Fran

A weak currency is a sign of a weak economy,
and a weak economy leads to a weak nation.

— H. Ross Perot

Pension & Retirement Investing

Slow and steady wins the Race!

We came late to the retirement race but are *determined* to catch up!

$25 a day, each day, every day - Whew! I think I can, I think I can... I know I can!

Just $25 saved each day and tucked away into a retirement account for 40 years is $365,000.

But... compounded annually at 8% results in a retirement nest egg of $2,380,358.00.
Now that's a cushy retirement!

KNL

Chapter 19

Pension & Retirement Investments:

Plan Now to Enjoy Later!

Powerball and Mega Millions lottery tickets or hitting the million dollar jackpot on the "wheel of fortune" at the local casino (which my ex-brother-in-law actually did) are some people's view of retirement savings. They think they will never be able to save enough from their hard earned salaries to ever dream of retiring. Think again. It can be done – one hard earned dollar at a time!

It's never too early to start thinking about the future. Only you can effectively pick out the right kind of savings plan that best matches your retirement goals. Financial advisors can help select pension and retirement plans that are suitable to your needs; but at the end of the day, it is your money so you must be the ultimate decision maker!

Retirement investing encompasses many different financial products and types of investing. The most marketed and wide spread retirement investment vehicles include: Pension Plans, 401(k) Plans, Company Stock, IRAs, Annuities, and Life Insurance.

401(k) and Company Retirement Plans

Many employers offer their employees retirement plans under the heading of a 401(k) Plan. A name designated under federal income tax codes. A 401(k) Plan is a deferred taxable investment account which means the tax is owed upon withdrawal of the funds. Normally, two types of plans exist at a company depending on which plan the company chooses. It is considered an added benefit of working for that particular company as not all companies offer 401(k) Plans.

The first is a straight forward 401(k) whereby the employee is the sole contributor; and, the second is a plan whereby the employer matches part or all of the monies the employee puts into the deferred taxable investment account.

Two Types of 401(k) Plans:

1. **Straight Forward 401(k) Plan** (the employee is the sole contributor).

2. **Matching 401(k) Plan** (employer matches part or all of the monies the employee puts into the deferred taxable investment account).

Two drawbacks to investing in 401(k) Plans are the following. First, you may have a limited number of investment options. And second, you will be subject to the employer's plan rules and may not be able to invest in things you understand or would like to invest in. Third, you may not be able to withdraw your funds without penalties and tax consequences.

The 401(k) Double Whammy: A 54 year old surveyor, during the Great Recession (as some have coined this last financial crisis) needed to withdraw money from his 401(k) Plan at his former employer to live on because he lost his job. His employer, a small family business like so many in the Midwest, was forced to lay him and other employees off in an attempt to keep their doors open for business. Shortly there-after, the company proceeded to go out of business due to the lack of promised federal stimulus money which was slated to repair our country's bridges, roads, highways, etc. The money never made it in time to keep the workers in place. He has been unsuccessful in finding similar employment or even somewhat suitable employment that uses his skills. Part-time surveying jobs are the maximum that he can find. He couldn't make ends meet on $450 a week unemployment benefits (which lasted 2½ years) and was forced to withdraw from his only savings – his old company's 401(k) Plan. Mortgage payments, car insurance, food, health care insurance, etc. eroded what little savings he had in short order. Little did he know that the IRS, operating under the U.S. federal government, even under these circumstances, was standing by ready to take its share of his withdrawn funds from his 401(k) Plan as current income / taxable salary. The federal government couldn't even cut him a break by taxing it at a lower rate of long-term investment / capital gains income. Instead they taxed him at the highest rate of ordinary income. The old "Rob Peter to give to Paul, you might ask?" Absolutely.

The *Double Whammy* came because he was not yet 59½. At age 59½, you may be eligible to withdraw funds without penalties but you will still incur a higher tax rate on these withdrawn funds. To cover the taxes he owed from early withdrawal on his 401(k), he charged his taxes to lower interest bearing charge cards. These credit cards' low APRs (Annual Percentage Rates) changed and the rates began to ratchet up. After 2 years and still unemployed, his charge cards ramped up. The low 3% APR suddenly rocketed to a 9% APR. Once he maxed out his credit cards, he used his debit card to pay for the taxes owed on his 401(k) withdrawals. He signed up for a regular, systematic payment of his taxes on a debit card at his local Walmart. With this program, he incurred penalties, interest and taxes because the timely debit card payments weren't monitored correctly. He thought he could set up the direct debit transaction and nothing would go wrong. But *Murphy's Law* kicked in. (If something can go wrong, it will). Some payments were paid while others were not. Call it computer error or call it human error. Whichever it was, taxes and penalties grew on his debit accounts and charge card accounts until he was forced to look at the possibility of filing for bankruptcy.

What can You do with an old 401(k) Plan?

If you have a 401(k) or 403(b) left at a former employer and are not sure what to do with the funds, don't fret. Since your 401(k) assets are often a significant portion of your retirement savings, it is very important that you weigh the pros and cons of your investment options.

Generally, you have *four* choices readily available to you:

1. Leave the assets in a previous employer's plan.

2. Roll over the assets into an IRA.

3. Roll over the assets to a new employer's workplace savings plan (if it is allowed).

4. Cash out or withdraw the funds.

Check your previous employer's rules for retirement plan assets regarding former employees. Most companies allow you to keep your retirement savings in the company plan after you leave the firm. This might make sense, particularly if you've been laid off or fired abruptly! Your money continues to grow in a tax-deferred account while it provides you time to really explore other employment options, stress free. Some benefits to leaving your assets in an old plan include: penalty-free with-drawals in case you leave your job in or after the year you reached age 55 and expect to start taking such withdrawals before turning age 59½. Also, discounted or "institutionally" priced investments in your old plan may not be able to be rolled over into an IRA.

If you want to roll the 401(k) into an IRA, you are allowed to do this. Insist on a *direct* rollover to a financial institution so you are not penalized. The reason for this is because if the check is made payable to you personally, your employer must first withhold 20% of the rolled over amount for the IRS, even if you indicate that you intend to roll it over into an IRA within 60 days. Only upon filing your income tax return, can you then receive credit for the 20% withheld by your employer. Keep it simple! Always ask for a *direct rollover* so it goes directly from one institution to another institution. That way, it keeps you (as the middle man) out of the transfer.

An IRA enables your investments to grow tax deferred, just like your 401(k). Also, an IRA could provide many more investment options than a typical employer 401(k) Plan. In addition, IRAs allow penalty-free withdrawals for a first-time home purchase or qualified education expenses if you are under the age of 59½.

Cashing out is usually never a good option and should be done only as a last resort because of the penalties normally associated with doing this. If you tap into your 401(k) as in the *Double Whammy Example* before the age of 59½, generally you will be subject to both ordinary income taxes and a 10% early withdrawal penalty!

Always evaluate the underlying fees and expenses of the investment options in your 401(k) versus an IRA. All plans differ. There could be quarterly administrative fees for managing the account, as well.

Company Stock

As a rule of thumb, the key to smart investing is diversification. Never have a disproportionate amount in any one investment category or vehicle. The reason for this is simple. When one investment goes up, another normally goes down and vice versa. From an academic view point, if you were completely diversified – you would neither make money nor lose money. Therefore the idea is to diversify and hedge the downside risk while allowing for upside on your investments. Basically, choose your investments wisely and choose types of investments that do not overlap with each other. For instance, don't have a portfolio that only consists of one stock, namely the company you work for.

Whatever retirement investment you choose that makes the most sense for your particular retirement needs and desires, make sure you monitor your accounts and investments. Turning a blind eye and filing it away for the future could spell disaster for your retirement nest egg. At least, on a quarterly basis, review all retirement accounts and documents. Make a schedule of when you can change allocations in your 401(k) Plan. Each employer plan is different. The plan you have might specify that changes to allocations can only be made every certain number of weeks, quarters, or it could even be yearly. Make sure there isn't a *"nest egg" sabotager* ticking away that is ready to go off to ruin one or more of your investments. Watch the market news on television or listen to it on the radio. Read magazines and newspapers which track your particular investments. You never know when a company has hit a speed bump with their current and future earnings and is headed for a downfall. Turning a blind eye could set you back years from your retirement. Insurance companies aren't immune to having payout difficulties to their policy owners either. Companies that hold your retirement plan can go bankrupt and your employee retirement plan can be changed drastically.

Platinum Tip: *Don't put all your eggs into one basket or all your "nest egg" into one stock.*

Many people sink their entire bonuses into what they know best – the company they work for. In fact, companies sometimes pressure employees to purchase *company stock* or invest in *partnership funds* to build up the firm's own capital base. This tactic helps companies grow and have a stronger capital structure. If the company goes under, however, you (the employee) are wiped out financially. Case in point: Enron.

The Enron Case: Enron was a high flying energy company which was growing by leaps and bounds. One of my personal friends became an energy trader. He moved his family over from London, faithfully invested every bonus he had for four years back into the company, because it seemed like a safe and smart investment. After all, who knew the company better than he? Unfortunately, people at the top of Enron did not convey the full truth about the company to its employees. When the company collapsed like a 'house of cards' virtually overnight, the employees who put all their hard earned salaries (bonuses) back into the firm lost everything! Four years of hard work went down the drain! Four years of their lives, four years of sacrifice, and four years of potential retirement savings lost forever. They had to pick up the pieces, brush off the self-pity, and start all over again. This time moving once again to another country that would hire a trader with the scarlet letter of Enron displayed on his resume. Although entirely not his fault, nor the fault of many other innocent employees, these employees became victims of the Enron fiasco, lost all their company stock, and in many cases, their life savings.

Net Unrealized Appreciation

Holding company stock in your firm's savings account could also produce a *net unrealized appreciation* (NUA), if you withdraw these funds. Special tax treatment may apply to highly appreciated company stock if you move the stock from your workplace savings account into a regular (taxable) brokerage account. If you leave your company before retirement, consider making a rollover to an IRA to postpone paying the taxes until retirement age. You may wish to consult with either a financial advisor or tax advisor regarding your individual situation.

Pension Plans

Pensions and pension funds are just one of many types of retirement investment vehicles. Pensions come in a variety of shapes and sizes.

IRAs

Traditional IRAs (Individual Retirement Accounts) are *tax-deferred*, *self-directed* accounts. Remember, tax deferred does not mean tax exempt. It simply means the tax owed is put off into a future point in time when the money is withdrawn. *Self-directed* means either you or an investment advisor (of your choosing) will manage the investment of the assets in your IRA. This could be a good thing or a bad thing depending on the investments you select over time. You could also lose your entire savings in an IRA if you select investments that go down in value. Or, you can make a fortune with deferred taxes if you choose the right strategies and investments. With an IRA, you direct your financial future. There are two types of IRAs: a **Roth IRA** and a **Traditional IRA**.

1. **Roth IRA**

    A. Can provide federal tax-free withdrawals, provided certain conditions are met. However, your tax contributions are not tax-deductible like a Traditional IRA.

    B. Can convert assets from a Traditional IRA to a Roth IRA. However, then you will pay the taxes upon conversion. (*Caveat Emptor or Buyer Beware* when changing from a traditional IRA to a Roth IRA!)

2. **Traditional IRA**

    A. Offers tax-deferred savings and your contributions are tax-deductible.

    B. Early withdrawal can lead to penalties and immediate taxable liability on the funds taken out except for certain circumstances. *(Again, Caveat Emptor or Buyer Beware!)*

An IRA enables your investments to grow tax deferred until the age of 70½. Then you are required to take the minimum yearly required distribution from a Traditional IRA, but *not* a Roth IRA. If you don't, you will incur a large penalty from the IRS.

Insurance Products geared towards Retirement

Insurance products geared for retirement savings come in a variety of different product types. The three primary types include: Life Insurance, Annuities, and Hybrids of the two. *Long-term care policies* can also be used to protect hard earned assets from going towards ever increasing healthcare costs.

Life Insurance

Life Insurance can be broken down into *two* primary categories: **Whole-Life** and **Term-Life**. Life Insurance policies will state on the actual policy whether it is whole-life or term-life. This distinction is very important as the premium amount paid on a monthly, semi-annual, or annual basis will be dramatically different depending on the type of policy that is taken out. Age, condition of health, smoker vs. non-smoker, lifestyle, race, gender, etc. can all determine the amount of your premiums.

Two Primary Types of Life Insurance

1. **Term-Life Insurance** – insures the purchaser of the policy for a *specific time* period and expires thereafter.

2. **Full-Life Insurance** – insures the purchaser of the policy through their *entire life* and is redeemed upon death.

Whole-Life

Basically, a straight vanilla ***Whole-Life Insurance Policy*** insures the person's life who takes out the policy and pays the premium on the policy. Once the person dies, the person named as a benefactor, receives the value of the policy. A husband might take out a policy on himself so that if he dies, his wife and children will receive money to live on after his untimely death. Certain types of death, however, could make it impossible to collect on the insured person. Many times suicide, certain occupations, and hobbies such as an airplane pilot could exclude the insured person unless pre-approved by the insurance company. *Caveat Emptor – Buyer Beware!*

Many companies also take out basic life insurance policies on employees that they term as *Key Men*. Key Men (and naturally Key Women) are people that are so important to the livelihood of the company that the insurance pays for the loss of business to the company in the event that employee dies while an employee of that firm.

Term-Life

A ***Term-Life Insurance Policy*** is essentially the same as the Whole-Life Insurance Policy except for one key ingredient. A Term-Life is valid for a specific time period. These policies are normally cheaper than a Whole-Life Policy because insurance companies research the probability of life expectancy. Charts are made up which show statistically the age you will "meet your maker" depending on lifestyle and genetics. If you are a smoker, drinker, male, female, race comes into play as well because certain diseases are more prone to develop amongst certain groups of people.

Annuities

Annuities in recent years have received a bad rap because investors didn't know what they were purchasing and felt they lost money through these investment vehicles. An annuity is basically a stream of payments similar to Social Security. You pay into the policy (or program as with Social Security) for years and at retirement you receive a stream of payments in which to live on for the rest of your life. If you die at an early age, that stream of payments never gets paid but the insurance company has made a huge profit from you paying your policy premium. If you die at a ripe old age, you the investor are the smart and lucky one and you will receive all of the payments due to you.

Hybrids

Hybrids are a combination of an annuity and a life insurance policy. An example of this is a structure that my husband and I invested in personally. This particular hybrid is structured as follows: a savings plan which is funded with after tax money, which then is invested and grows tax free. Upon retirement the savings can be withdrawn and taxed as a long-term gain or capital investment (the lowest tax rate for investments), and becomes an annuity stream upon retirement. In the event, the insured person passes away, the hybrid also acts as a normal life insurance policy, whereby the beneficiary receives a full payment of the face value of the policy upon the death of the insured excluding the money originally invested in the policy. Large insurance companies such as Northwestern Mutual offer these types of policies.

> **Platinum Tip**: *Want to leave a sizeable "nest egg" to your favorite charity, niece or nephew but you think you don't have enough money to do it? Think again! You can easily take out an insurance policy and place them as the beneficiary. This will enable you to bequeath a very sizeable "nest egg."*

Reckless Spending & Financial Pitfalls

Many people close to retirement become too reckless with their life savings. Spending temptations and financial pitfalls always arise. It is all too easy to walk unsuspectingly onto a money snatching land mine or sink into a "money pit investment." Fixer upper houses can potentially devastate an otherwise sound retirement plan, if you don't analyze the full extent of the costs involved with the renovation project. Lusting after that new automobile that you know you really deserve but don't need (especially after seeing the television ad that says that you do) can also destroy your otherwise sound savings plan. A hybrid life insurance policy can afford a pretty fail safe retirement plan in case you make a bad investment decision or purchase along the road to retirement. (Provided the insurance company doesn't go out of business.)

Keeping up Appearances

Maintaining a certain lifestyle or trying to keep up certain appearances to friends and people in the community can not only zap discretionary income but also eat away at your hard earned *nest egg* that was put away for retirement or an absolute emergency. Be independent and strong. Keep with your overall retirement, savings, and emergency fund plans.

So you don't have the latest fashion fad or trend this season. It's ok. Another fashion craze will come around soon enough. Who knows, next year's fashion trend might even become a classic that stays for years to come in your wardrobe – instead of being out of date in 6 months' time like the latest fashion fad!

Get Rich Quick Schemes

At this time in your life it is not the time for get rich quick schemes. Be wary. Remember the old saying, "If it sounds too good to be true, it probably is." There will always be the next big thing to invest in. My father was always investing in get-rich-quick schemes much to my mother's chagrin. Each time he would make a little extra cash or lost the entire investment. It was a losing man's game. He probably would have been better off just working hard at his normal job, investing prudently, and using his free time for relaxation and family time, instead of investing in every fly-by-night scheme that came his way. Every generation experiences the "Charlatan" that comes to town. My grandfather sunk money into a goldmine in Colorado when the owner of the mine came to his town in Iowa. My father also invested in tire repair kits, invested in oil and gas wells amongst other things as get rich quick "investments." The apple never falls far from the tree!

Be careful not to fall for every infomercial that guarantees you that you can walk away from your current job just by buying their product. The only person they are really helping is their own bottom line. Most of these ads always appear either on the weekend or late at night after you have had a couple of drinks and are feeling most vulnerable. You wake up in the middle of the night, unable to go back to sleep and begin to self-analyze yourself and your financial inadequacies, faults, and failures. Because they offer a quick fix solution to your problem, you figure what do I have to lose?! Remember your loss is their gain.

Most of these get rich quick schemes are about seizing the moment. While timing is everything in life, many of these seize the moment investing schemes look good at 3 am in the morning but suddenly look like a bad idea the next morning after you realize you just used your credit card to purchase some scheme to get-rich-quickly and receive virtually nothing in return. Or when you wake up, roll over in bed, and gaze upon the financial disaster that is lying next to you in bed and wonder – What was I thinking! And how do I escape this embarrassing situation unscathed. Did I really visit the Chapel of the Bells in Las Vegas last night or was it that wicked tequila in the Margarita that made me say, "I do!" That quick divorce could be very costly.

Another lesson my father taught me about investing, "If the train leaves the station, don't worry and don't chase it, another will arrive soon." In this case, father knew best. He had always been a value investor, not wanting to overpay for stocks and that strategy paid him handsomely over the years.

Retirement G-Goals

Although your libido might be decreasing at retirement age, your wants, desires and needs for financial gratification will surely not be decreasing. This time in your life should bring fulfillment to all your other fantasies that turn on your *Financial G-Spot!* Write down a list of your personal *G-Goals* (*gratification goals*). Everybody has different goals in life. Some people want to retire early, give back, pay it forward, or do charity work. Others want to see the world. Some enjoy working and feel the only way they'll exit the office is, "to carry me out in a pine box." Others hate to work and count the years, weeks, days and hours until they begin to collect Social Security. Whichever category you fall under, you need to set your goals high and aim for the sky. Some of these *G-Goals* could very well include those outlined below.

- Early Retirement
- Ditch the older Model and go for a newer Model (This could be a car or a significant other!)
- Travel the World
- Move to Paradise
- Start a new Life
- Etc., Etc., Etc.!

At different stages and ages of your life, you might find different things that bring you happiness, fulfillment and *G-Goal Gratification*. Others find that financial gratification can be just as important in your retirement years as in your early adulthood. However, everyone changes their mind along the bumpy road of life as to what exactly brings them bliss and happiness. But one thing is for certain, a sound retirement plan will help you attain those goals.

It's never too late to Invest for Retirement

You have been squirreling away money into CDs and community bank savings accounts every month. You're counting the days, not years until retirement and joyfully checking off the boxes on the calendar. You've added up your total social security monthly benefits checks that you will receive for the year and your pension benefits. You've checked and triple checked the Medicare or Medicaid amounts you are entitled to in addition to your normal health insurance plan. The mortgage on your house is paid for or nearly paid for. So why worry?

Rising health care costs can zap your squirreled away "nest egg" in the course of a few years. As an example, my grandmother at age 98 had to re-strategize her retirement savings and spending plan. After a fall, she needed more care and had to move out of her house and into an assisted living facility. Immediately the bills began to mound: caregivers, healthcare bills, food, lodging, transportation, etc, etc. The righting was on the wall. She would outlive her retirement savings if she didn't more evenly match her inflow (interest earned) to her outflow (bills and expenditures). Being a young adult during the Great Depression and living through many wars, she never trusted the stock market. Now, however, she had to take a leap of faith. Prudent, wise, timely and conservative investment strategies for her age have proved a success; nearly matching her dividend and interest income and social security checks to her monthly expenditures. Now years later, she is still successfully investing. It just goes to prove – you are never too old nor is it too late to invest for retirement!

Plan now to enjoy Later

Plan your retirement now. Review your plans at least once a year. Make modifications when necessary ... and have fun later!

Platinum Tip: *Plan now and save regularly so you can have fun later!*

The early bird catches the worm.

—Anonymous

Save now ... Relax later!

—Karen & Fran

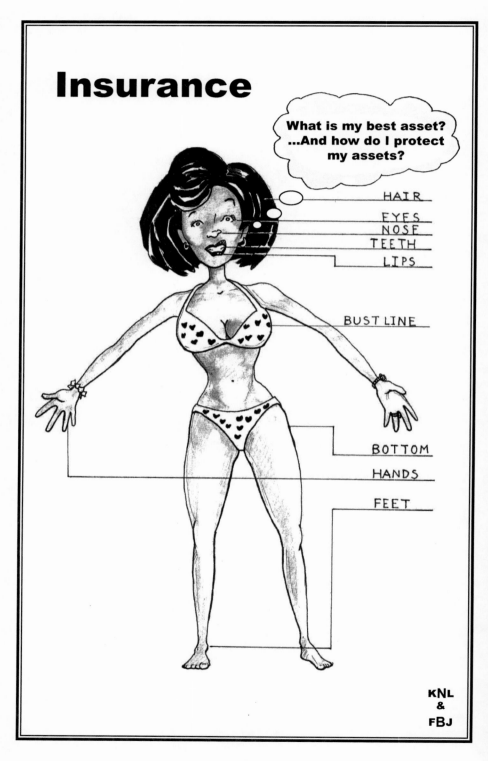

Chapter 20

Insurance:

What is your best Asset?

What is your most important asset? Some women would say their cleavage, smile, back, hands or feet while others would say their brains. You might find the answer to be very different to an insurer, however.

According to Lloyd's of London, the insurer of the mega rich and famous, many movie stars and singers insure everything from their vocal chords to their sexy gams. Celebrities who depend heavily on one or several aspects of their body to bring in future revenue know that without that precious asset their career could fade quickly. Examples of famous individuals who have taken insuring their body parts quite seriously include the following, just to name a few. Betty Grable back in 1940 reportedly insured her legs for $1 million. Mariah Carey more recently, however, insured her legs for a whopping $1 billion! Jennifer Lopez insured her derriere for $300 million. America Ferrara of *Ugly Betty* fame insured her smile for $10 million. Ken Dodd, on the other hand, insured his teeth for a measly $6 million. Rock singer Bruce Springsteen insured his voice several years back for $5 million. Angela Mount, a top wine expert, insured her taste buds for $16 million. Soccer player, David Beckham insured his feet for $70 million while Michael Flatley of *Riverdance* and *Lord of the Dance* fame, insured his feet for $40 million.

Disability Insurance

If you become disabled and are not able to go to work, you will probably not receive your weekly or monthly paycheck. This could be financially devastating because you will probably have to tap into your investments or rainy day savings accounts in order to meet your financial obligations. When no new money is coming in and money already saved is going out, it can be a double whammy financially! Loss of income and disability insurance could be a sensible choice.

Isn't it ironic that we insure many other situations by taking out home insurance, car insurance, life insurance: but, we women (who are notorious worry warts) fail to insure our own *physical welfare*. How can we provide for our children if we become suddenly paralyzed from an accident or become bedridden from a debilitating disease? Women in particular fail to realize the importance of insuring themselves against the loss of income. Since women are becoming more and more the primary breadwinner in many family units, it is vital to protect yourself in case you are no longer "employable."

Basically, there are *two* sources of income:

- People at Work, *and*
- Money at Work

According to Burt Herman, founder of the Herman Agency in Oak Brook, Illinois, "For most working people your most valuable asset is your earned income. What typically happens when you become disabled? You tap into your investments for living expenses thereby jeopardizing your "nest egg." When you are disabled, you are no longer adding to your savings while you are depleting your assets. You have to consider, how long will your savings last? Then what will you do to survive? Even if you think you have enough savings to maintain your standard of living for a while, wouldn't it make more sense to insure yourself against such a big exposure? You insure your home, automobile, jewelry and even other people." Case in point, you insure perfect strangers to protect them in case of an auto accident that is your fault. Home insurance insures visitors coming to and from your home should they slip on an icy walkway, porch, driveway, or become injured somewhere else on your property. But, your single biggest exposure is most likely loss of income due to a prolonged disability. This quite often goes uninsured and could potentially be devastating to your "financial well-being."

Example 1: A very famous actress and comedienne, Lucille Ball, began her career as a model. She was stricken with rheumatoid arthritis very young in her career and was laid up for almost two years in her late teens while trying to recover. She lost a great deal of her earned income as a model and because of this ailment ultimately became an actress and comedienne. Women in that time period did not even have *disability insurance* on their radar but today we do! *Disability insurance* can be taken out very easily.

Example 2: A very good English friend of mine had the perfect life: founder of a start-up computer and software company, newly married, and owner of a lovely home. He figured he was young, immortal, and indestructible because of his military background and rugged constitution. His distinguished military career included being in England's version of the Green Beret and fighting in the Falkland Islands. An avid rugby player and golfer, he faced back surgery for a degenerative disc. Believing in his country and their NHS (National Healthcare System) he opted for surgery through the NHS instead of private pay.

Unfortunately, he became permanently disabled as a result of spinal surgery gone awry. Luckily for him, he did have *disability insurance*. Not only did he face huge medical costs; but in addition, a complete lifestyle adjustment due to his disability. Medications, more surgery, tailoring his house to be safer and more user friendly for his medical needs, outfitting his car and business office have also all taken their toll on his family and his wallet. At least since he had purchased *disability insurance*, the expenses he incurred were partially offset by the disability policy he had taken out.

Mortgage Disability Insurance

Did you know that you can buy insurance to protect your home from being taken away from you and your family by creditors in the event that you or your spouse become disabled and can no longer make the mortgage payments? By taking out a *mortgage disability insurance policy* you can sleep well at night knowing that your monthly mortgage payments will be taken care of. The monthly premiums can even be included in your regular mortgage payment.

Disability Trends

We live harder, work harder, and play harder than ever before. As a consequence, there has been a dramatic increase in disabling injuries and illnesses. In the past 25 years, the number of severely disabled people ages 17-44 has increased 400%. While the number of people with protection has also increased, most Americans still have a disability income protection gap. This is alarming when you consider in a year's time, chances are only 1 in 1,200 that you will need fire insurance (generally considered a necessity for homeowners) but your chances are 1 in 8 that you will be sick, injured or killed!

Life Insurance

Most women lack *life insurance* policies in their overall investment portfolios. *Life insurance* policies come in two forms: *Term-Life* or *Whole-Life*.

Traditionally, life insurance companies went after a certain type of customer: healthy, middle-aged, non-smoking *males*. The reason is simple. Men, historically, were known as the main breadwinners in a household or family; so therefore, insurance companies targeted men when selling their products.

Today, however, times have changed dramatically (and for the better!). Women are also now considered breadwinners in families and households as well. In many cases, women are the sole breadwinner for the family or household. Some studies show that as much as 64 percent of American women carry no life insurance. And, those that do often carry only about half as much coverage as men do.

If you have children, a husband, elderly parents or pets that you would like to insure that they are kept in the same way in which they have become accustomed to, you can do this through either a *term-life* or a *whole-life* policy.

Term-life policies are normally less expensive to take out and only run for a specific time period, for example 20 or 30 years. If you don't pass away during the duration of the policy, the policy will expire and become worthless. It is similar to purchasing an *option* on your life as it has an expiration date. For example, a 25 year old, healthy woman could purchase a $200,000.00, *term-life* insurance policy for under $12.00 a month. Just for comparison's sake, a $200,000, *term-life* policy for a 45 year old woman would run $18.00 a month. This is simply because of the age factor. (Rates will vary. This is purely an example to demonstrate how age affects a policy.)

Women, in general, can purchase policies for less money than their male counterparts. The reason being, a woman's life expectancy is longer than a man's. And … men think they are the stronger of the species? Not according to the Darwinian Theory that only the strongest survive. Women throughout the centuries have proven to be the strongest and last the longest!

Platinum Tip: *Life insurance policies can be used as an estate planning tool to leave your heirs more money than they would have normally received. A stay at home mom can leave her children a sizeable lump sum of money by taking out a "term-life" insurance policy for just a few dollars a month.*

Many women and their husbands don't value the "stay at home person" who is really the organizer, grocery shopper, daycare giver for children or elderly parents, maid, chauffer, chef, dog walker, etc. In reality, if that "stay at home person" passed away, someone else would have to be hired and paid a handsome salary to fill the many roles that the "stay at home person" has played. This would create a *huge* financial void in the family household income. The moral of this story is never, never underestimate the value of a "stay at home person."

Whole-life insurance policies are policies that insure you until you pass away (or as my father said, pushing up daisies). For this reason, they are more expensive to purchase because they will not expire, provided you pay your premiums on time and you do not do anything that could jeopardize your policy. Make sure that you always (read the fine print) of your policy for loopholes on how the insurance company can escape paying you when you try to file a claim!

Life insurance is a wonderful asset in your overall portfolio. Some people don't like to think about their mortality. But, let's face it and embrace it! There are only two things certain in this world, according to Benjamin Franklin: death and taxes. And besides, the ancient Egyptians got it right when they planned for the longer life after life. In fact, the lovely Egyptian Hachetzu went to the afterlife complete with all her cosmetics (henna, etc.), servants, and jewelry. Who says you can't take it with you! And have a happy thereafter!

Platinum Tip: *Life insurance policies can be used by your heirs to help pay off the tax burden incurred from estate inheritance tax. Your broker, financial planner or insurance agent will be happy to provide you with information on structuring insurance policies for your estate.*

In your lifetime, you may, for simplicity sake, earn $100,000 a year. You could, however, take out a $2,000,000.00 *whole-life* or *term-life* policy to protect your loved ones, favorite pooch, and heirs. Imagine how long it would take you to actually amass that same $2,000,000.00 in your lifetime. Think of all those Starbuck cappuccinos you would have to forgo and all those designer shoes and handbags you would never get to relish and take care if you attempted to save all that money!

Example:

Salary before Taxes:	$100,000.00
Taxes:	- $ 40,000.00
Salary after Taxes:	$ 60,000.00
Living Expenses:	- $ a lot
Savings:	*not much left!*

And then, you have living expenses and no spending allowance? All work and no play money makes for a very dull and boring life! How is it then possible to accumulate those types of assets on your salary? Simple! You take out a *life insurance policy*. If you are the type of person who eagerly rewrites your will with the changing of the moon cycles – a will as an estate planning tool may be of no value to you and you should not dedicate any money towards it because the lawyer fees you incur might be more than your inheritable "nest egg". Perhaps, however, you are forward thinking and tend not to sway from decisions you have made. You would like to leave a legacy in the form of a scholarship in your name to your favorite alma matter, a donation to your favorite charity or money to your favorite niece or nephew, elderly parents, children, pets, etc. A life insurance policy could well be a good financial instrument to help you accomplish this goal as part of your overall portfolio. You can simply place a beneficiary on the policy that you take out.

Although you might think that you have left your relatives a sizeable pot of gold. Tax authorities might also like their share and become an "heir" as well. Many estates are left owing large inheritance taxes. A life insurance policy could be used to pay the tax burden due on your estate. This will insure that the money you bequeathed and thought you were leaving to your beloveds is really there once the tax bill is paid.

Mortgage Life Insurance

Did you know that you can buy an insurance policy that will protect your family's primary asset, namely your house, in the event the primary breadwinner dies in the family? By taking out a mortgage life insurance policy, it will enable you to pay off your house mortgage, should the unthinkable happen to either you or your beloved. The monthly premiums can be included in your regular mortgage payment (so you never forget to pay it!). In addition, policies can be joint or in an individual's name.

What is your best Asset?

No matter what you believe to be your most valuable asset: be it a body part, your home or an automobile, make sure you insure it and insure it well! By doing this, you will not only sleep better at night but you will also not get those unbecoming worry lines etched across your forehead by stressing whether you are underinsured or not. Insure now and forever rest in peace!

Terms used in the Insurance World

The following terms are commonly used in the world of insurance. Although there are many more, knowing these terms will make you seem less of a novice and appear more astute!

Annuitant – The investor who contributes money to the plan (annuity) in one lump sum or in periodic payments. At a future date, the annuitant begins receiving regular income distributions.

Annuity – A contract between an individual and an insurance company. Annuities are usually purchased for retirement income.

Auto Insurance – Insurance needed as the owner of a car to financially protect yourself and others. Auto insurance can include: collision, theft, liability, etc.

Disability Insurance – Insurance that covers the risk of losing earned income due to illness.

Fixed Annuity – Guarantees a minimum rate of return when the individual elects to receive income. The payout is determined by the account's value and the annuitant's life expectancy.

Health Insurance – Health insurance can range from hospitalization, dental, doctor's office visits, HMO, rehabilitation, optical, etc. Policies can and do vary greatly! Always read the fine print! People should obtain supplementary health insurance which covers areas not covered by Medicare and Medicaid. (Medicare and Medicaid are governmental programs offered to people at a certain age, income or circumstance.)

Home Owner's Policy – This policy covers your home and its contents. It may also cover someone "tripping on a banana peel" that was strategically placed on your front walkway, damage from a storm, renters, a teenage son crashing into the wall of your garage from putting the car in drive instead of reverse, and so on. Check with your insurance agent to modify the policy to cover your specific needs.

Liability Insurance – Sometimes liability insurance is included as a section under Automobile Insurance. This type of insurance protects you from hurting someone or something.

Life Annuity – This type of annuity carries no death benefit. All benefits end when the annuitant dies, even if there is a surviving spouse.

Life Insurance – Can be an insurance policy for either Whole-Life or Term-Life.

Long-term Care Insurance –This medical insurance policy pays a specific amount per day towards the care of a person by a care giver.

Term-Life Insurance – A life insurance policy written to cover a specified period of time as compared to a whole life insurance policy.

Umbrella Policy – Insurance which covers situations excluded by liability policies or other policies.

Whole-Life – Also referred to as Full-Life can be taken out as a financial plan for a survivor's needs.

I don't want to tell you how much insurance I carry with the Prudential, but all I can say is: when I go, they go too.

— Jack Benny

Fun is like life insurance;
the older you get,
the more it costs.

— Kin Hubbard (American Journalist)

There are worse things in life than death.
Have you ever spent an evening
with an insurance salesman?

— Woody Allen

Chapter 21

Real Estate:

Where most Millionaires are born!

*"Ninety percent of all millionaires become so
through owning real estate."*

— Andrew Carnegie, industrialist tycoon

*"Do you mean to tell me Katie Scarlett O'Hara, that Tara,
that land doesn't mean anything to you?
Why, land is the only thing in the world worth..."*

— Gerald O'Hara in the film Gone with the Wind

Your home can be the biggest asset in your portfolio. In fact, it can be the largest purchase you will ever make in your lifetime. If purchased correctly, it can be your retirement nest egg. Purchased incorrectly, it can become your worst nightmare. You could face foreclosure or even worse, it can send you completely into bankruptcy. However, if you play your cards right and invest in real estate correctly; you too can amass a fortune in real estate like Leona Helmsley, Donald Trump, William Mack, Stephen Schwartzman, and Stephen Ross (to name a few).

Types of Properties

Basically, real estate can be broken down into five categories, ranging from *Complete Perfection* to a *Complete Tear Down*. The five categories are defined as follows: Complete Tear Down, Fixer Upper, Money Pit, Hidden Gem, and Complete Perfection.

Complete Tear Down – Buy this for the land value only. The house or building needs to be bulldozed. The house has been through a fire, flood, earthquake, tornado, or hurricane. Or, through lack of maintenance and upkeep, the house or building needs to be raised and removed from the property. Even duct tape couldn't fix this structure!

Fixer Upper – A diamond in the rough, expect to put in new baths, upgraded kitchen appliances and cabinetry, plumbing and electrical wiring may need to either be modified or be entirely removed and replaced. Lead paint might be present. Mold could be lurking in the walls behind the sheet rock. Fumigation of termites, other creepy crawlers, and critters might be required. Make sure the building is structurally sound. Hire a GC (General Contractor) or a Home Building Inspector to review the project before you make a written offer. This will give you a ball park budget as to the money that will be needed to carry out the modifications you wish to do and make an educated decision if they are feasible or not! If you are planning to fix it up and sell it, make sure you put pen to paper and see if the numbers will show a profit and not a loss on the project.

Money Pit – This money vortex keeps sucking your hard earned money out of your pocket book and into a diabolic vortex of bills. The structure just keeps needing repairs, even after you fix it up! Just when you thought everything was fixed, the chandelier hanging from the ceiling crashes on the floor due to rotten beams above the newly painted ceiling. Check out the films *The Money Pit* or *It's a Wonderful Life* and you will see two prime Hollywood examples showcasing the "Money Pit" category.

Hidden Gem – A mansion, located in a bad neighborhood yet still considered a grand house, could be considered a *hidden gem*. Also, a house with a gorgeous interior, located in a wonderful neighborhood, but suffers from ugly curb appeal could also constitute as a *hidden gem*. Because of the undesirability hanging over the salability of the house, you might be able to scoop up your dream house for a song! You sometimes have to look outside the box to unlock the value in a property. Consider the house in the undesirable neighborhood. Could this house be transported and reassembled on another piece of land that you like?

Complete Perfection – You have found your dream home! The place you want to live the rest of your life. Price, in this instance, is not as imperative. It's all about quality of life, where you feel your best and where you feel at home. Everything works and is in great condition.

Supply & Demand vs. the Housing Market

The *Housing Market* and real estate in general are greatly controlled and affected by *supply & demand*. The relationship between real estate and *supply & demand* is outlined below.

The Function of Supply & Demand: How it affects Real Estate Prices

↑ Supply goes up; it becomes a Buyer's Market

↓ Supply goes down; it becomes a Seller's Market

↓ Supply goes down, demand goes up = Seller's Market, Price goes up

↑ Supply goes up, demand goes down = Buyer's Market, Price goes down

---

Buyer's Market

If you are attempting to sell a property in a *Buyer's Market*, it can be semi- to very illiquid to sell. You will face difficulty in trying to sell your property. In this particular market cycle, supply outstrips demand, thereby depressing prices even further. The buyer has all the advantage when negotiating a satisfactory purchase price. The seller, disadvantaged by the downward pressure on housing prices and over supply of houses on the market has a great disadvantage in the negotiation process. Many sellers, if they are not forced to sell, will choose to take the property off the market until the market comes back in their favor.

Seller's Market

In a *Seller's Market*, your property will be viewed like candy in a candy store to all home buyers. Supply of housing is limited and buyers are abundant. The buyer has a disadvantage in this market. It is much harder for the buyer to negotiate a better price on a home. In fact, buyers could face the possibility of not being able to negotiate a price reduction. Instead, buyers will be forced to bid over the asking price. (In England, this phenomenon is known as *gazump* or *gazumping*. The contracted price was raised after a formal lower offer was already accepted.) Some parts of California also experienced their own type of *gazumping* as buyers scrambled to out-bid each other for the same piece of real estate in the last housing boom. Typically, in this part of the market cycle, prices of real estate continue to soar, giving the buyer less home for their dollars spent.

A perfect example is the most recent *Housing Bubble & Collapse.* This boom and bust picked up great momentum in the early years of 2000-2007 and culminated in a spectacular collapse of property prices from 2007-2009. Some areas bottomed first and have already rebounded significantly. While some parts of the country have managed to come back faster than others, other areas of the country and parts of the real estate market are only gradually inching up in price and will still take considerable time to completely rebound to pre-crash prices.

The Pendulum Example

You can think of *supply & demand* in a simple way, by looking at the pendulum of a grandfather clock. When the pendulum of a clock swings too far in either direction, it snaps back like a rubber band correcting the market and forcing it to go back to normalcy. When the pendulum is in the center, the market is neutral. This is neither a *Buyer's* nor a *Seller's Market.* When the pendulum is swung too far to the right (becoming a *Seller's Market*), at some point gravity takes over and will force the pendulum to swing just as far in the opposite direction to the left (becoming a *Buyer's Market*) thus over-correcting itself. As the frenzy of dumping, foreclosures, short sales, and seller's just walking away from their properties because they are upside down on their mortgages subsides, normalcy will re-enter the marketplace. This will move the pendulum back to center position – to a neutral market.

Pendulum Example

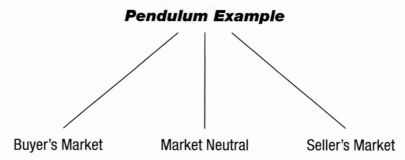

| Buyer's Market | Market Neutral | Seller's Market |

Platinum Tip: *Sometimes it can make more sense to rent instead of purchasing a home, especially if it is a second home. Look at all the maintenance expenses, property taxes and interest charged on a mortgage that you would be paying before you purchase. Compare these expenses to a rental or lease amount on the same property. It might be in your favor to rent instead of purchasing the property.*

Location, Location, Location

Location is one of the most important factors to look at when purchasing any piece of real estate. The location will determine a major portion of the purchase price. Location will also dictate what you hope to sell it for: the better the location, the higher the price. The mantra in real estate has always been that location determines the value of a property. For example, an acre of farmland in western Kansas is valued at a fraction of what an acre on the Upper East Side in New York City would be. Unless of course, you hit oil in Kansas and own the mineral rights. Then it could be a toss-up!

If you are looking at selling your property, it could be worth your while to hire a real estate appraiser to see if the value they place on your property is the same as the your realtor's listing price. The buyer, unless they are an "all cash" buyer, will have to take out a mortgage to purchase your property and it must appraise out by the buyer's lending institution in order for the buyer to be able to obtain a mortgage. Your house will have to pass the home inspector's criteria for a purchaser to take out many types of loans as well.

> **Platinum Tip:** *Location, Location, Location! If you can't remember all three at least remember one.*

Price

Price is naturally another major factor in both buying and selling real estate. "Everything will sell for a price" is a saying that seems to always hold true. At some point a buyer will step in and scoop up a property if it is considered cheap enough.

If your property is priced too high, you will be sitting on it for many years to come. If it is priced too cheaply, it will sell too fast and you will wish you had priced it higher. You have to weigh your opportunity costs as well to help determine what price you need to place on the real estate you wish to sell. If a better investment comes along, you might wish to sell your piece of real estate for a smaller profit in order to take advantage of a more lucrative investment.

Buy low and sell high. Sounds simple, right? Just like stocks, the same holds true for real estate. Also, just like the stock market goes up and down, so does the housing market.

Want to become a Real Estate Tycoon?

Do you believe that real estate could be your avenue towards wealth and prosperity? All you need is a little bit of luck, intelligence, education, street smarts and the capability of buying low and selling higher. This will help you become the millionaire you always knew you could be. There are plenty of seminars and classes that teach how to become a successful landlord by putting very little down, renting out the property (or properties), and over a 20-30 year period amass a portfolio of real estate to catapult you into becoming the next real estate tycoon. It can and has been done! And you can do it too. Carpe diem: *Seize the day!*

Terms used in Real Estate

The following terms are commonly used in the world of real estate. Although there are many more, knowing these terms will help you navigate through the process of buying, selling, renting, or leasing your dream home.

Appreciation – an increase in value.

ARM (Adjustable Rate Mortgage) – a financing technique in which the lender can raise or lower the interest rate according to a set index.

Balloon Payment – a single large payment made at maturity to pay the debt in full.

Buyer or Purchaser – the buyer of real estate / the purchaser of real estate.

Buyer's Market – the supply of available properties exceeds the demand.

Capital Gain – the difference between the price at which you bought an investment property and the price at which you sold the investment property, less improvements made, and less any other money spent on the real estate project.

Capital Loss – in regards to the buying and selling of real estate, a capital loss is the amount by which the proceeds from the sale of a property are less than the cost of acquiring it. If the property is sold after owning it for one year and one day it is considered to be a long-term capital loss. If the property is sold before one year, the loss is considered a short-term capital loss.

Closing – final settlement between the buyer and seller. The date on which title passes from the seller to the buyer.

Depreciation – a loss in value for any reason. Depreciation can be used as a tax deduction.

Fixed Rate Mortgage – a loan secured by real estate that has the same rate of interest for the life of the loan.

Foreclosure – a court process that transfers title of real property. A foreclosure is used as security for the debt as a means of paying the debt. This causes an involuntary sale of the property.

Investor – purchases real estate in the hopes of making a profit.

Landlord – the owner of rental real estate.

Lease – does not convey ownership but does convey possession and use for a period of time for compensation.

Leasee – A "Leasee" is a tenant or lease holder and is the party given a lease.

Leasor – A "Leasor" is the landlord or owner and is the party granting a lease.

Mortgage – a written agreement that pledges property as security for payment of a debt.

Open Listing – an employment contract given to any number of brokers who work simultaneously to sell the owner's property.

Option (Option to Buy or to Sell) – a right or privilege to purchase or lease real property at a specified price during a designated period for a specified amount.

Owner – owner of real estate, real property.

Rental – pay a specific amount of money for the use of space as designated by a lease agreement.

Renter – a person who does not own, but leases the space.

Sale Lease Back – a finance arrangement in which an investor purchases property that is owned and used by a business, while simultaneously leasing back the property to the business by the buyer or the investor.

Seller – the seller of real estate. The seller is the owner of real estate who is trying to sell their real estate.

Seller's Market – the demand for available properties exceeds the supply of those for sale.

Short Sale – the sale of a property generating a price below the mortgage amount. This requires approval by the mortgagor.

Single Agent – a broker who represents either the seller or the buyer in a real estate transaction, but does not represent both at the same time.

Transaction Broker – a licensee who has limited representation to the buyer and seller in a transaction. Instead of being a single agent, the licensee is working for the contract.

Truth-in-Lending Act – a federal law that requires lenders to inform consumers of the exact credit costs before consumers make their purchases.

Valid Contract – an agreement that is binding on all parties.

Zoning – a government or municipal power classifies real property for usage and specific purposes.

Buying real estate is not only the best way,
the quickest way, the safest way,
but the only way to become wealthy.

— *Marshall Field*

It's tangible, it's solid, it's beautiful.
It's artistic, from my standpoint, and I just love real estate.

— *Donald Trump*

The major fortunes in America have been made in land.

— *John D. Rockefeller*

Buy on the fringe and wait. Buy land near a growing city!
Buy real estate when other people want to sell. Hold what you buy!

— *John Jacob Astor*

Real estate cannot be lost or stolen, nor can it be carried away.
Purchased with common sense, paid for in full,
and managed with reasonable care,
it is about the safest investment in the world.

—*Franklin D. Roosevelt*

Valuing Other Assets

A Tiffany leaded, stained glass lamp stuffed in the attic of my beloved, great aunt Gertrude's? Could I have hit the Jack Pot?

Is it only a mass-produced copy bought at Woolworth or Target?

Garage Sale Sticker Price: $10

Flea Market Would Fetch: $20

Or a good imitation by a semi-notable artist?

Estate Sale Price Tag: $250

Dealer Bid Price: $350

I think this could be the *real deal!* A one-of-a-kind, Tiffany stained glass lamp signed by the master!

Christies' or Sotheby's Auction House Hammer Price: Priceless

One Person's Junk is another Woman's Treasure!

KNL

Chapter 22

Valuing other Assets:

Jewelry, Antiques, Automobiles, and More!
...and other Collectibles you may have around the House

Jewelry as an Asset Class

Most jewelry has a resale market value. Men often pay their secret lovers, prostitutes, and hidden girlfriends with jewelry as opposed to money because they don't want the obvious paper trail. This technique is used quite often in London, England. New bejeweled watches, rings and necklaces (never or gently used) show up in antique stores and jewelry markets all the time. Some expensive pieces also find their way to these stores and markets through divorce settlements, from jewelry stores who couldn't sell their merchandise at the marked up retail price or because the person who received the present didn't want to keep it and wanted the cash instead. There are many different reasons people sell their jewelry. The smart, sexy, savvy woman should know how to buy and resell her jewels wisely. Look to antique shops featuring jewelry, estate jewelry dealers and markets, pawn stores, etc.

Auction houses such as Christie's, Sotheby's, Dreweatts, and Bonhams just to name a few sell jewelry in their estate jewelry sales, very high end jewelry sales, and even household contents sales. In fact, Christies and Sotheby's globally have numerous auctions year round specializing in just jewelry. Sometimes you can snag a deal and some-times not. Make sure you do your research before you bid.

Diamonds: *"Diamond or Pear Shape ... These rocks don't lose their shape! ... Diamonds are a girl's best friend."* We all can recite the lyrics (written by Jule Styne and Leo Robin) to this infamous song originally sung by Carol Channing in the Broadway production of *Gentlemen Prefer Blondes* in 1949 and then epitomized by Marilyn Monroe as Lorelei in the 1953 Hollywood rendition of *Gentlemen Prefer Blondes*. In reality, however, the lyrics have great meaning and still hold true! Diamonds have great value and can be a girl's best friend because they are traded just like other commodities. (Refer to **Chapter 15: Commodities** for greater detail.) Diamonds are priced according to the "4 Cs:" carat weight, color, clarity, and the cut. The *Rapaport* updates jewelers and traders of diamonds on the current price, according to the "4 Cs." Consumers can easily find price information by accessing *Blue-Nile.com*. Diamond exchanges are very active in many cities around the globe such as New York, Brussels, and Amsterdam. Many times you can get a better price on jewelry in the districts that they operate. It is like buying from a wholesaler or middleman. Likewise, you can sell your jewelry in a Diamond or Jewelry District. One such district is located in New York City on 47th Street between 5th and 6th Avenues. Also, Hatton Garden (a section of Holborn in London) has been operating as London's jewelry quarter since the middle-ages and is the center of the U.K. diamond trade. No matter which jewelry quarter, district, or street you choose around the globe to visit, just remember to be well versed on the "4 Cs" and practice your bartering skills. They will come in handy!

Over the last ten years, diamond prices tripled in value (depending on the "4 Cs" of course!) especially in the better quality and larger diamonds of the over 10 carat category. During this last financial crisis, however, prices fell more than 30% but are still trading at substantial gains due to the fear in the marketplace and demand from Chinese and Indian investors. Like gold, there is still that notion that a diamond is an investment you can take with you in case of an emergency.

Remember the story of the Russian Imperial Romanov family in the early 1900s? When the entire royal Romanov family (including the Tsar) was executed, the last to die were Tatiana, Olga and Maria because they had sewn all their jewels inside their clothing thereby protecting them to a certain extent. The women were smart because they knew that the over 2 pounds (1.3 kilograms) of diamonds that were sewn into their clothing would be worth a great deal of money no matter which country they ended up in. When the family was captured and shot to death, stories say that it took many rounds of ammunition to kill the women and girls because the bullets were bouncing off the jewels sewn inside their clothes. Some had to be stabbed after the shooting in the end to insure death.

Gold & Silver: "Silver and gold, silver and gold ... ," this beloved song sung by Burl Ives in the children's made for television Christmas special *Frosty the Snowman* conjures up not only fanciful memories of good times and yesteryears but also emphasizes the value placed on commodities that even children can comprehend. The ancient Egyptian pharaohs clad almost everything in the precious metal. Not only does it not rust or corrode, it is very pliable and can be transformed into a currency basis as well. When the wise men from the East were searching out the baby Jesus they brought gold, frankincense and myrrh because they were considered to be precious commodities. The British pound sterling (GBP) as it is still referred to today takes its root back to Anglo-Saxon England when 240 silver pennies equated to one pound weight of silver. In the U.S. silver certificates were redeemable in the same face value as the silver coins and the U.S. was minting coins such as real silver dollars, silver half dollars, and silver dimes. Gold reserves were also once used to back both the U.S. dollar and the British pound. During the Nixon presidency in 1971 all that changed. Most currencies dropped precious metal backing, currencies were allowed to float, and the U.S. became the international reserve currency.

There are signs up all over the Diamond District in New York City these days saying "We buy gold." They are willing to buy your used and out of fashion gold jewelry by the ounce. The reason is simple, gold is trading at extremely lofty levels which some are calling a bubble and could be the next one to burst! At this price it makes sense to re-evaluate pieces in your collection that you keep but never wear. You could make a sizeable profit off the pieces or at least hopefully make back the money once spent on a piece you no longer wear.

The Silver Vault in London is a sight to behold! An underground vault and maize of silver dealers, specializing in antique and modern silver pieces of every sort can be found there. If you love silver, you will truly enjoy this find. Since English pieces of silver are all hallmarked by date and silversmith / maker / retailer, it is much more difficult to get ripped off when purchasing and selling antique English silver. The antique silver market in the United Kingdom is much more active than in the U.S. or the continent of Europe due in part to the stringent hallmarks. If you find a family heirloom tucked away in your great Aunt's attic that is English silver such as a Paul Storr, Garrard, or Barnard piece or sold by the infamous retailer Rundell, Bridge and Rundell (the royal goldsmith years ago) from London; you may have hit the jackpot. Or if your family antique silver has the stamp Tiffany on it from the United States, your family heirloom could be worth a sizeable fortune!

Antiques

Most antiques have value. Some have significant value due to the maker, scarcity or type of antique. The *Antiques Road Show* has brought this form of resale to "Main Street." The *Antiques Road Show* airs on television and travels from city to city throughout the U.S. and England. People bring their treasures to the show to have the appraiser view and give an estimate as to the value of their antique.

You can also call an auction house or antique dealer in your area to get an estimate on the value of that priceless piece of furniture or porcelain heirloom that you inherited from your great, great aunt (twice removed) and see once and for all what that priceless keepsake is now worth and could fetch at auction!

Auction houses are a great place to look at future sales of period pieces ranging from antiquity to the current times; "old masters" to reproduction paintings, stone and copper age items to modern. These houses offer very interesting and educational classes and provide a great opportunity to meet new people.

Never overlook a good garage sale, yard sale or estate sale. They are virtually the same thing but are called differently in each community. The antique dealers scour the newspapers for the most prospective addresses to cash in on lucrative finds. The dealers normally show up hours before the sale begins. You will always find the best pieces early on in the sale before everything is picked over.

Automobiles

Automobiles in general are considered a *depreciating asset*. While they are still considered an asset on the balance sheet of an accountant, they normally depreciate in value over the years and normally need to be replaced.

Some classic automobiles, however, can significantly *appreciate* in value. Naturally, this depends on specific factors including: the condition, number made, model year, and automobile type. For example, Ferraris, Corvettes, and certain Jaguars and Mustangs from the 1960s continue to entice the automobile lover and can create a cult like frenzy around the automobile auctions and car shows. Although certain years reap better prices due to many factors outlined previously, the real factor that can catapult the resale price tag of a specific car into the stratosphere is namely, having been previously owned by someone famous. An iconic movie star, gangster or politician will rocket the price tag of the car. Even though you may own the exact same car, if Joe Schmo owned it instead of John F. Kennedy or James Dean the price tag will be completely different. Other price factors come into play such as if only a few were made or survived in good shape over the years or if the particular model style of that automobile was extremely beloved by people.

Automobiles can trade over book value when new as well. Some of the bond traders I know, aside from trading bonds, are known to "flip" a hot automobile. This is done by placing a down deposit with a car dealer on a car when the model is just announced. The car gets rave reviews and incites demand. People will pay way over the book value of the car when it rolls into the showroom at the dealer just to show off that they have the newest and hottest car in town.

Wine

Wine cellars are all the rage now. Some wines even become cult wines like Screaming Eagle and fetch exorbitant prices. Reds can be kept normally longer in a well-designed wine cellar than whites. To find wines that will increase in value demand a lot of reading, education and tasting on behalf of the collector. Read *Wine Spectator* (a magazine devoted to wines) and follow the wine auctions if you want to be a serious wine collector. Wines can be bought and sold just like many other commodity type products.

Collectors' Items

One woman's junk is another woman's treasure! Beauty is in the eye of the beholder especially when it comes to collecting. You would be surprised just what is collected these days as a hobby. Certain Barbie dolls can fetch a very vivacious price plus GI Joe and Ken dolls a handsome price as well. Fiesta Ware (dishes) in certain colors and pieces – like a covered tea pot in red from the 1930s-1940s – can be sold for quite a bit of money. Even pennies, nickels, dimes, and quarters with specific dates and mint marks can be worth a small fortune. These are just a few items that can be found readily in the basement or attic of a relative's home (collecting dust and mildew) that deserve a second look.

Before you take a dumpster to haul out all the things you view as trash either around your house or your elderly parents' or grandparents' houses – think twice. Make sure you go on line to see what some of these "treasures" could actually be worth. Go to a local flee market, peruse collectors' ads in newspapers who want to buy certain collectables in your area or call in a professional dealer for pricing. It could really be worth your while!

Platinum Tip: *Dealing in antiques and collectibles can be treated as a hobby or as a profession, depending on how much money you make from it and satisfaction it brings.*

According to an ancient folktale,
King Solomon commissioned a jeweler
to make a ring with an inscription,
the words of which would be meaningful to him
whatever his mood, happy or sad.
The jeweler brought him one with the words,
"This too shall pass."

— King Solomon

One woman's junk can be worth a treasure!

— Karen & Fran

Mirror, Mirror on the Wall... Whose Portfolio is the *fairest* of them All?

KNL

Part 3

Accentuate the Positive & Eliminate the Negative!

Once you have gone shopping to accumulate that diversified "wardrobe" of assets, it's time to look at yourself in the mirror and see if all the items you have purchased not only suit you but enhance your portfolio's physique. Maximize your best assets and minimize your worst. This is often times easier said than done, but not so for the smart, sexy, and savvy investor!

Nip & Tuck your Portfolio

Surgeon: First let's peel back the layers of the patient to see what we are dealing with here.

Nurse: Eh gads, what a mess!

Surgeon: Ok. Scalpel. Let's see if we can make a beauty out of this beast.

Nurse: Scalpel.

Surgeon: Let's do a little liposuction on the stock area. With the excess fat removed, we will use it to plump up the gold section.

Nurse: And what about those?

Surgeon: Good spot nurse. And while we are at it, might as well perk up those two saggy, stodgy bonds in the portfolio and replace them with some perkier, well-rounded, high performance ETN ones!

KNL

Chapter 23

Nip & Tuck your Way to a Well-Rounded Portfolio

A restaurant in downtown Sarasota, Florida called *Two Senoritas* was going through a major renovation. On the outside it read during the construction, "Even a Senorita needs a lift now and then." This is very applicable to what we must do to keep our portfolio in fine running condition: a rebalancing or *nip & tuck* of your assets are necessary every now and then. Perhaps you are top heavy in the financial stock area and bottom heavy in another type of asset. Your portfolio has gone pear shaped just like your body! The securities and overall performance in your once high flying investment account have lost their youthful glow. The returns are now sluggish, lackluster, and exhibiting signs of sagging returns. A quick rebalance of your overall portfolio can help you defy gravity (just like the latest *va-va-voom bra*)! When it comes to "seeking alpha" style profits, a few sexy "in" stocks may be just what the doctor ordered in order to kick start that lackluster portfolio once again and keep you "in the game."

A call to your local "portfolio doctor," a good financial advisor, might be just the remedy in order to discuss how to get that youthfulness and stride back in your portfolio. Beauty creams and age spot removers can't be applied as a quick fix this time. However, the use of options such as buying a call on a stock that is going nowhere fast in your portfolio can be applied as a temporary fix, similar to that quick fix spot remover that you have stored in your bathroom medicine cabinet.

Visualize putting your portfolio on a weight scale. How does it size up? Is it flabby in some areas? Too much muscle in another? And, is it overall too fat or too skinny? Be careful of the quick fix that later ends in a disastrous and too extreme *nip & tuck* that leaves you and your portfolio looking like The Joker in *Batman* with permanent financial scars that you can never fix. We've all seen the botched jobs on women's faces from poor cosmetic surgeons. The same botched up job can just as easily happen to your once normal looking portfolio if you choose the wrong expert. You also don't want the bad Botox injection that leaves your portfolio (we've all seen it happen on the foreheads of both men and women alike) in a temporary paralysis!

Platinum Tip: *As critical as you are to yourself in the mirror, make sure you are just as critical with every investment decision you make. Choose whether you want a permanent fix or a temporary "band-aid" to the problem at hand.*

Check out the credentials of your financial advisor the same way as you would any doctor or surgeon you would entrust with your life as this too is a vital part of your life, it's your life's savings! Make sure you have a good rapport and can talk easily and frankly with your advisor, just as you would with a doctor or surgeon and be able to tell them your portfolio's ailments or wishes. A full service broker is more like the old fashioned doctor you grew up with that takes the time to try to assess your needs and then administers the cure to your ailment.

Have you ever woken up in the middle of the night about 3:00 am? Yep, then you've seen all the self-help infomercials coming to your emotional rescue. Everything from diet doctors, beauty remedies, and the newest, fangled gym equipment fill the airwaves. Who said the old fashioned snake oil remedies that you could swallow or rub on to cure anything from TB (tuberculosis) to the common cold is any different than what we are encountering through infomercials today. The traveling doctors on the back of a wagon in the 1800s selling the latest "cure all" is still very much alive and well in infomercial land. These ads are ready and willing to rescue you from anything unsatisfactory that you have or believe you might have. Until you turned on the channel, you didn't realize that you were considered obese, old, and flabby but thanks to the infomercial they have pointed out all your faults. But lucky for you, they also have provided a proven method to solve your problems for a price!

So too, the unscrupulous financial advisor, and the false rumors started by traders, salesmen and analysts in the marketplace to try to get you to buy, sell or hold a product just in order for them to make a profit off of you are no different in many respects to the infomercial of today or the snake oil salesman from the 1800s. This different style of Wall Street infomercial called "heard on the street" and broadcast in the media will find fault with the securities you hold in your portfolio, scare you into acting on the problem, and will offer solutions to fix your problems by buying their product and services.

Mirror, Mirror on the Wall

Mirror, mirror on the wall … who's the smartest, sexiest, and savviest of them all? The investor who has a healthy, diversified portfolio that is increasing in value each year is who! It is *not* the portfolio that is too skinny from under investing or too bloated by excessive poor security selections. What should you do to keep your portfolio looking its best?

1. Look over your portfolio as you would yourself in the mirror.
2. Look at what assets are performing to your liking and what are not.
3. Evaluate what you would like the overall body of your portfolio to look like.
4. Modify your investments by either buying another asset class to diversify your current holdings or selling assets that no longer belong or suit your portfolio's needs. Rev up your portfolio by selling securities that have lack luster returns, have become boring, or out of fashion. Substitute in their place more desirable assets.
5. Purchase or sell options, only if you are comfortable doing so, to improve or protect your best assets and overall portfolio performance.

The Youthful verses the Mature Portfolio

You don't have to be youthful to be beautiful: what looks pretty on the outside may be unhealthy on the inside. In summary, a little adjustment here and there can add a more attractive appearance and youthful glow to your overall assets, net worth, and (in the end) self-worth that you attach to yourself. Just like your own beauty, the beautiful performance of your portfolio, comes from within – it is the individual asset's performance and how well each asset works together with the other assets that creates the beautiful portfolio.

Platinum Tip: *Just like a fine bottle of wine that gets better over the years, so too, your portfolio should develop, become more complex and mature over time. Don't be afraid, embrace it, and be proud!*

In the end, it is up to you to decide whether a full blown face lift, tummy tuck or liposuction treatment is needed on your portfolio. If you decide that drastic action is required, you might need to sell everything in your portfolio and start all over again.

Perhaps, however, only minor actions are needed to slightly tweak your portfolio. You will have to make that decision. Sometimes no decision is a better decision. Sometimes procrastination does pay off. Have you ever sold a stock that was treading water only to find that 3 months later the stock was up 25% from where you had purchased it?

The "Band-Aid" Solution

If you only need a slight fix on your portfolio and you overall like the stocks you have purchased for the long-term, a call option could be the right medicine. Much like the latest beauty cream you can quickly slather on to protect yourself from the free radicals in the market place, the purchase of a call option as mentioned previously might be a quick fix, but it might not be right for your individual circumstances. Another quick fix could be a put option. A put option can act similar to an age defying miracle youth pill (much like Resveratrol™) that can reverse the hazardous effects of a failing stock by providing a way out when the underlying security is declining. Basically, it counteracts the problem at hand and reverses the negative effects. (Refer to **Chapter 16: Futures, Derivatives and Options** if you want to learn more about this subject.)

The Well-Rounded Portfolio

In portfolio and investing terms, the well-rounded portfolio is a sensible, balanced approach to investing. This is called *diversification* on Wall Street. Hypothetically speaking, if you are diversified (own a little of everything) some securities would go up in value while others would go down in value. In an academic sense, true diversification would mean that your portfolio would remain flat. The negatives would negate the positives and vice versa. In another words, your overall net gain or loss would never go up or down. This is true *diversification*.

Because you can never pick all winners, it is wise to use *some* diversification in order to help limit your downside risk. It would not be prudent, however, to be *completely* diversified as many would have you believe on their television market shows and newsletters. Why would you invest? You might as well just sit on a whole pile of cash or stuff it in your mattress because you would get the same return.

Obviously no one, not even Warren Buffet or Bill Gates can own everything to be fully and completely diversified nor would they want to entirely. They therefore attempt to diversify their assets wisely and choose amongst specific asset classes that they believe will outperform the market or at least keep pace with the rate of inflation.

Nip and Tuck your Way to a Well-Rounded Portfolio

If you follow this chapter's advice on *nip & tucking* your way to a well-rounded portfolio, you will be a successful investor. Have you already followed the advice in this chapter? Congratulations are in order! You have now made your portfolio as fit and fabulous as you are!

Where is it Going ...when You're Gone?

John, do you know how much we scrimped and saved our entire lives just so that never-do-well son of ours could spend all our hard earned money! Now look where it got us! John Doe Jr. hasn't even given me flowers for Mother's Day - Not that he ever did!

Instead of keeping a job, settling down and marrying a nice girl, John Jr. insists on spending our money on alcohol, drugs, and chasing sleazy women!

Harriet, calm yourself! You are supposed to be resting in peace! These are our retirement years. Just imagine we are laying on a beach somewhere soaking up the sun!

Don't worry, everything is under control. If our son, John Jr., doesn't straighten up by age 35; according to our will and trust, our life savings will go to our favorite Pet Charity instead. After all, Fluffy our cat was always more of a son to us than John Jr. ever was! Why... Fluffy even brought you home a mouse for Mother's Day.

Rest easy Harriet, rest easy - I've got it all under control.

RIP
Mrs. John Doe
Age 85

RIP
Mr. John Doe
Age 85

KNL

Chapter 24

Where is it Going when You're Gone?

Estate Planning: Wills, Trusts & Greed

Now that you've earned financial freedom and success, you must address the issues of estate planning to insure your wishes are carried out and that your hard earned money goes to the places you intended it to go. If you don't do proper estate planning, your long lost uncle (Uncle Sam) could be the one inheriting your estate instead of your children, grand-children, or your favorite charity.

Estate planning is affected by both federal and state laws. Federal and state laws establish legal parameters that allow for certain types of estate planning. Both federal and state laws can be tweaked and changed entirely from year to year so you will have to stay on top of all the changes made to them. For instance, recent history has shown great fluctuations in the federal taxes imposed on estates, ranging from 0% to 55%, depending on Washington leadership and the government's need for money. The government is greedy and becomes your partner in death as in life. As Mark Twain once said, "Nothing is certain except death and taxes."

Federal and state taxation rules and exemptions also affect estate planning. Taxation rules and allowable exemption amounts change from year to year and can differ widely from state to state. Consult with a tax professional or try to keep abreast of new and current rules via the internet, radio, television, and print news stories.

Estate planning should also be structured to suit the specific individual's needs based on family dynamics. Family dynamics such as disabilities, blended families, irresponsible children, and the like are all discussed in this chapter.

Examples of Estate Planning

Examples of different family dynamics and estate planning techniques and strategies are described below:

Example 1: Irresponsible Children, "Challenging" Heirs

Mr. Smith has three very irresponsible and immature grown children. Mr. Smith sets up his estate that he worked so hard to attain so that no one child receives any principle on the estate until the youngest son reaches age 60. The reason Mr. Smith set up his will and trust to read this way is because Mr. Smith is afraid his children will recklessly destroy their inheritances. The children have been known in the past to be the quintessential "trust fund babies" who indulge heavily in gambling, spending sprees, and give handouts to unsavory friends. Mr. Smith is hoping (in his afterlife) that his grown children will finally have the maturity to better handle their inheritance and safeguard it for future generations. One son is now 39, another 43, and the oldest son 48. The estate attorney and bank helped Mr. Smith set up his trust so that Mr. Smith's three grown, but still financially irresponsible children, would only receive interest each year on their inheritance and would finally receive the principle when the youngest son reached age 60.

Example 2: Good Kid, Bad Kid

Mrs. Brown is a single mom, who divorced the children's father 20 years ago. She received a large divorce settlement which she successfully invested in Apple stock twenty years ago. She now has a considerable estate consisting of cash, stocks, and real estate. Mrs. Brown has one very responsible daughter, Lucy, who has successfully completed graduate school and has a wonderful career. However, her son, Charlie who is 24 years old, causes her constant grief and sleepless nights. She would like to reward her daughter, but protect her son from himself. The estate is divided equally: 50 percent given to Lucy and 50 percent given to Charlie. However, the trust is structured so that Lucy upon the death of Mrs. Brown is given her entire 50 percent inheritance immediately. Charlie, on the other hand, is only given interest on the principle each quarter from the bank that is the custodian for the trust. Within 10 years of Mrs. Brown's death, Charlie will inherit the entire principal due him provided he demonstrates he has straightened up.

Example 3: Keep Control beyond the Grave

Are you a control freak? You can still control your children from the grave. Say that your son earns $30,000 a year, you can make a matching salary inheritance by structuring your trust to give him an amount equal to his last year's salary. If he chooses to do nothing, he receives nothing. If he works hard and earns more, he receives more from the trust.

Example 4: You never Know, Who goes First

Everyone thought Sam would die before Sara. Sam was chronically ill suffering from a form of leukemia. Sam, being the good, responsible and loving husband and father, set up a trust and will to handle all assets in the estate, essentially placing all assets under Sara's name. Sara suddenly died of a heart attack. The estate planning was in a tail spin! Sara's will and trust bequeathed everything to her four children and eight grandchildren but excluded her husband Sam of 45 years. This was due to Sam, believing he would die first. Sam now found himself at the mercy of his children and grandchildren for continuing his lifestyle. He is now attempting to downsize because his greedy children have decided to upsize their lifestyle from their lucky inheritance. Only one child has agreed to help Sam in his hour of need.

Example 5: No One gets my Money

Mrs. Courvoisier has her own ideas about her demise and estate planning! She does not wish anyone to benefit from her demise but instead wishes that the entirety of her estate will go to various charities. Not wanting any lawyers to benefit from her estate planning by charging fees for their services in structuring her charitable giving plan, Mrs. Courvoisier simply and frugally requests her beloved charities to provide her with a simple form that legally enables her estate to pass swiftly to them.

Example 6: Use of a Beneficiary

A simple way of avoiding legal costs and angry relatives is designating a beneficiary or beneficiaries on all your financial documents. Simply name a beneficiary or beneficiaries on your IRA accounts, pension accounts, savings accounts, 401(k) accounts, brokerage accounts, and any other accounts you may have.

Mary and George who are married with no children have used this effective and low cost method to address their estate planning needs. The survivor inherits all. This is a good example of the *KISS Principle*: Keep it simple stupid!

Example 7: Providing for Fluffy

Want to protect and provide continual care to your pampered pet and best friend? You don't want your beloved Fluffy to go to the pound and face being put down after you are gone! So how do you ensure that your loyal companion will live happily ever after? Easily!!! You set up a trust that ensures for your pet's individual well-being and care. It would be a good idea to pick out a friend or relative who not only loves your pet but will care for them for years to come. You will also need to provide that person with an annual stipend in your will to ensure that they can financially take care of your Fluffy in the manner of which Fluffy became accustomed to under your love and care. The most well-known example of this is Leona Helmsley. She designated a significant portion of her estate to ensure that her beloved pooch Trouble was well taken care of.

Community Property State

One of the first questions to ask is whether you live in a *community property state* or a state that uses *Dowagers Rights* to determine inheritance rights. Currently, there are 9 community property states: Arizona, California, Idaho, Louisiana, Nevada, New Mexico, Texas, Washington, and Wisconsin. If you live in a community property state, you own 50% of everything held by you. Your spouse can only make financial provisions for their 50%. (Refer to **Chapter 7: Love & Marriage** for additional information.) The rule of *Dowagers Rights* (that gives the surviving spouse a certain percentage of the total marital estate upon the deceased spouse) does not apply in community property states. The state you live in dictates to a larger degree what kind of a plan you must make. You should ask for legal advice from a proper estate planning lawyer in order to better understand your inheritance rights. And, what exactly are the legal parameters of estate planning in your specific state of residence.

Platinum Tip: *Many wealth management advisors try to solicit business by offering tickets to attend a free dinner and seminar on estate planning. Depending on the speaker and their knowledge of estate planning, it could be worthwhile attending one of these to learn some of the basics of the estate planning process in your state. And hey, if you don't learn anything, at least you might meet some interesting people and get a free dinner in any case.*

Probate vs. Estate Planning

Which is better? Generally, people try to avoid probate. Probate can be very long, expensive, complicated, and exhausting for heirs. In addition, the spouse can be deeply, financially burdened because all the assets – including checking accounts – can be held up in probate for years, depending on the state.

In states where probate can be an expensive, complicated, and drawn out process, lawyers often recommend setting up a trust to avoid probate. Whatever assets are placed in a trust with a will supporting the trust will help avoid the estate going to probate. Caution, however, if you are creating a trust or trusts, make sure that all the accounts and anything titled is in the name of the trust. All checking accounts, real estate holdings, time share properties, and even your car should be titled in the name of the trust. IRAs can be an exception to this rule, however.

Platinum Tip: *If anything is titled; it should go into a trust provided you have been smart, savvy, and created one.*

Often people have real estate in multiple states, countries and U.S. territories; problems can arise in a state, country or territory which is not your primary residence. It is also usually suggested that trusts are created for the elderly, the care of a disabled child, or the financial care of a blended family (especially when it's a second or third marriage). Often a trust can also help if there is an incapacitated adult or one who has recently been diagnosed with Alzheimer's or Dementia.

If your significant other is an international business person or in the military overseas – watch out! There may be assets hidden in countries you can't pronounce or spell. Finding the assets can be like following a treasure map. With so many twists and turns, legal costs, and years gone by in the discovery process – you may never be able to claim the assets once your spouse is deceased. Having a well-defined trust will keep you from trying to reconstruct your fortune and having it held up in probate.

Power of Attorney

There are different types of *Power of Attorney* which should not be confused. Basically, the powers are defined as either being: *general* or *limited*. When dealing with elderly parents and grandparents, a *Power of Health or Healthcare* and also a *Durable Power of Attorney* are normally recommended to enable you to act on behalf of your beloved relative. A *Durable Power of Attorney* is effective until the grantor dies. Whereas a *Limited Power of Attorney* may only be in charge of managing the assets during a specific time period, life event such as surgery, or it could be limited to having a limited amount of given responsibility by that individual. A *General Power of Attorney* has a wider reaching given responsibility than a *Limited Power of Attorney.*

Due to unforeseen circumstances, the person given the responsibility may die, become incapacitated, or may not want to be in charge of your estate while you are still alive. Then what? Make sure your estate has a designated secondary person or entity in place to ensure that your bills are paid. You wouldn't want at age 98 to be placed on a curb corner with only a few of your belongings because the rest of your belongings have been repossessed while your son (John Doe Jr.) was in charge of your estate as Power of Attorney, now would you?!

Selection of your Fiduciary

Selecting a good fiduciary should center on the primary question of, "Who is the best person to handle the estate?" This could be either a family member or a non-family member such as a good friend or a trust facility at a bank or brokerage facility.

A common mistake when selecting a Power of Attorney or Power of Healthcare, however, happens when the person who is given the Power of Attorney or any fiduciary role are often kept in the fiduciary position even if it is not in the best interests of the trust. Although it might be fine today, it could pose a problem later on. People must look at what's good for the present and also into the future. Often, a family member or ineffective investment advisor is kept on despite being inappropriate for the position. In fact, many people choose a non-family entity such as a bank to be the fiduciary. One must always ask, "Is this the best person to manage the trust or estate?" Unfortunately, many people have "challenging heirs." We are talking about the ones who have done very little with their own lives. So, why would you suddenly put them in charge?

Family Ties

What defines a family and who are the people you feel responsible for? Families today are diverse. They span many ethnicities, religions, and sexes. In addition, many families consider a family pet to be part of the family, a housekeeper, or a friend who becomes more of a family member than just a friend, etc. Today, there are many gay couples who are adopting children and are also legally married in one state, but, not legally married in another.

Blended families, due to the increased rate of divorces, usually have different goals when dispersing wealth. They also must contend with a wide variety of heirs with various pecking orders. Also, children from various marriages and financial infidelities place different goals and responsibilities on individuals writing up their estate plans.

Financial Infidelity in Estate Planning

Beware of financial infidelity in estate planning. An example of this is when a man meets with his wife and lawyer to draft an estate plan. Then, after the meeting the man calls the lawyer up discretely to discuss a way to secretly leave a girlfriend some money, a house in Monte Carlo, or a yacht docked in Longboat Key, Florida. Or, several wills may have been drawn up unbeknownst to you by either your parents or your beloved. The only will you saw, however, is now trumped by another will which was discovered after their demise. (Refer to **Chapter 9: Financial Infidelity** to learn more on this topic.) Financial infidelity can continue beyond the grave!

Life Insurance

Life insurance is also sometimes used as a component in estate planning. Life insurance is often offered by investment advisors and insurance agents. It can be used as a means to pay estate taxes on large estates or as a straight inheritance. Life insurance comes in a variety of packages. (Refer to **Chapter 20: Insurance** for more details.)

Platinum Tip: *Place all legal documents and other valuables in either a safe deposit box or a home safe that is protected from natural disaster, fire, petty theft, and prying eyes. Make sure an attorney, trusted friend, or relative knows where you placed these documents so they are easy to find upon your death. Otherwise, people will have to hunt for the hidden treasure!*

Your Forever Plan

In summary, the goal with estate planning is to make "The Estate Plan" your "Forever Plan." Decide and designate where it's going when you're gone. Discuss your plan with those close to you, particularly those who are involved in your healthcare and well-being. Be prepared to tweak and change your "Forever Plan" as needed. This way, you can rest easy and peacefully later!

Don't be overly concerned about your heirs.
Usually, unearned funds do more harm than good.

— Gerald M. Loeb, 1900 - 1974
(predicted the 1929 Crash as quoted by E.F. Hutton,
"The Battle for Investment Survival")

Chapter 25

Conclusion:

Think Rich! Get Rich! Stay Rich!

Think Rich!

Many a mentor has told their prodigy – dream like the person who is your boss! Look like the person you admire most; and, take on the positive attributes you admire most in that person.

Will you be an entrepreneur, manager, vice president, CEO or owner of a *Fortune 500* company? You can if you put old barriers behind you and focus on the positive. If friends or relatives try to put you down by saying you are dreaming or that you don't have the education or skill set, don't think you are alone. It happens to everyone. Get new friends who are supportive and surround yourself with people who will encourage and help you to succeed. Admittedly, it can be difficult to make a relative stop being negative towards you. You can select one of four choices when dealing with an unsupportive relative: 1) you can secretively prove them wrong, 2) you can confront them and tell them to be more supportive, 3) you can just stop seeing them as often, or 4) you can decide not to talk about your dreams and aspirations with them. Negative people are joy takers and will try to steal your bliss. Many are simply jealous or figure if they don't have the tenacity or skill set to accomplish their own goals and dreams, you shouldn't be able to either.

Many people hit hard obstacles in their lives but don't have the will to get over the hurdle and succeed. Instead they settle for complacency and mediocrity. But you don't have to. You are bright, ambitious and have the ability to succeed at anything you put your mind to!

We want you to internalize this thought process as well as this strategy. Visualize yourself richer. Now think about the goals you wish to accomplish that will make you richer. Envision the strategies you will use to attain each of these goals that you have set for yourself. Now, think of the tasks that will enable you to achieve each strategy.

Also examine, where you want to be in your life and your career at this moment and in the future. Have a heart to heart with yourself. Envision your life, your career and your love life 1 year from now, 5 years from now, and 10 years from now. Create goals, strategies and tasks to achieve this. Yes, this might be the time in your life to chase your dreams and really go for it!

And finally, where do you want to be in your love life? (If it is a romantic dream you are most interested in, you will have to wait for our next book to come out!) Now is the time in your life to start living your dreams! Seize the day! And, go for it! Just keep your eye on the ball and stay focused on obtaining your dream of a happy, loving and fulfilling relationship. It might mean putting a 110 percent effort into saving and changing the relationship you are in or finding a new one. Whichever the case, you can succeed at nearly anything you really put your mind to!

Platinum Tip: *You don't have a business unless you have or can find a problem to solve.*

Get Rich!

"If you throw enough mud against a tree, something sticks!" is an old saying. Invest in yourself, your education, and keep trying different investment ideas and strategies. Never give up! You might have to readjust and refine them, but in the end you will succeed. Just keep trying and never give up. We know you're motivated because it took motivation to read this book. That proves you have ambition and the will to succeed. Now you just need to apply your skills, determination and use the knowledge you obtained from this book to help you *get rich*! If you don't rocket to the moon, don't get discouraged. After all, slow and steady wins the race too! (Just remember the *Choo Choo Train* diagram and explanation in **Chapter 1: Finding your Financial Center** and also the *Marathon* illustration at the beginning of **Chapter 19: Pension & Retirement Investing**.

Be careful with "get-rich-quick schemes" because they normally only make the owner of the company wealthy! If the money making scheme seems too good to be true, it probably is. Instead, stay within your area of expertise. Whether it happens to be real estate, stocks, bonds, commodities, or buying and selling collectibles and antiques that you have an interest in and feel you can master the expertise to excel in that area – the choice is yours!

Stay Rich!

You may think that to *stay rich* is easy but it is not! Think how many movie stars, financial wizards, rock stars, sports stars, and lottery winners have all made and lost their considerable fortunes. Donald Trump, Mike Tyson, and Michael Jackson are just three examples but there are many, many more.

Some obstacles to keep you from *staying rich* include:

- **Taxes.** Remember it is not what you earn, it's what you keep.

- **Greedy Relatives.** Long lost relatives always manage to appear at opportunistic times. Beware of their motives. Parents can put the guilt trip on. Your spouse or partner may have a very dysfunctional family and are constantly requiring financial help. Sometimes tuff love is the best policy. If you keep giving hand-outs, why should they not continue to ask for more?

- **Insurance.** Always protect yourself and your property against not only natural disasters but other people.

- **Health Issues.** Medical expenses can quickly zap your savings, cause you financial distress, and harm your financial goals. By eating a healthy diet, exercising, and getting routine medical check-ups, you can avert many catastrophic (to your pocket book) health issues. A stitch in time…saves nine!

- **Bad Investments.** All investments start out good and then can turn bad. Learn to bail out of an investment early on if it doesn't feel right. This will save you time, money, aggravation, and legal expenses. Sometimes a little woman's intuition can pay off. If it feels wrong, don't do it.

Live in the moment. You *are rich* in so many aspects of your life and can continue to *stay rich* in your money matters, your career and your love life! "Could have, would have, should have" need to be kept out of your vocabulary and replaced by **Think Rich! Get Rich! Stay Rich!**

Think Rich, Get Rich, and Stay Rich!

Every female has her own unique way of thinking and problem solving, her own unique strengths and weaknesses, and her own unique set of goals in life that she wishes to obtain. Every smart, sexy, and savvy gal, however, harnesses her own uniqueness and uses it to implement smart, sexy, and savvy investment strategies to cover her through the good times and bad times. She looks at financial products that will individually suit her needs, are uniquely right for her purposes, and investment parameters.

Just because Jane Doe is buying or selling a specific security doesn't mean that you (the smart, sexy, savvy investor) too should do the same. After all, Jane Doe may be investing for sport as opposed to investing for a profit and with her future in mind. She might be investing in stocks the same way as betting on a horse in a race. Instead of analyzing the performance of the horse (or stock) she might be attracted to the pretty colors that the jockey is wearing. Or, she might place a bet because she likes the name of the horse (or stock) entitled, *"Luck be a Lady Tonight"*.

Although "lady luck" can sometimes deliver, be smart, sexy, savvy, and don't count on it. Instead, invest wisely and with logic and thought behind it. Do your homework, watch financial television shows, read business and financial newspapers and magazines, and listen to market programs on the radio that pertain to what you would like to invest in. Broaden your investment horizons and your financial thinking. Go to online financial websites like *Yahoo! finance* and the like. You don't have to go it alone. If you need help, there are plenty of astute financial advisers who will help you manage your money.

But do stay involved, don't be too passive. You are the boss and the captain of your finances and your own financial destiny. The harder you work at achieving your goals, the more fortunate and blessed you will find yourself to be.

Good luck! And may you always **Think Rich! Get Rich!** *and* **Stay Rich!**

Platinum Tip: *Live in the present but prepare for the future!*

Do it! Move It! Make it happen!
— Anonymous

No one ever sat their way to success.
— H. J. Brown

Confidence is the hinge on the door to success.
— Fortune Cookie

Never, never, never give up.
— Winston Churchill

Wall Street Jargon

Wall Street Jargon

Bear Market - declining securities out number advancing securities for an extended period of time.

Beating the Market or Average - your particular security or your overall portfolio as compared to the overall market in which it trades in is performing better than the overall average of that market.

Blue Chips - considered to be top quality securities. Blue chip stocks normally provide investors with a secure dividend as well. (These are not the potato chips that Jet Blue Airlines serves on their flights.)

Bulls & Bears - refer to the investors in the market and the market makers. They are either positive "bullish" or they are negative "bearish" in their outlook on the market or of a particular sector or security.

Bulls make Money, Bears make Money, but Pigs get Slaughtered - you can make money being both bullish and bearish but don't get too greedy or you could lose your entire investment.

Bull Market - advancers out number decliners for an extended period of time.

Buy Low, Sell High - the best way to make a profit on a long position. Buy the security at a low price and sell the security for a high price. The difference of the two prices is the amount of money you made on the transaction.

Cut your Losses - sell the security for a loss because you think the security has further room on the down side to fall.

Dead Cat Bounce - when the market is supposed to rebound the next day after a large decline but instead barely moves in price.

Dogs of the Dow - the worst performing stocks listed on the Dow Jones Industrial Average for the year.

Don't fight the Fed - never bet against Federal Reserve policies. If the Fed is easing rates it means there is more liquidity in the market place. If the Fed is tightening, it means that there will be less liquidity in the market place. The Fed will move the market with its policy making.

Don't get Greedy - don't get greedy, take some money off the table. Sell part of your position.

Heard on the Street - heard a rumor about a security or company, etc. that will affect the market value or price of a security.

Hedgies - an endearing name used for hedge funds.

In the Black - you are making money.

In the Money - you are making money.

In the Money Trade - you are making money at this particular time.

In the Red - you are losing money.

Income Producer - a stock or bond that is purchased primarily for the dividend or yield.

January Effect - as January goes so goes the market trend for the year – either up or down. If the first few trading days are positive, the entire month of January will most likely be positive. If the whole month ends on a positive note, then the entire year will end on a positive note.

Junk or Junk Status - the status or credit rating of the security is considered very low quality / grade and is thereby deemed junk. It is still tradable and many investors make huge fortunes off of trading junk bonds for example, Michael Milken.

Large-Caps - large companies that are well funded and have a large capitalization.

Longs - an investor who is long or who owns a particular security. Longs are betting that the price will go up in value. They are long the overall market.

Market Gyrations - sudden ups and downs of price in the overall market average.

Market Maker or Make a Market - is generally a "floor" trader who maintains firm bid and offer prices in a given security by standing ready to buy or sell round lots at publicly quoted prices. A dealer is called a market maker in the OTC Market and a specialist is a market maker on the exchanges.

Market Rally - the market goes up. This can be for part of a trading day or for a longer period of time over days, weeks or years.

Mid-Caps - mid-sized companies that have a mid-sized capitalization.

Mr. Market - a term used to personify the overall market because the market can often feel as though it is angry at its investors and punishes them or is happy and content with its investors and rewards them.

Never catch a falling Knife - you may think a security has backed away from its highs and is now considered a bargain to invest in. The security, however, may keep falling in price and it will metaphorically "cut you like a knife" as it slips through your grasp.

Out of the Money Trade - you are losing money at this particular time.

Paper Gain or Loss - a security has gone up or down in value or price but it is only a paper gain or paper loss until it is sold.

Pink Sheets - over the counter securities used to be listed on pink sheets of paper. The name is still used today to define small companies traded on the open market and not an exchange. Normally, these are very small companies.

Pull the Trigger - buy or sell.

Range Bound - the security or market trades in a range. It will hit a certain benchmark, ceiling or floor and retrace those numbers again and again.

Shorts - an investor who is short or does not own a particular security but is betting that the price will go down. They can be short the overall market. (Shorts are not a reference to clothing on Wall Street.)

Sideways Action - the price goes practically nowhere. It neither goes up nor down much.

Small-Caps - small companies which could or could not be well capitalized.

Smart Money - usually refers to institutional (very large) investors who can sway the price of a security just because of the large volume either purchased or sold. Retail (small investors) will try to observe where the smart money are placing their bets and whether they are long or short the overall market.

Street Smart - your education is not learned through a university or college. Instead you are smart in the financial world because you picked it up the hard way by working on Wall Street.

Take your Money off the Table - sell the security and park the money in cash or cash equivalents. Downsize your exposure to risk by selling.

Tanking - the market or a particular security experiences a significant drop in price. Generally, if the market falls a huge amount, it is considered to be "tanking."

The Street - refers to Wall Street, not necessarily only the physical location anymore because investment banks are scattered throughout the world.

The Trend is your Friend - follow the trend of the overall market either up or down and you are more likely to make money because it is being friendly towards you.

Trade Up - purchase a better quality name or credit rating. (This does not refer to "trading up" to a better boyfriend or husband.)

Wall Street - a slang name for the financial district in lower Manhattan where many of the exchanges were located near or on Wall Street. Now, however, it refers to the global investment community at large.

Whipsawed - when you are caught in volatile price movements that go up and down and you continuously make losing trades as prices rise and fall because you get the direction of the movement wrong. The term is also used in technical analysis and refers to misleading signals in the chart trends of markets or of particular securities.

Widows' and Orphans' Stocks - securities comprising mainly of large-cap stocks and preferreds (preferred stocks) which are considered stable, will go up moderately in value over time, and are good income producers.

A-Z Guide of Financial Terms

*Note: If an abbreviation or abbreviated form of a term
is normally used in the financial world that abbreviated form
is written in front of the terminology.*

Terms used in the Financial World:

Acquisition - this is when one company takes over the controlling interest in another company. It can be either a hostile takeover or a mutually agreed upon takeover.

ADR (American Depositary Receipt) - a negotiable certificate representing a given number of shares of stock in a foreign corporation. It is bought and sold in the American security markets, just as stock is traded.

Aggressive Investment Strategy - a method of portfolio allocation and management aimed at achieving maximum return. Aggressive investors place a high percentage of their investable assets in equity securities and a far lower percentage in safer debt securities and cash equivalents, and they pursue aggressive policies including margin trading, arbitrage, and option trading.

Arbitrage - profiting from differences in price when the same security, currency, or commodity is traded on two or more markets.

Ask - the term "ask" is used in conjunction with "bid and ask." It means the selling price. The trader is offering to sell or is "asking" for a specific price.

Asset(s) - can be real estate, businesses, and paper assets such as stocks bonds and mutual funds.

Asset Management - the managing of client accounts at a brokerage house, bank, or savings institution.

Auction Market - system by which securities are bought and sold through brokers on the securities exchanges, as distinguished from over-the-counter market, where trades are negotiated. For example, the New York Stock Exchange is a double auction system or two-sided market where many buyers and many sellers come together. Not just one auctioneer and many buyers.

Bear - an investor who acts on the belief that a security or the market is falling or will fall. A "bear" is a person who has a pessimistic view on the market or a particular security.

Bear Market - denoted by a prolonged period of falling prices. Bear markets in stocks are normally brought on by the anticipation of declining economic activity, and a bear market in bonds is normally caused by rising interest rates.

Bearer Bond - a bond that is payable to the one physically possessing it. Coupons are physically attached to the paper bond certificate, which the bondholder sends in or presents on the interest date for payment.

Bid - an indication by an investor, a trader, or a dealer of a willingness to buy a security at a certain price.

Blue Chip Stock - think blue blood or crème de la crème. This type of stock is a common stock of a nationally known company that has a long record of profit growth and dividend payment. It also has a reputation for quality management, products, and services. Examples include: IBM, GE, and Du Pont.

Bond - simply stated, a bond is an "I Owe You". It is a form of debt or debt instrument. Types of bonds include: municipals, government issued treasuries, corporate bonds, savings bonds, and Eurobonds, bearer bonds, etc.

Bond Quote - price at which the last sale and purchase of a particular bond took place.

Book Entry - securities that are not represented by a certificate. Instead, they are merely recorded on customer's accounts. No certificates change hands.

Book Value - the value at which an asset is carried on a balance sheet. It is also the net asset value of a company's securities. The Book Value can be a guide in selecting underpriced stocks and is an indication of the ultimate value of securities in liquidation.

Boutique Investment Bank - a small, specialized brokerage firm that deals with a limited clientele and offers a limited product line.

Broker - an individual or a firm that charges a fee or commission for executing buy or sell orders submitted by another individual or a firm.

Broker / Dealer - Most brokerage firms operate both as brokers and as principals, therefore the term broker/dealer is commonly used. A broker acts as an intermediary between a buyer and seller. A person who specializes in stocks, bonds, commodities or options and acts as an agent. They must be registered with the exchange where the securities are traded. A dealer acts as a principal in a security transaction and can be an individual or a firm. Principals (dealers) trade for their own account.

Bull - an investor who acts on the belief that a security or the market is rising or will rise. Bulls are optimistic on the economy, an individual security or the market as a whole.

Bull Market - denoted by a prolonged rise in the prices of stocks, bonds, or commodities. Bull markets can last a few months or many years.

Calls - short for call options. A call option grants the right to buy a specific number of shares at a specified price by a fixed date.

Capital Gain - the difference between the price at which you bought an investment and the price at which you sold the investment; less improvements made and other money invested in the investment.

Capital Loss - In regards to the buying and selling of securities, a capital loss is the amount by which the proceeds from the sale of a security are less than the cost of acquiring it. If the security is sold after holding it (owning it) for one year and one day it is considered to be a long-term capital loss. If the security is sold before one year, the loss is considered a short-term capital loss.

Cash - Currency, some savings accounts, money market funds, and some certificates of deposit are included in cash investments.

Cash Account - an account in which the customer is required by the SEC's Regulation T (Reg-T) to pay in full for securities purchased not later than two days after the standard payment period set by the NASD's Uniform Practice Code.

Cash Dividend - money paid to a corporation's stockholders out of the corporation's current earnings or accumulated profits. The board of directors must declare all dividends.

CBOE (Chicago Board Options Exchange) - the first national exchange based in Chicago for the trading of listed options (puts and calls). The CBOE is also well known for its VIX Index which is a measure of fear in the economy and market place. CBOE is also a publicly traded stock listed on the NASDAQ Exchange.

CD (Certificate of Deposit) - a debt instrument issued by a bank that usually pays interest. Individual CDs start as low as $100. Maturities range from a few weeks to many years. Make sure to shop for rates and maturity dates on CDs as they vary!

Close - the price of the last transactions for a particular security on a particular day.

Commercial Paper - short-term debt obligations issued normally by banks and corporations with maturities ranging less than one year. They are unsecured and usually discounted, although some are interest-bearing. Normally issued only by top-rated concerns and are nearly always backed by bank lines of credit.

Commodities - are tangible. Commodities include: precious and semi-precious metals such as gold, silver, and copper; food products such as orange juice, pork bellies, coffee, wheat and corn; natural resources such as gas, oil, timber, and cotton; and, precious and semi-precious stones like diamonds, etc. are just some examples of commodities.

Common Stock - equity issued by a company that gives the investor ownership in the company. Stocks may or may not pay the shareholder a dividend. Stocks can be traded on many domestic and international exchanges. A share price can go up or down depending on economic and individual company conditions.

Corporation - the most common form of business organization, in which the total worth of an organization is divided into shares of stock. Each share of stock represents a unit of ownership. A corporation is characterized by a continuous life span and its owners' limited liability.

Cost Basis - the original price (purchase price) of an asset, used in determining capital gains.

Depression - a saying exists that describes a depression quite well. A recession is when your neighbor is out of work and a depression is when you're out of work! The best example is the Great Depression of the 1930's that was centered in Europe and the United States.

Derivative - a financial instrument whose value is based on another security.

Discount Broker - Traditionally, a discount broker only executed trades and did not offer advice on which securities should be bought or sold. Today, however, many discount brokers offer a much wider range of services to their clients.

Diversified Investment Company or Strategy - a mutual fund or unit trust that invests in a wide range of securities.

Dividend - a distribution of a corporation's earnings. Dividends may be in the form of cash, stock, or property. The board of directors must declare all dividends.

Dividend Yield - The yield on a dividend is the annual rate of return on a common or preferred stock investment. The yield is calculated by dividing the annual dividend by the stock's purchase price.

DJCA (Dow Jones Composite Average) - a market indicator composed of the 65 stocks that make up the Dow Jones Industrial, Transportation, and Utilities Average.

DJIA (Dow Jones Industrial Average) - a market indicator composed of the Dow Jones Industrial stocks.

Dow Jones (Dow Jones Industrial Average or DJIA) - is a price-weighted average of 30 actively traded blue chip stocks that are comprised mainly of industrial companies. It is the oldest and most widely quoted of all the market indicators.

Dow Jones Average - is the most widely quoted and oldest measure of the change in stock prices. Each of the four averages is based on the price of a limited number of stocks in a particular category.

DTC (Depository Trust Corporation) - a clearing house and repository where stock and bond certificates are exchanged primarily electronically. The DTC is a member of the Federal Reserve System and is owned by most of the brokerage houses on Wall Street and the New York Stock Exchange (NYSE).

Economist - a paid professional whose work is to study, analyze and often predict facts about the economy.

Equity - stock ownership interest possessed by shareholders in a corporation.

ETFs (Exchange Traded Funds) - families of funds that are traded on the exchange similar to stocks. ETFs can focus on a specific market sector (i.e. energy, utilities, financials, etc.), or countries (i.e. U.S., Canada, Spain, etc.) or can be much more broad based in their scope (i.e. global equities). SPDRs, Vanguard, and iShares are just a few examples.

Ex-Dividend - a stock with a dividend trades ex-dividend. The dividend can be paid monthly, quarterly or yearly. A company can even declare a special one off dividend to reward its shareholders. The interval between the announcement of the dividend and the payment of the dividend is referred to as trading ex-dividend. An investor who buys shares during that interval is not entitled to the dividend because it trades "ex," "not," or "without" the dividend. Normally, a stock's price moves up by the dollar amount of the dividend as the ex-dividend date approaches, then falls by the amount of the dividend after that date.

Exchange - an organization, association, or group of persons that maintains or provides a marketplace in which securities can be bought and sold. An exchange does not have to be a physical place, and many strictly electronic exchanges do business around the world. Examples include: NYSE and NASDAQ.

FDIC (Federal Deposit Insurance Corporation) - This federal agency established in 1933 guarantees (up to $300,000) funds on deposit in member banks. The agency provides deposit insurance for member banks and prevents bank and thrift failures.

Full-Service Broker - a broker or brokerage firm that provides a wide range of services to its clients. Full-service broker commissions are normally higher than those of a discount broker because of the broader range of services they provide.

Futures - Futures Contracts are agreements to either buy or sell a specific amount of a commodity or financial instrument at a particular price on a stipulated *future* date.

GNP (Gross National Product) - total value of goods and services produced in the U.S. economy over a particular period of time, usually one year. It is a primary indicator of the status of the economy. The GNP is made up of consumer and government purchases, private domestic and foreign investments in the U.S., and the total value of exports.

Growth Stock - is a relatively speculative issue that is believed to offer significant potential for capital gains. It often pays lower dividends and sells at a higher price/earnings ratio.

Hedge Fund - is an investment firm that uses a hedging strategy to offset investment risk. A perfect hedge completely eliminates a future gain or loss. Hedge funds can go long and short. "Hedgies" is a nickname given to hedge funds.

Holding Period - a time period signifying how long the owner possesses a security. It starts the day after a purchase and ends on the day of the sale.

Income Producing Stock or Bond - is a stock or bond that is purchased primarily for the dividend or yield.

Interest - the cost of using money, expressed as a rate per period of time, usually one year, in which case it is called an annual rate of interest. An interest can also mean a share, right or title in a property.

Investment Advisor - provides investment advice for a fee. They are registered with the SEC (Securities and Exchange Commission) and abide by the rules of the Investment Advisers Act.

Investment Bank - a firm that acts as underwriter or agent, that serves as an intermediary between an issuer of securities and the investing public. Aside from their investment banking functions, most investment banks also maintain broker/dealer operations, serve both wholesale and retail clients in a brokerage and advisory capacity, and offer a growing number of related financial services.

IPO (Initial Public Offering) - a corporation's first sale of common stock to the public.

Leverage - doing more with less.

Liabilities - are what you owe. Examples include: credit card debt, school loans, medical bills, automobile payments and leases, law suits, financial support of children and elderly parents, child support and alimony.

Liquidity - the ease with which an asset can be converted to cash in the marketplace. A large number of buyers and sellers and a high volume of trading activity provide high liquidity.

Long - a long position in a portfolio. You own the security and are thereby long the position.

Long-term Gain - the profit earned on the sale of a capital asset that has been owned for more than 12 months.

Long-term Loss - the losses incurred on the sale of a capital asset that has been owned for more than 12 months.

Maturity or Maturity Date - is the date on which the principal amount of a note, bond or other debt instrument becomes due and payable. Also, it is when an installment loan must be paid in full.

Mergers - combining two or more companies, either through a pooling of interests, a purchase or a consolidation.

Momentum Stock - relates to the rate of acceleration of the price or volume of a stock.

Money Market - the securities market that deals in short-term debt instruments and negotiable certificates of deposit. Money market instruments are considered to be safe and very liquid forms of debt that mature in less than 1 year. Treasury bills and commercial paper make up the bulk of money market instruments.

Money Market Account - also called Money Market Deposit Accounts. These accounts are normally insured by the FDIC and invested in short-term debt instruments. They are market-sensitive bank accounts and available to depositors at any time without penalty.

Municipal Bond - refers to a debt obligation of a state or local government entity. Many receive tax-exempt status from federal, state or local taxes.

Mutual Fund - operated by an investment company that raises money from shareholders and invests these funds in various investment securities. Mutual Funds offer investors diversification and professional management. Management fees are common. Funds may invest aggressively or conservatively.

NASDAQ (National Association of Securities Dealers Automated Quotation System) - the NASDAQ is primarily made up of technology and technology related stocks.

Net Asset Value - of a mutual fund is the market value of a fund share, also called the bid price. No-load funds, the NAV, offering price or market price is what the investor pays to purchase the shares. The NAV is calculated by most funds after the close of the exchanges each day by taking the closing market value of all securities owned plus all other assets such as cash, subtracting all liabilities, then dividing the result (total net assets) by the total number of shares outstanding.

Net Change - calculated as the difference between the last trading price on a stock, bond, commodity, or mutual fund from one day to the next.

Non-diversified Investment Company / Strategy - a portfolio management strategy that seeks to concentrate investments in a particular industry or geographic area in hopes of achieving higher returns.

Non-Farm Payroll - used as a lagging market indicator and includes all employment outside of farming.

NYSE (New York Stock Exchange) - the largest and oldest stock exchange in the United States. Started in 1792 and located at 11 Wall Street in New York City, it is also referred to as the Big Board and The Exchange.

Offer - an offer to buy or to sell.

Options - An option gives the purchaser the right to buy or sell in exchange for an agreed upon amount within an agreed upon amount of time. If the right is not exercised within this specified period, the option expires and the option buyer loses the money.

OTC (Over-the-Counter) and OTC Market - the term used to describe a security traded with the telephone-linked and computer-connected OTC Market rather than through an exchange.

Outstanding Stock - are equity securities issued by a corporation and in the hands of the public.

Paper Gain - refers to an unrealized capital gain in an investment or portfolio. These profits become realized only when the securities are sold.

Paper Loss - the loss is only recorded on paper because the security has not really been sold.

Passive Income - income you are not working for. Examples include: businesses you invest in, royalties, rental real estate investments, etc.

P/E Ratio (Price-to-Earnings Ratio) - is used as a measure of a stock's performance. It is calculated by dividing the stock's current market price by its earnings per share.

Penny Stock - can be high risk but also high reward. It can also be high risk and no reward. Penny stocks are normally small companies and considered a riskier investment.

Pension Plan - is a contract between an individual and an employer, labor union, government entity, or other institution that provides for the distribution of pension benefits at retirement.

Pink Sheets - listing of very small companies and are normally considered to be a risky investment.

Portfolio Income - income derived from paper assets such as stocks, bonds, mutual funds, cash investments, etc.

Portfolio Income Statement - clearly shows your profits and losses from your market investments by a monthly, quarterly, semi-annual or annual basis and sent to you by your investment advisor or stock broker.

Preferred Stock - an equity security that represents ownership in a corporation. It is issued with a stated dividend which must be paid before the dividends are paid to common stock holders. Common stock holder's rights are subordinate in a company bankruptcy to preferred stock holder's rights. However, it generally carries no voting rights. Preferred stock can also be retired.

Price - This can refer to the purchase "bid price" or the sale "ask price". These are normally different and provide for a "spread" (difference) in between the two prices.

Private Placement - It is an offering which complies with Reg-D under the Securities Act and is solely for a very small group of investors.

Public Offering - is the sale of an issue of common stock, either by a corporation going public or by offering of additional shares.

Puts - a contract that gives the owner the right to sell an investment at a specified price and within a specified time.

Rating Services - the three major rating agencies in the U.S. include: Moody's, S&P, and Fitch.

Realized Gain - the amount a tax payer earns when he sells an asset.

Realized Loss - the amount a tax payer loses when he sells an asset.

Recession - a general economic decline lasting from 6 to 18 months. A saying exists that describes a recession quite well. A recession is when your neighbor is out of work and a depression is when you're out of work.

Reg. T (Regulation T) - was set up under the SEC. Currently sets the loan value of a marginal security and payment deadline beyond regular settlement.

Return - can be a gain or loss.

Risk (Risk / Reward) - Every reward carries a risk and some are greater than others.

ROI (Return on Investment) - The profit or loss on an investment and is often expressed as an annual percentage rate.

Rule of 72 - to find the number of years required to double your money given a specific interest rate, divide the compound return into 72. The answer is the approximate number of years that it will take for your investment to double. For example: At a 4% interest rate, divide 4 into 72 and you get 18 years.

Russell - The Russell averages range in size from 1,000 to 5,000 companies, depending on which average it is. Examples include: Russell 1000, Russell 2000, Russell 5000, etc.

Russell 2000 - most commonly quoted average on CNBC and Bloomberg of all the Russell averages. The index has 2000 different companies listed. These companies are normally smaller in size than those listed on the S&P or the DOW.

S & P (Standard & Poor's Stock Index) - Standard & Poor's produces a number of stock indexes.

S & P 500 (The Standard & Poor's 500 Index) - the most commonly mentioned S & P index on financial programs and is a much broader range index than the S & P 100. The S & P 500 is a stock index comprised of 500 companies. As a comparison, the S& P 100 is a value weighted index composed of 100 blue-chip stocks (high quality stocks).

SEC (Securities and Exchange Commission) - the Commission created by Congress to regulate the securities markets and to protect investors.

Secondary Market - is the market in which securities are bought and sold after they are offered to the public for the first time. A security first makes its debut on the "red carpet" as an IPO and then trades on the secondary market.

Settlement Date - the date in which an executed order between a buyer and a brokerage firm must be finalized with payment.

Short - means to "short" a position or sell a position they don't necessarily own because they think that the price will go down. This takes place when someone or some entity sells a security short to purchase it again later at a lower price in order to make a profit. There are "naked shorts" and "covered shorts".

Short-term Gain - is a gain on a capital asset where the holding period is less than one year. Ordinary income tax rules apply.

Short-term Loss - is a loss on a capital asset where the holding period was for less than one year. A short-term loss can offset a short-term capital gain.

SIPC (Securities Investor Protection Corporation) - amongst other things it protects the customer's assets held by a brokerage firm against a bankruptcy or default up to $500,000 for cash and securities.

Specialist - a stock exchange member who stands ready to quote and trade certain securities either for his own account or for customer accounts. The specialist's role is to maintain a fair and orderly market in the stocks for which he is responsible.

Speculation - trading a security with a higher than average risk in return for a higher than average profit potential.

Speculative Stock or Security - is a stock or security with a higher than average risk.

Speculator - an investor who speculates or trades with higher than average risk.

Spread - the difference between the "bid price" and the "ask price". The "bid" is the price the broker/dealer is willing to pay for the security. The "ask" is the "asking price" that the broker/dealer is will to sell the security for.

Stock - equity or ownership in a corporation. Can be common or preferred.

Stock Certificate - written evidence of ownership in a corporation.

Stockbroker - a licensed professional who sells stocks and acts as a dealer and receives a commission for services.

Stockholder - a person or entity that holds shares (of any amount) in a corporation.

Stock Quote - a list of representative prices bid and asked for a stock during a particular trading day. Stock quotes are listed in the financial press and most daily newspapers.

Stock Split - an increase in the number of a corporation's outstanding shares. This decreases the stock's par value. However, the market value of the total number of shares remains the same.

Suitability - a determination made by a registered representative as to whether a particular security matches a customer's objectives and financial capability. The representative must have enough information about the customer to make this judgment.

Supply & Demand - the total amount of goods or services available for purchase by consumers in contrast to the demand desired by consumers.

Tax Rate - the amount of taxes you pay is dependent upon which tax bracket you are in. Each tax bracket carries with it a different percentage levied by the government.

Ticker Symbol - the name "ticker symbol" derived from stock symbols that used to be on actual "ticker tape" produced by a ticker tape machine.

Ticker Tape - What you see on CNBC and Bloomberg stations is today's modern version of the ticker tape. To see a true ticker tape machine, take a tour of the New York Stock Exchange.

Trade Date - is the date you buy or sell a security.

Treasury Bill(s) - a marketable U.S. government debt security with a maturity of less than one year.

Treasury Bond(s) - a marketable U.S. government debt security with a maturity of 10 or more years.

Treasury Note(s) - a marketable U.S. government debt security with a maturity of 1 to 10 years.

Trend - can go either up or down and normally lasts for a while. "The Trend is your Friend" is a saying that is used by many investors and means that if you follow the trend that is in place, either up or down, you will make money.

Trend Line - a tool used by technical analysts to trace a security's movement by connecting the lows in an upward trend or the rally highs in a downward trend.

Valuation - how a security is valued.

Value - what is the price, what is it worth in today's market.

Value Investor or Investing - selecting stocks of undervalued companies evidenced by low stock prices relative to earnings.

VIX (Volatility Index) - used as a trading tool. It measures the volatility in the marketplace. Not just used anymore as a gauge to assess market sentiment but can actually be traded as any other index.

Volatility - the magnitude and frequency of changes in the price of a security within a given period.

Warrants - a security, usually issued together with a bond or preferred stock that gives the holder the right to purchase a proportionate amount of common stock at a specified price at a later date in time.

Yield - the rate of return on an investment, usually expressed as an annual percentage rate.

Yield Curve - a graphic representation of the projected or actual yields of fixed income securities in relation to their maturities.

YTM (Yield-to-Maturity) - represents the "rate of return" on a bond that accounts for the difference between the bond's purchase price and its proceeds upon maturity, including interest income.

Zero-Coupon Bond - a fixed income or debt security that doesn't pay interest (coupon) payments and is traded at a discount to the full face value amount upon maturity. Instead, the buyer of the security receives the rate of return through the appreciation of the security which is redeemed at face value on a specified maturity date. Zeros can be extremely volatile.

Sources

Books:

Charles Schwab's New Guide to Financial Independence by Charles Schwab. Copyright 1998, 2004 by The Charles Schwab Corporation. Published by Three Rivers Press, New York, NY.

Commodity Trader's Almanac 2011 by Jeffrey A. Hirsch & Yale Hirsch. Copyright 2011. Published by John Wiley & Sons, Inc., Hoboken, NJ.

Dictionary of Finance and Investment Terms (Third Edition) by John Downes & Jordan Elliot Goodman. Copyright 1991 by Barron's Educational Series, Inc., NY.

Difficult Conversations: How to Discuss What Matters Most 10th Anniversary Edition, written by and 1999 Copyright by Douglas Stone, Bruce Patton, Sheila Heen, and Roger Fisher. Published by Penguin Books by Penguin Group, NY, NY 2010.

How to make Money in Stocks (A winning System in Good Times or Bad) by William J. O'Neil. Revised First Edition, McGraw-Hill, Inc. Copyright 1991, 1998 by McGraw-Hill, Inc. Printed and bound by R. R. Donnelley & Sons.

In Business As In Life - You Don't Get What You Deserve, You Get What You Negotiate by Chester L. Karrass. Copyright 1996. Published by Stanford St. Press, Beverly Hills, CA in 1996.

Managed Futures in the Institutional Portfolio edited by Charles B. Epstein. Copyright 1992 by John Wiley & Sons, Inc. Published by John Wiley & Sons, Inc., NY.

Missed Fortune 101 by Douglas R. Andrew. Copyright 2005 by Douglas Andrew. Published by Warner Business Books, NY.

Real Money (Sane Investing in an Insane World) by James J. Cramer. Copyright 2005 by J. J. Cramer & Co. Published by Simon & Schuster, New York, NY.

Science of Getting Rich (The Empowered Woman's Guide to Success) by Wallace D. Wattles. Copyright Scorpio Moon Publishing, Toronto.

Security Analysis (The Classic 1934 Edition) by Benjamin Graham and David Dodd. Copyright 1934 and renewed 1962. Whittlesey House, McGraw-Hill Book Company, Inc., New York.

Small Stocks Big Profits by Gerald W. Perritt, Dearborn Financial Publishing, Inc., 1993). Copyright 1988 by Dow Jones – Irwin. Copyright by Gerald W. Perritt.

Stock Market Logic - (A Sophisticated Approach to Profits on Wall Street) by Norman G. Fosback. Copyright 1976, 1993 by The Institute for Econometric Research, Inc. Published by Dearborn Financial Publishing, Inc., Chicago, Illinois.

Stock Trader's Almanac 2011 by Jeffrey A. Hirsch & Yale Hirsch. Copyright 2011. Published by John Wiley & Sons, Inc., Hoboken, NJ.

The G Spot: And Other Recent Discoveries About Human Sexuality by Alice Kahn Ladas, Beverly Whipple and John D. Perry (July 1982). Published by Dell Publishing a division of Random House, Inc., New York, NY.

The Motley Fool UK Investment Guide (How the Fools beat the City's Wisemen and How you can Too) by David Berger with David and Tom Garner. Text copyright by The Motley Fool UK 1998. Boxtree 1998 an imprint of Macmillan Publishers LTD, Basingtoke and Oxford.

The New Options Market. (Strategies for profit by trading puts and calls on the Chicago Board Options Exchange and the American Stock Exchange) by Max G. Ansbacher. Walker and Company, New York. Copyright 1975 by Max G. Ansbacher. Published in U.S. in 1975 by the Walker Publishing Company, Inc., published in Canada by Fitzhenry & Whiteside, Ltd. Toronto.

The Next Great Bubble Boom (How to Profit from the Greatest Boom in History: 2005-2009) by Harry S. Dent, Jr. Copyright 2004 by Harry S. Dent, Jr. Published by Free Press, NY.

Timing the Market (How to Profit in the Stock Market using the Yield Curve, Technical Analysis, and Cultural Indicators) by Deborah Weir. Copyright 2006 by Deborah J. Wier. Published by John Wiley & Sons, Inc. Hoboken, NJ.

Understanding Wall Street (2nd Edition) by Jeffrey B. Little and Lucien Rhodes. Copyright 1987 by Jeffrey B. Little. Published by Liberty Hall Press.

Your Money Personality (What It Is and How You Can Profit from It) by Kathleen Gurney, Ph.D. Copyright 1988 by Kathleen Gurney, Ph.D. Second Edition, published by Financial Psychology Corporation.

Illustrations, Charts and Graphs:

Illustrations and text by Karen L. Neilinger with help on the illustrations and graphics by Alpha Graphics, Greenwich, CT.

Illustrations and text by Karen L. Neilinger and Francine J. Blum with hand sketched illustrations by Trevor Denham, CA.

Internet Articles:

"Bag-lady Syndrome" defined by www.urbandictionary.com.

"Commanding Heights: The German Hyperinflation," 1923 on PBS, www.pbs.org.

"Diamonds - An Investor's Best Friend?" by Siemond Chan with Yahoo! Finance – Thursday, May 16, 2013 2:28 PM EDT, Yahoo Finance 5/25/13.

"Even Financially Successful Women Fear Becoming Bag Ladies, New Study Finds," article by Beth Greenfield, Shine Staff. Shine. yahoo.com. Friday, March 29, 2013.

"Fear Becoming a 'Bag Lady' Someday? Many Others Do, Too," article by Amy Langfield, TODAY contributor, NBC News, published Monday, April 2013, 1:07pm ET.

"Forbes Woman and the National Endowment for Financial Education 2011 Online Poll," article on Forbes.com.

"Hyperinflation in the Weimar Republic," www.wikipedia.org.

"The Bag Lady Syndrome: 3 Ways I Fight the Fear," article by Maria Niles, February 8, 2011, on www.blogher.com.

"What to do with an old 401 (k)," article by Fidelity, on www.fidelity.com/viewpoints/401k-options.

"Women Fear Becoming 'Bag Ladies Even When They're Financially Secure," Says Study by Emma Gray. The Huffington Post, posted 3/28/2013 2:15pm EDT.

"Women, Money and Power and Study," article and study by Allianz Life Insurance Company of North America, 2013.

Some Definitions sourced from www.Investopedia.com.

Some Historical Events sourced from www.Wikipedia.org.

Some Lyrics sourced from www.Lyricsmode.com.

Some Quotes sourced from www. BrainyQuotes.com.

Magazine Articles, Newspaper Articles, and Pamphlets:

"Carol Ross Joynt: Debt Becomes Her," by Carol Ross Joynt, CNN correspondent. Vogue Magazine, March 2011 edition. Article adapted from the book Innocent Spouse: A Memoir. Copyright 2011 by Carol Joynt. Media, LLC.

"Dealing with Debt," by Thomas S. Caldwell, C.M., Caldwell Securities Ltd, Toronto, January 2004.

"Divorce of Patricia Kluge," article by Geraldine Fabrikant, The New York Times, September 30, 2011.

"How Common is Financial Infidelity," by Jennifer Saranow Schultz, The New York Times, Febuary 24, 2011.

"I should have known Better: How a Financial Pro Lost his House," article by Carl Richards, The New York Times, section F1, Wednesday, November 9, 2011, F1.

"REITs and hybrid mREITs", by Pargon Report.

"TD Ameritrade Options Guide. Are Options Right For You?" by Investools from TD Ameritrade Holding Corp. Copyright 2011, TD Ameritrade IP Company, Inc.

"When Life Insurance Is an Investment," by Peter C. Katt, CFP, Journal of Financial Planning, July 2011.

WISERWoman, A Quarterly Newsletter from the Women's Institute for a Secure Retirement, Spring/Summer 2001, 1920 N. Street, NW, Suite 300, Washington, DC.

Other Sources:

Our great thanks and appreciation goes out to these top professionals who shared with us their valuable time and expertise during the writing of our book.

Francis B. Dowling, Financial Representative, Northwestern Mutual, Hamden, Connecticut.

Burton Herman, CLU, LUTCF, Founder of the Herman Agency, Herman Agency, Inc., Oak Brook, Illinois.

Larry Herman, JD, CPA, CLU, CHFC, Herman Agency, Inc., Oak Brook, Illinois.